CONTAINING NATIONALISM

CONTAINING NATIONALISM

MICHAEL HECHTER

OXFORD
UNIVERSITY PRESS

OXFORD
UNIVERSITY PRESS

Great Clarendon Street, Oxford OX2 6DP

Oxford University Press is a department of the University of Oxford.
It furthers the University's objective of excellence in research, scholarship,
and education by publishing worldwide in

Oxford New York

Athens Auckland Bangkok Bogotá Buenos Aires Calcutta
Cape Town Chennai Dar es Salaam Delhi Florence Hong Kong Istanbul
Karachi Kuala Lumpur Madrid Melbourne Mexico City Mumbai
Nairobi Paris São Paulo Singapore Taipei Tokyo Toronto Warsaw
and associated companies in Berlin Ibadan

Oxford is a registered trade mark of Oxford University Press
in the UK and certain other countries

Published in the United States
by Oxford University Press Inc., New York

British Library Cataloguing in Publication Data
Data available

Library of Congress Cataloging in Publication Data
Hechter, Michael.
Containing nationalism / Michael Hechter.
Includes bibliographical references and index.
ISBN 0-19-829742-4
1. Nationalism. I. Title.
JC311.H383 2000 320.54–dc21 99-048960

ISBN 0-19-829742-4

1 3 5 7 9 10 8 6 4 2

Typeset by Best-set Typesetter Ltd., Hong Kong
Printed in Great Britain
on acid-free paper by
Biddles Ltd
Guildford and King's Lynn

for Eliana
O matre pulchra filia pulchrior.
(Horace)

ACKNOWLEDGEMENTS

THIS book first began to take shape during a series of lectures on nationalism I presented during Trinity Term 1996 at the University of Oxford. Although the number of undergraduates at these lectures dwindled rapidly as the lures of summer approached, it was heartening that my colleagues Erica Benner and Lars-Eric Cederman saw fit to attend regularly and remained engaged with the issues.

The final manuscript was a long time in coming. In part, writing a book on nationalism in these times has been rather like trying to hit a rapidly moving target. Almost every day the morning paper would trumpet new headlines about nationalism, and I was impelled to discern what their deeper implications, if any, might be. As the onrush of headlines never quit, the enterprise became increasingly daunting. The book was also difficult to write on account of the seriousness of the topic. Too many lives have been sacrificed in the name of nationalism; this gives would-be analysts a special obligation to try and get matters right.

In this attempt, I have received a great deal of help. Debra Friedman's multiple readings, astute editorial advice, and constant intellectual support were essential at all stages of the project. The research assistance of Wade Roberts and Nobuyuki Takahashi was little short of exemplary. A number of people read all or parts of the manuscript and were kind enough to give me their unvarnished reactions: Yoram Barzel, Daniel Bell, Johannes Berger, William Brustein, Sun-Ki Chai, Hartmut Esser, John A. Hall, Oscar Hechter, Edgar Kiser, Alexander Motyl, David Schmidtz, and Pierre van den Berghe. I am deeply grateful to them all. In addition, several anonymous reviewers provided trenchant comments on previous drafts of the text. Bernard Grofman offered me valuable advice on electoral systems, as did Timur Kuran on Ottoman history. Much as I am tempted to blame these commentators for the book's shortcomings, I alone take full responsibility for its faults.

I was fortunate to have been invited to present various parts of the book at colloquia and conferences at Cornell University (Robert Gibbons), the Hong Kong University of Science and Technology (Andrew Walder), the University of Minnesota (William Brustein), the University of Mannheim (Hartmut Esser), New York University (Guillermina Jasso), the London School of Economics (Anthony Smith), the Royal Swedish Academy of Sciences (Peter Hedström and Richard Swedberg), the University of Leipzig (Karl-Dieter Opp), the University of Wisconsin (Crawford Young and Mark Beissinger), and the University of Washington. Finally, some of the material in this book was presented as the 1999 Maxwell Cummings Lecture at McGill University (Axel Van Den Berg and Hudson Meadwell).

Evan Kimble and Karen Erickson helped with the graphics. Last, a research professorship from the College of Social and Behavioral Sciences of the University of Arizona enabled me to complete the manuscript.

I would like to acknowledge the previously published material that appears in this book. Table 3.1 first appeared in Michael H. Fischer, *Indirect Rule in India* (New Delhi: Oxford University Press, 1991 p. 8). Figure 3.2 first appeared in Mark Brayshay, Phillip Harrison, and Brian Chalkley's 'Knowledge, Nationhood and Governance: the Speed of the Royal Post in Early-Modern England.' *Journal of Historical Geography*, Vol. 24, 1988. And Figure 6.1 first appeared in an article by Sam Cole, 'Cultural Accounting in Small Economies', *Regional Studies*, Vol. 27, 1993.

M.H.

Seattle
June 1999

CONTENTS

LIST OF FIGURES

LIST OF TABLES

The happiest nations have no history.
(George Eliot)

CHAPTER 1

Nationalist Puzzles

ONE Sunday morning not long ago, I walked to the Fremont farmer's market in Seattle to buy some local produce. The most bohemian neighbourhood in town, Fremont is a throwback to the informality and insouciance of the counterculture of the 1960s. At the south-western edge of the market, just beyond the tatty displays of cast-off furniture and second-hand clothes, loomed a large bronze statue of a man peering intently toward the horizon. The man was V. I. Lenin. During the past year a local entrepreneur had rescued the statue from a garbage dump in a small Russian town and brought it home to Seattle. One can only imagine the reaction of the town's officials when they learnt of his interest in shipping this relic of socialist realism half-way around the world. Why the statue ended up in Fremont is a mystery to me. In any case, some prankster had placed a red rubber traffic cone on top of Lenin's hat. This small embellishment radically altered the statue's appearance: what had originally been an intense revolutionary firebrand now had become a harmless dunce. Lenin's fate in Seattle's Fremont district is but one small reflection of a sea-change that has jolted world politics.

As the founder of the first socialist state, Lenin symbolized the hopes of the most successful branch of the international workers' movement. For most of the twentieth century, political movements based on class—in particular, socialism and communism—were regarded as the principal threat to domestic and international order by friends and foes alike. A mere sixty years ago, the spectre of political upheaval was so substantial that the United States enacted a welter of New Deal social policies, vastly extending the government's provision of public goods, to keep revolution at bay. Considerably more extensive welfare states were constructed in Western Europe to allay similar anxieties. Pitched battles for and against unions grabbed the headlines. John L. Lewis, Harry Bridges, Jimmy Hoffa, and other lords of labour played major roles in American politics until the 1970s.

Since then, the salience of class politics seems to have waned, and not just in the United States.[1] One sign is the long secular downturn in the power of trade unions. The proportion of the American labour force in unions has been declining since 1935; it stands at about 17 per cent today. How many Americans nowadays can remember the name of a single labour leader? Even in Britain, arguably the most class-ridden society in the world, Tony Blair succeeded in severing the unions' sway over the Labour Party by repealing Clause Four of its constitution in 1995. The most momentous indicator of the demise of class politics, of course, is the collapse of the Soviet Union and its client states in 1989. When I was a child, schools held mandatory air-raid drills to protect us from the communist peril; now, only the most perspicacious American schoolchildren know the slightest thing about communism. The subject has become relegated to history. All told, the working class in industrial societies has refused to play its foreordained role in a revolutionary drama. The traffic cone and the whimsical placement of Lenin's statue in Fremont mutely signify all this and more.

This is not to imply that there has been an end to ideology. While the politics of class has been retreating into the wings, the politics of ethnicity has been moving into the limelight. The increasing salience of ethnicity is evident in domains as distinct as popular culture and world politics. Hollywood stars once hid their distinctive ethnic origins by adopting Anglo-Saxon names; now ethnically distinct names are à la mode. Disney's animated films—probably the only cultural experience shared by American children—used to portray their ethnically distinct characters as willing participants in the melting pot; recently, however, assertive ethnic identity has come to reign. *Dumbo's* helpful, if mocking, crows have been superseded by a strident Simba from *The Lion King* (Rothstein 1997).

Popular culture has taken its cue from broad political trends. Nationalism and its close cousin, ethnicity, currently are the most potent political forces in the world. To appreciate how times have changed, consider the world in 1994. During that year, eighteen of the twenty-three wars being fought were based on nationalist or ethnic challenges to states. About three-quarters of the world's refugees were fleeing from, or were displaced by, ethnic or nationalist conflicts. And eight of the thirteen United Nations peace-keeping operations were designed to separate the protagonists in ethno-political conflicts (Gurr 1994: 350). If anything, this trend became even more pronounced subsequently.

The advent of computer-mediated communication, which lowers the costs of collective action, may exacerbate this kind of conflict.[2] Whereas broadcast media formerly were controlled by governments in most countries, and by large corporations elsewhere, new communications technologies permit individuals and social movements to set up their own broadcast media. Both Oaxacan *Zapatistas* and Kosovar nationalists have used digital communications technology to air their political grievances to an international audience. As result, they have been able to attract manpower and finances from supporters far afield. No such possibility existed for their historical forebears. Hence digital communication may weaken the power of states and could result in even more nationalism in the future (Castells 1997: 254–5, 257).[3]

Of course, these developments have not gone unheeded. A mountain of new articles and books and at least two new scholarly journals devoted to nationalism have appeared recently. As a result, our knowledge of nationalist movements and conflicts in a large number of specific countries and historical periods has been significantly extended.

Yet we know very little about nationalism in general. Despite this latest flurry of scholarly attention, a number of basic questions remain. This book focuses on three of them. There is much agreement that nationalism is a creature of the last two centuries, but no consensus about the causes of its modernity. Similarly, everyone recognizes that nationalism is much more prevalent in some

countries (Canada) than others (the United States), but the reasons
for this difference are controversial.[4] Last, since nationalism is frequently associated with terrible violence, is there any means of
containing its dark side? These three questions motivate the
present book.

Some deny that general questions of this sort are meaningful, let
alone answerable (Hall 1993; Calhoun 1997). On this view, since
every instance of nationalism is rooted in a particular time and
place, it can only understood in its historicity. If nationalism is
socially constructed not by the analyst, but created by people and
responded to by them over time, then any attempt to abstract away
from these particularities is bound to fail. I do not deny that
nationalism is a social construction. But I contend that exploring
the conditions under which this social construction takes place is
fruitful.[5]

There have been few such explorations, however. This penum-
bra in the literature of nationalism arises for a number of reasons.
Historical case studies rather than comparative analyses tend to
dominate the literature. Although several important comparative
studies do exist, they have not yielded satisfactory answers to these
questions. Such answers have not been forthcoming because the
very meaning of nationalism is controversial.

Accordingly, tedious though it may appear to be, the first step
in any attempt to analyse the general causes and consequences of
nationalism is to define the term. Just what does nationalism entail?
The phenomena described as nationalist make up a bewildering
pot-pourri of cultural and political events. On the cultural side the
list includes the establishment of folk festivals[6] and the production
of works of art,[7] literature,[8] music,[9] and even dress (Bogatyrev
1971), celebrating the virtues of a host of nations.[10] Even the academic disciplines of archaeology and palaeoanthropology have
been pressed into service to glorify the origins of various peoples.[11]

If nationalism is part and parcel of much modern culture, nationalist politics ranges from the mundane to the violent. Consider the
mundane. Prior to all athletic and many cultural events, audiences
in the United States stand to sing 'The Stars and Stripes Forever'.
Presumably this practice evolved to encourage immigrants having
a multitude of cultural loyalties to 'become American'. Is there any

more sacred American symbol than the United States flag? Campaigning and voting for legal nationalist parties are perhaps the most common nationalist political activities.

But violence is often a by-product of nationalism, as well. Sadly, here too there is no shortage of examples—the Israelites' fabled resistance at Masada, the Greek triumph against the Persians at Marathon, Joan of Arc's heroism against the English, old European Holocausts, new ones in the former Yugoslavia and in Rwanda and Burundi, and the politics of 'terrorism' in Ireland, Israel, and Sri Lanka. The scale of current nationalist violence is far greater than may be commonly appreciated. For example, more than 30,000 Tamils have been killed since 1983 in the Sri Lankan civil war:

> For the past five years, most of the Tamils' fighting has been done by an army composed largely of young women and schoolchildren. One of the bloodiest civil wars in recent history has been waged by boys and girls as young as 14: youngsters raised with a death wish and obsessed with martyrdom . . . There are at least 3,000 Tigresses now fighting on the rebel side . . . What has kept the Sri Lankan government at bay in recent years . . . has been a steady stream of devastating suicide attacks, either in battle or in strikes against government installations or political leaders. Hundreds of Tamils have died in this way. Many have been female; nearly all have been in their teens or early twenties . . . (McGirk 1995).[12]

Given this congeries of referents, defining nationalism is no easy task.

Nationalism Defined

The term 'nationalism' first appeared in 1774 in a text written by Herder (Alter 1989: 7); ever since, it has been used to describe a bewildering mix of phenomena. Commentators frequently complain that nationalism embraces so many dissimilar meanings that the very concept is muddled. Thus, the editors of the most comprehensive reader on the topic aver that 'perhaps the central difficulty in the study of nations and nationalism has been the problem of finding adequate and agreed definitions of the key concepts, nation and nationalism' (Hutchinson and Smith 1994: 4). For another expert 'the plethora of phenomena which may be sub-sumed under the term "nationalism" suggests that it is one of the most ambiguous concepts in the present-day vocabulary of polit-ical and analytical thought' (Alter 1989: 4). This ambiguity makes the study of nationalism particularly appealing to writers whose motivations are primarily political rather than analytical.[13] If people cannot agree on a definition of nationalism, it can be no surprise that they offer quite different assessments of it—particularly what its causes are, if it is retrograde or noble, or if it is a form of politics that is here to stay.

Our ability to understand nationalism is not quite so feeble as these complaints might suggest, however. Despite the many state-ments to the contrary, there is more consensus in the scholarly lit-erature than is commonly perceived. Nationalism is, above all, political (Breuilly 1993). The literary, musical, and artistic aspects of nationalism may be eminently worthy of study, but they ultimately are not responsible for the growing interest in the subject.[14]

Yet even if the scope of nationalism is limited to the realm of politics, a major definitional hurdle still lingers. The reason is that the story of nationalism has two quite different political aspects. It begins as Sleeping Beauty, an uplifting tale of the victory of the common people against the corrupt monarchical forces of the *ancien régime*. Thus in his allegorical painting of the French Revolution of 1830, *Liberty Leading the People at the Barricades*, Delacroix places the tricolour in Liberty's hand as she emerges half-naked from the barricade. By the twentieth century, however, nationalism transmogrifies into Frankenstein's monster, animating a rogues' gallery of xenophobic and even genocidal social move-ments (Minogue 1967: 7).

Since no single term can possibly encompass such a Janus-faced phenomenon, distinctions are often made between types. Proba-bly the most popular distinction is between Western and Eastern (Oriental) types of nationalism (Kohn 1944; Plamenatz 1976), but many other distinctions—like that between civic and particularis-tic nationalism (Greenfeld 1992)—have been advanced, as well. At the end of the day, most of the existing typologies of nationalism rest on thinly disguised normative criteria: they merely distinguish between good nationalisms and malign ones (Billig 1995; Chatterjee 1993).

The problem with this kind of definitional strategy is that there is nothing either good or bad, but thinking makes it so. An adequate definition of nationalism ought to accommodate all the different storylines; it should be capable of encompassing both its liberal and illiberal varieties. At the same time, it ought to exclude phenomena that are not specific to nationalism. Any definition that is useful for explanatory purposes must rest, therefore, on analytical rather than normative foundations.

The situation is far from hopeless because a broad consensus does exist in the scholarly literature concerning one particular analytical definition. It has long been held that nationalism consists of political activities that aim to make the boundaries of the nation—a culturally distinctive collectivity aspiring to self-governance—coterminous with those of the state.[15] By the state, I refer to the set of specialized institutions that is responsible for producing order, justice, social welfare, and defence in a territorially bounded society (North 1981; Poggi 1978; Weber [1922] 1978: 905). Nationalism thus, directly or indirectly, entails the pursuit of national self-determination.

This definition is not optimal, however, because it begs an important question about the timing of nationalism. Since the state is such a Johnny-come-lately—the vast majority of societies in history have managed to do without it—defining nationalism in terms of the state confines it to the modern world by fiat. That nationalism is only to be found in the modern era is something that deserves explanation in its own right. Accordingly, nationalism is better defined as *collective action designed to render the boundaries of the nation congruent with those of its governance unit.*

This congruence can be attained by fundamentally dissimilar policies, however. Nation and governance unit can be made congruent by enacting inclusive policies that seek to incorporate the members of culturally diverse groups in the polity on an equal basis. *E pluribus unum*, the motto found on United States coins, precisely expresses this inclusive nationalist strategy.

Alternatively, nation and governance unit can be made congruent by enacting exclusive policies that limit full membership in the polity to individuals from one or more favoured nations. Exclusive nationalist strategies include the enactment of restrictions on immigration or citizenship, famously proposed by the 'integral nationalist' Maurras ([1954] 1970), as well as more draconian policies such as ethnic cleansing and outright genocide. Sleeping Beauty and Frankenstein's monster can both find a home within the scope of the present definition.

One aspect of this definition deserves further comment. If nationalism is collective action designed to achieve a particular end, then how can that end be discerned empirically? Whereas the motives of individual participants in nationalist movements are largely inscrutable,[16] every social movement, or political party, attempts to recruit followers on the basis of goals that are widely advertised. It follows that groups seeking to advance the congruence of nation and governance unit (say, by promoting national sovereignty) are unambiguously nationalist.[17] Still, nationalism is a variable, not a constant. To the degree that a given group aims for something less than complete sovereignty—or for goals that are quite irrelevant to its attainment—then it is perforce less nationalist.[18]

Definitions work by setting boundaries around concepts: an all-inclusive definition is futile.[19] Like all definitions, this one excludes certain phenomena from its purview. The question to ask of any definition is whether it excludes the right elements for the purposes at hand. Whereas the present definition is not historically exclusive—it does not restrict nationalism to the modern era, for example—it is admittedly substantively exclusive. It limits nationalism to the realm of politics. According to this definition, therefore, the mere expression of nationalist ideology or sentiment in verbal, musical, or symbolic form—as occurs frequently in sixteenth-century Europe (Marcu 1976), to say nothing of other places and times—does not qualify as nationalism in the absence of a social movement whose stated goal is the attainment of national self-determination.[20]

Nationalism must be distinguished from other political phenomena with which it is sometimes conflated. Nationalism of the state-building variety (further discussed in Chapter 4) is different from garden-variety *imperialism*, which occurs when central rulers expand their control into areas occupied by one or more distinct cultural groups, but then make no subsequent attempt to meld the resulting mix into a single cultural entity. Imperialism is not a type of nationalism because empires are purposively multinational. Likewise, nationalism is different from *regionalism*, which entails collective action designed to change the existing balance of rights and resources between the centre and the authorities or citizens of a given region. When such centre–periphery bargaining occurs without a demand for peripheral sovereignty,[21] then it too fails to qualify as a type of nationalism.

As so defined, nationalism appears to be straightforward. But this is a mistaken impression. The present definition rests on two concepts, the *governance unit* and the *nation*, both of which are problematic.

The Governance Unit

By governance unit, I refer to *that territorial unit which is responsible for providing the bulk of social order and other collective goods—including protection from confiscation, justice and welfare—to its members*. Since governance units are also responsible for producing these collective goods, it follows that they must have the capacity to extract the revenue and other resources necessary to defray this production. In much theoretical writing the governance unit is simply called a *state*. Indeed, many governance units are states.

But far from all of them. My use of the qualifier 'the bulk of' highlights the difficulty of precisely determining just what the governance unit in a society may be. For simple hunter-gatherer societies, the matter is clear: the local group is the relevant unit (Johnson and Earle 1987).[22] Similarly, in classic feudalism the mantle of governance falls to the manor. In contrast, governance in advanced societies is carried out in much larger and geographically extensive units. Sometimes, as in France, the governance unit is the central state: its agencies are largely responsible for the supply and allocation of the relevant collective goods throughout the whole country. Thus it is often said that at any given hour in any given day, every student in a French school is learning exactly the same lesson.

In many other complex societies, however, governance tasks are carried out simultaneously in different territorial units. Since governance in federal systems always involves more than one level of decision-making, its locus is much more difficult to ascertain. In the United States, for example, the Federal government is responsible for the provision of defence and, ultimately, of justice. But state governments are responsible for providing some collective goods (including higher education, freeway maintenance, and aid to dependent children), whereas still others (including policing, fire protection and elementary education) are the responsibility of municipalities, or even smaller units such as local school districts. Since the allocation of powers between various levels of government has always engendered intense political conflict, it is no easy task to determine where the bulk of governance occurs in a polity like the United States. Worse still, governance tasks are likely to change over time in federal systems. If the governance unit is subject to somewhat fluid boundaries, so too is the nation.

The Nation

Stemming from the Latin verb *nasci*, to be born, the term 'nation' originally designated a group of people who were born in the same place. In the European universities of the late Middle Ages, 'nations' were groups of students who came from the same region or country (for one description, see Woolfson 1999). Somewhat later, a primary and a secondary meaning evolved. In eighteenth-century France a nation came to mean the people of a given country, without distinction of rank and often in contrast to the ruling monarch. In 1789–93 the three French estates merged in the National Assembly, abolishing the economic and political prerogatives of noblemen and clergy. Nation came to be the slogan of liberal republicans who wished to modernize society and to rationalize its governance. The secondary meaning of 'nation' referred to a strange people. The King James Bible distinguished between the 'people' of Israel and the 'nations' of gentiles. Initially the two meanings were distinct. However the defeat of monarchies in Europe from 1789 to 1914 led to a blending of the two meanings, for many nations now were proclaimed sovereign (Kedourie 1960: 13–14; Rustow 1968). Today, the terms 'nation' and 'state' are often used interchangeably, but nationalism cannot be understood when the meanings of these two terms are not kept distinct (Akzin 1966).

There is, however, an underlying core definition of the nation that has been enunciated by nearly every eminent scholarly and political authority on nationalism. Whatever else it may consist of, the term *nation* refers to a relatively large group of genetically unrelated people with high solidarity. Thus:

John Stuart Mill: A portion of mankind may be said to constitute a Nationality, if they are united among themselves by common sympathies, which do not exist between them and any others—which make them co-operate with each other more willingly than with other people, desire to be under the same government, and desire that it should be government by themselves, or a portion of themselves, exclusively (Mill 1861: 287).

Ernest Renan: A nation is a grand solidarity constituted by the sentiment of sacrifices which one has made and those that one is disposed to make again ... The existence of a nation ... is an everyday plebiscite ... The desire of nations to be together is the only real criterion that must always be taken into account (Renan [1882] 1994: 7).

Max Weber: In the sense of those using the term at a given time, the concept undoubtedly means, above all, that one may exact from certain groups of men a specific sentiment of solidarity in the face of other groups. Thus, the concept belongs in the sphere of values. Yet, there is no agreement on how these groups should be delimited or about what concerted action should result from such solidarity (Weber [1922] 1978: 922).

Josef Stalin: A nation is a historically constituted, stable community of people ... (Stalin [1942] 1994: 20)

Hans Kohn: Nationalism is first and foremost a state of mind, an act of con-sciousness ... The collective or group consciousness can center around entirely different groups, of which some have a more permanent character—the family, the class, the clan, the caste, the village, the sect, the religion, etc.—whereas others are of a more or less passing character—schoolmates, a football team, or passengers on a ship. In each case, varying with its permanence, this group-consciousness will strive towards creating homogeneity within the group, a conformity and like-mindedness which will lead to and facilitate concerted and common action (Kohn 1944: 11).

Karl Deutsch: Membership in a [nation] essentially consists in wide complementarity of social communication. It consists in the ability to communicate more effectively, and over a wider range of subjects, with members of one large group than with outsiders.... People are held together 'from within' by this communicative efficiency, the complementarity of the communicative facilities acquired by their members. Such 'ethnic complementarity' is not merely subjective. At any moment, it exists as an objective fact, measurable by performance tests. Similar to a person's knowledge of a language, it is relatively independent of the whim of individuals. Only slowly can it be learned or forgotten. It is a characteristic of each individual, but it can only be exercised within the context of a group (Deutsch 1966: 97).

David Miller: Nationality answers one of the most pressing needs of the modern world, namely how to maintain solidarity among the populations of states that are large and anonymous, such that their citizens cannot possibly enjoy the kind of community that relies on kinship or face-to-face interaction ... In societies in which economic markets play a central role, there is a strong tendency towards social atomisation, where each person looks out for the interests of herself and her immediate social network. As a result, it is difficult to get them to agree to practices of redistribution from which they are not likely personally to benefit, and so forth. These problems can be avoided only where there exists large-scale solidarity, such that people feel themselves to be members of an overarching community, and to have social duties to act for the common good of that community, to help out other members when they are in need, etc. Nationality is *de facto* the main source of such solidarity (Miller 1994: 22).

These statements could be supplemented by many more of the same ilk; many of the most important students of nationalism have a remarkably common conception of the term 'nation'. They all agree that, among other things, a nation is a large solidary group. Evidently, not all solidary groups are nations, however.

The Distinguishing Features of Nations

What distinguishes nations from other kinds of solidary groups, such as families, voluntary associations, religions, and formal organizations? Mill (1861: 287) believed that the principal distinction lies in the nation's history as a community of fate: its members have an 'identity of political antecedents; the possession of a national history, and consequent community of recollections; collective pride and humiliation, pleasure and regret, connected with the same incidents in the past'. Likewise, it has often been argued (Armstrong 1982; Smith 1986) that national solidarity is a byproduct of long histories of ethnic distinctiveness, of the myths and symbols of ethnically distinct peoples. Following Kohn (1944) and Deutsch (1966), Anderson (1983) suggests that the solidarity of nations required the development of new communication technologies—among which 'print capitalism' takes pride of place—that promote interaction between parochial social groups formerly mired in purely local social networks. Stalin believed that the solidarity of nations is invariably produced by a conjunction of linguistic and other objective group characteristics: for him a nation is a community formed on the basis of a common language, territory, economic life, and psychological make-up manifested in a common culture.

The idea that nationality is necessarily owed to the existence of objective differentiae such as language and religion—one shared by Wilson and Stalin—has faded. None of these tangible group characteristics necessarily produces national solidarity: language is constitutive of national identity in some places but not in others, religion is constitutive of national identity in some places but not in others, and so forth.[23] Nowadays it is fashionable to insist on the intersubjectivity of nationality. Rather than the deterministic outcome of given social conditions, nations are increasingly regarded as entities that are socially constructed (Chatterjee 1993; Eley and Suny 1996a). On this view, certain kinds of social conditions indeed may be necessary for the emergence of nations, but without the leavening of the nationalist ideal the potential will be unrealized.

Far from a new insight, this subjectivist conception of nations—often counterposed to the ostensibly crude sociological view of these matters—actually has deep roots in classical sociological theory. For Weber ([1922] 1978: 922), 'If the concept of "nation" can in any way be defined unambiguously, it certainly cannot be stated in terms of empirical qualities common to those who count as members of the nation.' The source of nationhood, for Weber, is not to be found in the objective differentiae of language and religious practice that might happen to separate the members of two different groups, but in the intersubjective awareness that the salient intergroup differences, whatever they might be, are sufficient to demarcate two nations. Durkheim's ([1912] 1965) analysis of the concept of the sacred is strikingly reminiscent of Weber's ruminations about the nation. For Durkheim, the sacredness of an object does not lie in any of its objective features, but rather in the attitude of respect that individuals manifest in their dealings with it.

Despite this, territoriality is one objective criterion that does seem to be a necessary characteristic of the nation. The presence of a real or putative homeland is properly regarded as a defining feature of the nation.[24]

Nations tend to be larger than other kinds of solidary groups, save perhaps for religious ones. More than other kinds of solidary groups, nations have an elaborated sense of collective history: all have some socially sanctioned 'story' of the people, as revealed in oral and musical traditions, history textbooks, and other publicly available sources. This, in turn, implies the existence of some social recognition of the national category, which leads to an available social identity. Of course, this social identity need not be salient to all members. A minimal requirement for the self-consciousness of any kind of group is its members' awareness of at least one alternative group offering similar collective goods (such as protection from confiscation or predation). This suggests that nations are never found in isolation (Evans-Pritchard 1944; Sahlins 1989: 271).[25] Whereas large size and a sense of collective history are shared both by nations and ethnic groups, the last element, territoriality, is sufficient to distinguish nations from ethnic groups.

Nations therefore constitute a subset of ethnic groups. They are territorially concentrated ethnic groups (like the Quebecois and the Kurds), rather than ethnic groups—like American Jews, Algerians in France, and others often termed *minorities*—who are spatially dispersed in a given state.[26] Since nations are primarily concentrated in a territory they consider to be their homeland, they can pose a realistic threat of attaining sovereignty by becoming independent polities (Haas 1997).[27] The final advantage of the present definition is that it can accommodate the basic types of nationalism in history.

Types of Nationalism

It is widely appreciated that there are important differences between nationalist movements. Much effort has been made to create typologies that aim to capture some of the relevant distinctions (see, for example, Hall 1993). Most of these distinguish the liberal, culturally inclusive (Sleeping Beauty) nationalisms characteristic of Western Europe from the illiberal, culturally exclusive (Frankenstein's monster) nationalisms more often found elsewhere. Whereas these normative differences between nationalist movements have been enormously important in history, it is doubtful that they can be explained if the dimensions of nationalism are chosen on normative grounds. To explain why nationalism has taken such different forms in different societies, it is better to seek a typology that is derived from analytical considerations.

If nationalism is collective action designed to render the boundaries of the nation congruent with those of its governance unit, then a simple analytic typology of nationalism flows directly out of this definition (see Figure 1.1). Further, this typology helps account for the normative differences between types of nationalism.

State-building nationalism is the nationalism that is embodied in the attempt to assimilate or incorporate culturally distinctive territories in a given state. It is the result of the conscious efforts of central rulers to make a multicultural population culturally homogeneous. Thus, beginning in the sixteenth century and continuing into the twentieth, the rulers of England and France attempted—fitfully perhaps, and with more or less success—to foster homogeneity in their realms by inducing culturally distinctive populations in each country's Celtic regions to assimilate to their own culture. Since the rationale for state-building nationalism is often geopolitical—to secure borders from real or potential

State wants to expand and incorporate

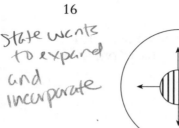

Territory resists incorporation

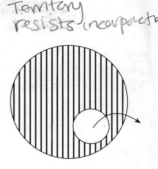

State-Building Nationalism

Peripheral Nationalism

State wants to extend boundaries

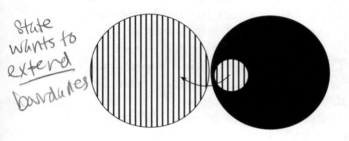

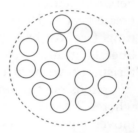

Irredentist Nationalism

Unification Nationalism

State wants to unify into a nation

state / nation boundaries are already congruent

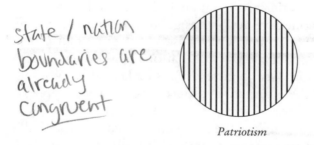

Patriotism

FIG. 1.1. The Types of Nationalism, and Patriotism

rivals—this kind of nationalism tends to be culturally inclusive. However, much less liberal means of skinning a culturally homogeneous cat have been resorted to in history, as well. Central rulers of a given culture also can unify their country by expelling culturally alien populations (as in the Spanish *Reconquista*), or by exterminating them (often the fate of the indigenous peoples of North America).

Peripheral nationalism occurs when a culturally distinctive territory resists incorporation into an expanding state, or attempts to secede and set up its own government (as in Quebec, Scotland and Catalonia). Often this type of nationalism is spurred by the very efforts at state-building nationalism described above.

Irredentist nationalism occurs with the attempt to extend the existing boundaries of a state by incorporating territories of an adjacent state occupied principally by co-nationals (as in the case of the Sudeten Germans).

Finally, *unification nationalism* involves the merger of a politically divided but culturally homogeneous territory into one state, as famously occurred in nineteenth-century Germany and Italy. In this case, the effort to render cultural and governance boundaries congruent requires the establishment of a new state encompassing the members of the nation. Whereas state-building nationalism tends to be culturally inclusive, unification nationalism is often culturally exclusive.[28]

Although *patriotism*—the desire to raise the prestige and power of one's own nation state relative to rivals in the international system—is often considered to be nationalistic, the present definition rules this usage out. Patriotism is no form of nationalism at all, for here the boundaries of the nation and governance unit are already congruent. This limitation is not, however, very damaging. Since few states, if any, qualify as nation states, patriotism (as defined in this book) hardly exists. Most of what passes as patriotism in common parlance implicitly advances the interests of one nation at the expense of others in multinational states. In the present framework, such activities are instances of state-building nationalism.

The preceding typology is not exhaustive. It has no place for nationalist movements—like Zionism and Mormonism—that resulted from the migration of religious groups to distant promised lands. Such movements have been exceedingly rare, however. Now that nationalism has been defined, and its main types distinguished, the following chapter will present an overview of the argument of the book.

CHAPTER 2

Causes of Nationalism

SINCE nationalism is such a powerful force in the modern world, and one that is too often implicated in terrible acts of violence, there is a pervasive interest in containing its dark side. Both states and international bodies like the United Nations currently invest considerable resources to this end. The efficacy of these interventions is questionable, however. Doubtless, we would be more confident about measures to contain nationalism if the conditions responsible for its development were better appreciated.

What might contain the dark side of nationalism? One solution is to grant nationalists their wish—self-determination.[1] Since doing so would set a precedent that might unravel most existing states, however, this idea is a non-starter. Short of granting self-determination, nationalism can be mitigated by intervening in three general processes. The first of these is nation-formation. As nations are the basis of nationalism, anything that decreases their salience perforce must reduce its scope. One means of containing nationalism, therefore, is by enacting measures that erode the social base of nations. This requires an appreciation of the underlying mechanisms responsible for group formation, group solidarity, and the development of national identity.

Yet the mere existence of nations has no necessary implications for nationalism. Nations that do not crave their own state apparatus pose no threat to the social order. Nationalism ultimately rests on the demand for national sovereignty. Hence a second means of containing nationalism is by reducing this demand. Conditions that lower the demand for sovereignty include the establishment of indirect rule and other state institutions that are responsive to the distinctive values of national groups.

A third means of containing nationalism is by raising the costs of collective action. This strategy can be effective, at least for a time, even if interventions in the first two processes have failed or not been attempted. The demand for sovereignty will not be very compelling if members of national groups face high costs of collective action. These costs tend vary both across time and between societies; they are largely determined by the state of available technology, the society's political institutions, and by the nature of the geopolitical environment.

If the principles underlying these three processes have been correctly identified, then it should be possible to answer three critical questions about nationalism. First, why has nationalism mostly been confined to the last two centuries of history? Second, what kinds of people tend to become nationalists? Last, what specific institutions are likely to effectively curtail nationalist excesses? This chapter provides an overview of the argument that is developed in greater detail in the remainder of the book.

The Formation of Groups

If the nation is a relatively large and territorially concentrated ethnic group with a sense of common history and a putative homeland, then how does it arise? As has been seen, the nation is a distinctive kind of large, solidary group. However, the existence of nations—like that of all solidary groups—is problematic. To understand the genesis of nations, therefore, the mechanisms responsible for the formation of any kind of group must first be understood.

Humans are often considered to be social animals.[2] Yet if people are inherently so sociable, then why is only the smallest of groups, the nuclear family, found in all human societies? Evolutionary theory provides a powerful answer to this question.[3] If people act in such a way as to maximize their genetic fitness, as evolutionary theory teaches us, then they will behave nepotistically and favour genetically proximate relatives over more distant ones. Under certain conditions people might even aid close kin at considerable personal expense.[4]

Whenever cooperation extends beyond networks of close kin and people act on the basis of charity, duty, or civic obligation, however, inclusive fitness cannot be the explanation.[5] The family is universal in human societies, but people do not necessarily form other kinds of groups because the costs of doing so sometimes outweigh the benefits.[6]

The principal benefit of group formation lies in the concentration of individually held resources. By pooling at least some of their own resources, people can provide themselves with jointly produced goods—including security from predation or confiscation, cooperative production of food, insurance from natural disasters, and greater access to information and mates—that they cannot produce through their own individual efforts. Pooling also encourages specialization, which enables such goods to be produced more efficiently. The demand for such joint goods serves as a focal point that enables otherwise disconnected individuals to imagine themselves in a common situation and, on this account, to identify a single course of action that their expectations of each other can converge on (Schelling 1960: 54).

Of course, producing joint goods entails cooperation. As Hobbes recognized long ago, this cooperation can be costly. The principal cost of forming a group is the subsequent loss of individual autonomy. To obtain the joint good that is the group's *raison d'être*, participants are obliged to comply with rules that are required to produce the given good. Sometimes this obligation conflicts with the member's other (more preferred) interests. Thus someone may prefer to spend an afternoon fishing rather than standing guard around the village perimeter. In addition, participation in groups often subjects people to invidious status ranking and other forms of competition. These costs of cooperation lead people to be wary of joining existing groups, let alone forming new ones.

Therefore group formation often occurs in the face of uncertainties of physical security and food production.[7] Perhaps the most fundamental kind of group is that formed to provide its members with mutual insurance.[8] A particularly apt example is provided by the !Kung San of the Kalahari, whose desert environment makes them especially dependent on water. During rainy seasons, when water is plentiful, nuclear families scatter in mutual isolation. During dry seasons, however, water is only available in water-holes. To gain access to water in dry seasons, therefore, individual families are compelled to cluster around water-holes and enter into social relations with one another, forming temporary multiple-family groups (Johnson and Earle 1987: 38–54).[9]

Elsewhere, people living in riverine areas subject to periodic flooding benefit from irrigation, another kind of joint good. This may help explain why the first civilizations arose in the riverine areas of the Fertile Crescent (Pfeiffer 1977). Similarly, long-standing common property resource institutions arise in uncertain environments in Switzerland, Japan, Spain, and the Philippines (Ostrom 1990). In the Swiss mountain commons, the location and timing of rainfall is unpredictable (Netting 1981). In medieval Valencia, which established irrigation systems, erratic rainfall is also a major source of uncertainty (Glick 1970).

These are some of the kinds of conditions that foster group formation, but the resulting groups will have more or less solidarity.

The Determinants of Group Solidarity

The greater the proportion of each member's resources contributed to the group's ends, the greater the group's solidarity (Hechter 1987: 18). Solidarity may be necessary for group maintenance, but it is also insufficient—even highly solidary groups can succumb to the predation of external enemies.

What accounts for variations in group solidarity? All members value the group's joint good (else why would they voluntarily join?), but it is more valuable to some members than others. The greater the value of the joint good, and the less it is available outside group boundaries, the more *dependent* members are on the group. Groups whose members, on average, are highly dependent can demand more of those members, in terms of corporate obligations, than those who are less dependent.

Even though they may place great value on the joint good, however, members none the less may prefer to free ride and consume the good without contributing to its production (Olson 1965). If they are contingent cooperators (Axelrod 1984; Bendor and Swistak 1997), they will demand assurances that their contribution will not be squandered by free riders or those who take more than their fair share. Both types of people will only be willing to help produce the joint good if they believe that others are unable to free ride. Hence maintaining a continuous supply of the joint good requires the establishment of social *controls*—monitoring and sanctioning institutions—that discourage free riding.[10] The purpose of these controls is not only to discourage members from free riding. They will not be instituted unless they also reduce the controller's ability to confiscate members' property (Barzel 1999). Despite this, the nature of these controls may be obscure to group members themselves.[11]

Now, however, a new problem arises.[12] Since these institutions of control are themselves collective goods, why would individuals ever establish them? Why, in other words, would anyone voluntarily seek to control other members? In some circumstances monitoring and sanctioning are not very costly activities and thus are well worth the effort. Visibility in the production and consumption of joint goods is one such condition. If the joint good is to be kept out of the hands of non-contributors, its production and distribution must be highly visible—otherwise, neither free riding (a production problem) nor overconsumption of the good (a distribution problem) can be precluded. Production visibility is at a maximum when individual effort can be well-measured by output assessment. Distribution visibility, however, is at a maximum when individuals must draw measurable shares of the joint good publicly from some central repository.

Many groups produce joint goods merely by pooling individual assets so that a common store, or bank, is created. The individual depositor then has a right to draw on some portion of the common pool as a private good in the event of the relevant need. In technologically primitive conditions, visibility is at a maximum when joint goods are collected and disbursed from some central place.[13] Under these conditions, all members will voluntarily take on this control burden in order to safeguard their investments (Hechter 1990*a*: 20).

Because social controls specify who has access to the joint good, they invariably establish social boundaries. The very act of keeping non-contributors from consuming the joint good establishes a kind of territoriality (Sack 1986: 59–60).[14] When production is based on cultivation, the territoriality extends from a social to a physical boundary.[15] The crucial point is that boundaries between groups initially flow from institutions of control rather than from already pre-established social identities. Hence, identities are derived from boundaries rather than vice versa. All told, then, variations in group solidarity are a function of dependence and control mechanisms. Groups with highly dependent members which have extensive control capacity will have the highest solidarity.

The implications of this discussion for the formation and solidarity of nations are clear. Nations, it will be recalled, are spatially concentrated groups that are perceived—both by outsiders and insiders—as distinctive. This cultural distinctiveness arises from the existence of certain common practices and beliefs—including, but not limited to, those involving language, religion, and mode of production most generally—that differ from those adopted by other groups in a given environment. According to the preceding analysis, nations form to preserve and promote these practices and beliefs in the face of rivals. *Thus the articulation and promotion of culturally distinctive institutions is the joint good that lies at the core of nation-formation.*

Once they are formed, however, nations are far from equally solidary. Since solidarity depends on the average of individuals' contributions to joint goods, then the greater the commonality of practices and beliefs in a given nation, the greater its solidarity. In the absence of collective action, specialized practices and beliefs evolve as adaptations to micro-ecologies. Even if they have the same language and religion, the members of a tribe who cultivate on a hillside are likely to have somewhat different agricultural practices—different ploughs or field systems—than the cultivators in a valley. Since micro-ecological variations lead to cultural differences, common practices and beliefs are initially found only in the smallest of groups.

The builders of nations must overcome these (relatively minor) cultural differences. They attempt to do so by promulgating an arbitrary set of culturally distinctive practices and beliefs, including some sanctioned story of the nation, as a standard to be adopted throughout the territory. Although this task is ultimately educational, it can proceed, in the absence of formal schools, on the basis of oral tradition or written texts. It only succeeds, however, to the degree that the target population is dependent on the nation-builders, and that these nation-builders have the capacity to monitor and sanction their dependants (see Chapter 6). These general principles help provide answers to the three questions posed at the beginning of this chapter.

Why is Nationalism Modern?

Most scholars agree that nationalism is a creature only of the past 200 years of history. For the vast bulk of time following the emergence of humankind—over 99 per cent of human history (Service 1975: 5)—people lived in small groups that engaged in hunting and gathering. Since hunting and gathering societies are small local groups numbering fifty or less (and often non-territorial, to boot) they cannot qualify as nations for these reasons alone. Nations are inconceivable prior to the neolithic revolution, which led to settled villages based on the domestication of plants and animals.

No doubt, the rise of agriculture was associated with firmer conceptions of property rights, and thus strengthened the territoriality of local groups. Since nations are large and pan-local, however, they require a setting that encourages such independent local groups to engage in routine, regular, and relatively non-competitive contact.[16] The exchange of wives and commodities was essential for the formation of pan-local groups. Ultimately, the establishment of multicultural agrarian empires, such as the Roman and Chinese, and later the Habsburg and Ottoman, provided the most favourable conditions for nation formation.[17] This is because the order imposed by imperial rule spurred military, cultural, and economic exchanges between localities. The size and scope of pan-local groups could substantially increase with the invention of printing (Anderson 1983), advances in transportation infrastructure (including the building of roads and harbours, and communications technology.[18] For all these reasons, industrialization provided an even greater impetus to nation formation.

Still, these purely technical conditions by themselves are insufficient to account for the emergence of nations. They do not necessarily preordain a sense of common history, a concept of the homeland, or any of the other aforementioned requirements of nationhood. National sentiments tend to be inculcated by schools. And universal public schooling is largely an invention of the nineteenth century, at least in Western Europe and its American and Australasian cultural offshoots.

If multicultural agrarian empires created the conditions for nation-formation, and if some of these empires are thousands of years old, why then is nationalism confined to the last two centuries of history? The answer is simple. Even when great agrarian empires afforded the conditions for the emergence of the first nations, they generally did not provide a strong motive for the development of nation*alism*. Missing was the demand for national self-determination.

It is not at all obvious why a nation would desire to have its own government. By definition, nations are culturally distinctive—more precisely, their members consider them to be so. This cultural distinctiveness is likely to be expressed in a complex stew of religious beliefs, as well as linguistic and consummatory practices. Thus, for breakfast the French hanker after butter croissants, the English cold toast, and the Cantonese congee. At a minimum, the existence of cultural distinctiveness suggests that individuals of a given nationality have certain values in common. No doubt, the prominence of these culturally specific values varies from person to person. Despite this, these individuals' value schedules will tend to have some common arguments derived from the national culture, in addition to other common arguments relating to wealth, power, and prestige (Hechter 1994*b*).

These distinctive values have implications for governance. In the final analysis, the rationale of any government is to provide citizens and subjects with collective goods entailed in the enactment of law, the protection of personal safety and public order, the protection of vested rights, the cultivation of hygienic, social-welfare, and cultural interests, and the organized armed protection against outside attack (Weber [1922] 1978: 905). Some of these goods (like garbage collection) are discrete; therefore their quality can be rather readily assessed. It is easy to perceive when goods of this kind are provided inadequately. Other collective goods (like education, justice, or defence), however, are neither very discrete, nor can their quality be so easily assessed. Such goods are better provided locally than centrally. When the goods are provided locally, it is more likely that the right mix of goods—the mix that is most consistent with the distinctive values of the nation—will be provided. Local provision also increases the accountability of the suppliers.

There is no motive for nationalism when the boundaries of the nation and the governance unit are congruent, for then the nation *already* has self-determination. This was the situation characteristic of the great agrarian empires prior to the nineteenth century. But how can this be? Surely these empires encompassed various nations within their borders. Hence, the boundaries between the polity and the nation could hardly have been congruent (McNeill 1986). If so, then nationalism should have been commonplace in premodern agrarian empires.

It is essential to avoid confusion at this point. The motive for nationalism only exists when the boundaries between the *governance unit* and the nation are not congruent. This implies nothing whatever about the congruence between the boundaries of the *state* and the nation, however. Under certain conditions the boundaries between the state and the nation can be non-congruent *without* providing a motive for nationalism. To understand why, we must look further into the structure of governance.

Recall that a governance unit is that agency providing the bulk of collective goods—including social order, protection from confiscation, dispute resolution, and welfare—directly to its own members. In the modern world, it is often assumed that governance units are states, the specialized political institutions responsible for ruling a bounded territory.

Not all states are governance units, however. In fact, prior to the last two centuries most states (including virtually all empires) were not governance units at all. Before the advent of modern commun-ications technology, no central ruler had the capacity to enforce his will on territories at a spatial remove. Empires and premodern states resorted to a mix of governance strategies throughout their realms. Regions closest at hand to the court often could be ruled directly by the centre (in feudal states, they often constituted the king's demesne). For regions at a distance, however, the centre was compelled to rely on some form of *indirect rule* (Chapter 3).

The basic idea behind indirect rule is simple enough.[19] Since the central ruler of a geographically extensive state cannot control far-flung territories and populations by himself, he is compelled to delegate authority to agents for this purpose.[20] This delegation of authority permits the central ruler to exert limited control over extensive territories and populations and provides him with the resources to defend and extend his territory in the event of war.

Although central rulers nominally claim ultimate authority throughout their realm, in more remote regions the agents typ-ically reserve the *de facto* right to govern their own territory as they choose. In return for this privilege, they compensate the central ruler (in tribute, taxes, or payments in kind) and accept the obligation to provide some level of military service in the event of war. The agents can be recruited from two quite different sources. Sometimes the ruler selects a culturally alien agent in reward for faithful service (as when Cromwell granted newly conquered lands in Ireland to his generals). At other times the traditional authority in the territory is selected as the central ruler's agent.

Why would such traditional authorities ever agree to surrender some of their sovereignty to the central ruler? To obtain protec-tion from rivals both near and far. Although the forms of indirect rule—its detailed institutional arrangements—vary enormously from Western European feudalism to colonial rule in Africa and Asia, this basic management strategy lies at the heart of all feudal, patrimonial, and colonial systems of rule prior to industrialization. Indeed, until the development of modern communications technology, some form of indirect rule was the *only* means of governing large territories and populations.

Indirect rule thwarts nationalism. It does so, however, on the basis of two distinct mechanisms. Whereas one mechanism inhibits nationalism by reducing the demand for sovereignty among the members of culturally distinct groups, the other merely increases the cost of collective action across the board. Both mechanisms lead to the same result. It follows that nationalism is most likely to emerge following the breakdown of indirect rule. Indirect rule can be eroded in two quite different ways: due to the rise of direct rule, and due to the collapse of the centre in a multinational empire.

The first cause of the breakdown of indirect rule is its replacement by direct rule (Chapter 4). Under direct rule, the centre assumes full responsibility for governing the entire polity.[21] Direct rule fosters economic change by standardizing coinage, weights, and measures, and by removing interregional barriers to trade and migration (Heckscher 1955; Wallerstein 1974: ch. 3). It facilitates communications, thereby extending the reach of markets. Urbanization and industrialization are spurred in its wake. At the same time, it brings about significant political changes, for it erodes the power of local authorities. By shifting dependence from local to central authorities, direct rule lays the groundwork for all types of nationalism. By destroying the previous basis of social order, direct rule encourages central authorities to engage in *state-building nationalism* (Chapter 4). To legitimize the new order, state-builders attempt to erode the base of peripheral nations by fostering cultural homogeneity through public education and other policies. At the same time, the growth of direct rule provides local authorities with a strong interest in mobilizing populations dependent on them to protect their extensive rights and prerogatives.[22] This interest often underlies *peripheral nationalism* (Chapter 5). Finally, the military success of states that have instituted direct rule offers an incentive for others to engage in *unification nationalism*.

Another source of weakened indirect rule results from the collapse of the centre in a multinational empire. Indirect rule is the outcome of a bargain between the central ruler and his distal agent, the local authority. Under the terms of this bargain, the local authority pays tribute to the central ruler in return for protection and other centrally provided goods. However, should the efficacy of the central ruler decline (say, as a result of his military defeat), the bargain loses value for the local authority. Given no substitute ruler, the local authority is likely to abrogate his part of the bargain.

In culturally distinct territories, this often brings nationalism in its wake. Since local authorities in a system of indirect rule already control the territory's administrative apparatus, they have resources that can be used to mobilize their dependants. Sometimes they can make credible claims to secede. Examples abound in the historical record. By demonstrating the military vulnerability of many European central rulers, Napoleon paved the way for nationalism from Spain in the west to the Balkans in the east. Most recently, the collapse of the Soviet Union in 1989 unleashed nationalism throughout much of its former empire.

Direct rule only becomes technically possible after the development (and adoption) of modern communications technology—roads, rail, steam engines and the other accoutrements of the industrial revolution. Due to technical limitations, however, no existing state fully employs direct rule, though France probably comes the closest to doing so. In so far as industrialization provides the technology necessary for the growth of direct rule, it indeed serves as a distal condition for the development of nationalism (as Gellner 1983 argues). But there is no necessary link between industrialization and nationalism: industrialized societies (like Switzerland and Canada) can adopt institutional arrangements that provide indirect rule in forms such as federation. All told, nationalism is only likely to come on to the historical stage with the rise of direct rule. This explains why nationalism is a creature of the last two centuries.

Who are the Nationalists?

Even when the boundaries of the nation and the governance unit are not congruent, this by no means foreordains nationalism. What is it about the location of these two boundaries that might motivate individuals to engage in collective action? Nationalism rests on the belief—or better yet, the ideal—that individual members of the nation would be better off with self-determination than without it.[23] By no means does this imply that the benefits of self-determination need be exclusively material, for people are also motivated to pursue ideal interests. Given the plasticity of individual values, is it possible to predict what kinds people will hew to the nationalist ideal? To some degree, yes (Chapter 6).

People who expect that their wealth, power, or prestige will increase from self-determination are those most likely to support nationalism (Hechter 1994*b*). To the degree that interests flow from one's position in the social structure, then certain kinds of people will be the usual suspects. First, consider local élites—indirect rulers, rival political entrepreneurs, and the culturally distinct intelligentsia—who face the growing power of a *strengthening* central state. As direct rule progresses, these people may deploy their resources to establish nationalist movements in hope of retaining their position. The greater their influence over subject populations, the more their ability to mount a nationalist challenge to the centre.[24]

Local élites who face a *declining* central state may grasp an opportunity to enhance their authority, as well. The purveyors of distinctive cultural goods—such as language and literature teachers and the clergy of a distinctive national religion—are especially likely to believe that national self-determination will redound to their personal benefit (Breton 1964).[25] Individuals in these circumstances imagine that their own prospects will improve if the rights to certain kinds of jobs—especially government jobs—are reserved for nationals (Johnson 1965: 178).[26]

The appeal of nationalism rests on the presumption that a government that is run by one's co-nationals will enact superior policies.[27] These policies may be preferable for material reasons, ideal ones, or some combination of the two. To the degree that a regional population has distinct preferences, self-determination is likely to increase citizens' welfare by encouraging policies that are responsive to these preferences.[28] Beyond this, however, it is possible to provide several more specific answers. For example, nationalism will have less appeal to the members of privileged groups in states with little redistribution; such regimes will be regarded as guarantors of their privilege. Thus Southern slaveholders were among the most steadfast supporters of the Confederacy. By the same token, the loyalty of privileged groups in states with extensive redistribution cannot be taken for granted. The secessionist Lega Nord of Italy argues that the taxes of rich northerners should not be diverted to the impoverished Mezzogiorno. Similar sentiments fuelled nationalism in oil-rich Scotland and Biafra. In addition, nationalism is likely to appeal to those who believe they are disadvantaged by virtue of their cultural distinctiveness.

Nationalism based on individual interests should wax and wane with personal circumstances. Therefore, it ought to be susceptible to shifts in state policy that accommodate nationalist demands or redress grievances. It also ought to be vulnerable to cooptation.

Whereas positing a link between nationalism and individual interest is unremarkable, the claim that nationalism may also flow from identity rather than from interest *tout court* is more controversial. On this view, individuals having a strong sense of national identity expect to reap net psychic benefits from sovereignty. Thus they may be willing to sacrifice material advantages to attain it (Calhoun 1991).[29] Since identities change much less readily than interests, such identity-based nationalism should not be so highly responsive to shifts in government policy.

It is not so much that life in a society dominated by one's conationals is invariably happy. Just the opposite. People dislike receiving poor treatment merely on account of a trait they are powerless to alter. This motivation is so strong that it helps explain the extremely high rates of social homogeneity that are typical of voluntary associations (Blau 1977).

Since the state is not a voluntary association, however, unhappy citizens cannot easily leave it in the face of discrimination, whether overt or subtle. Those lucky enough to belong to a nation with its own state can emigrate, if they are permitted to do so, if they qualify for citizenship in the destination state, and if they can bear the costs of moving. But, however costly, emigration is rarely an option for the members of stateless nations. Hence nationalism may be the best response to this limitation on exit. All things equal, therefore, nationalism should be more likely to emerge among the members of stateless nations, such as the Welsh, Palestinians, Kurds, and Uighurs, than among minorities—like the overseas Chinese, Armenians, Irish, and Jews (since the establishment of Israel)—whose nations already control an existing state.[30]

Social identity is that part of the individual's self-concept emanating from membership in groups. Complex societies afford people a wealth of different social identities to choose among (Simmel [1922] 1955a). They can identify with groups that crystallize on the basis of any number of characteristics, whether ascribed or achieved, including gender, nationality, class and sexual orientation. Why people identify with some of these groups at the expense of others is a question that has been intensively studied in social psychology. One leading view is that people attempt to increase their self-esteem by trying to achieve a positive social identity. Since social identities have differential prestige, it follows that the higher a given group's prestige, the more that membership in it contributes to individual self-esteem. Therefore, the stratification of cultural groups turns out to be a key determinant of the relative salience of social identities. Whereas interests stem largely from an *individual's* position in the social structure, identities stem largely from the position of their *group*. Imagine an industrial city in Quebec entirely composed of Roman Catholics. If most of the Francophones in this town are condemned to be workers in the local factories, and most of the Anglophones expect to become managers and professionals, then language will be a more salient social identity than religion in this city.

If the preceding analysis suggests some of the most common reasons why people may be attracted to nationalism, it offers no means of predicting either the emergence of nationalism or its intensity. In the first place, nationalism is parasitic on the demand for sovereignty (Chapter 7). In the second place, nationalism—like all other forms of collective action—is inhibited by free riding and other problems. Even though social scientists do not yet have an adequate understanding of collective action, some of its important determinants have been established (Hardin 1981; Lichbach 1995; Olson 1965; Udéhn 1996). Since sovereignty is a collective good, it will not tend to be produced unless the national group has adequate mechanisms of dependence and control. Beyond this, the intensity of nationalism cannot be determined independent of the tactical strategies undertaken by nationalist leaders.

What Institutions can Contain Nationalism?

Since violence is a too-frequent by-product of nationalist conflict, there is a pervasive interest in containing this aspect of nationalism. Are there any means of doing so? This depends on the sources of the violence. To the degree that violence is non-instrumental, then institutional interventions cannot reduce it (Hechter 1995). To the degree that violence is enacted strategically, however, the prognosis for containing nationalism is not nearly so pessimistic. Whereas some kinds of institutional arrangements provide incentives for intergroup conflict, others promote cooperation. Consociationalism, cantonalism, and federation all have been proposed as solutions to nationalist conflict, but none of them necessarily achieves this. That can only be done by institutions providing decentralized decision-making within multinational states (Chapter 8).

Finally, those multinational regimes that routinely comply with norms of procedural justice are less likely to witness nationalism. Whereas the subjects in traditional societies expect their rulers' behaviour to be constrained by custom rather than by formal criteria, direct rule leads to the establishment of state-wide defence, dispute-resolution, and welfare institutions (such as schools). Usually these are organized bureaucratically. At least in theory, bureaucracy heightens expectations that state-provided goods (including government jobs and access to universities) will be allocated on some culturally neutral basis. When these expectations are not met (for example, when government jobs or transfer payments consistently go to members of one nation at the expense of another), this gives members of the aggrieved group an interest in self-determination.[31] Following the erosion of central rule, concerns about intergroup distributive and procedural justice are likely to increase. People are wont to ask, 'If group X gains power, what assurance do we have that they will look after my interests and those of my family and friends?' This uncertainty increases their receptiveness to the nationalist ideal.

CHAPTER 3

Indirect Rule and the Absence of Nationalism

NEARLY everyone regards nationalism as a modern phenomenon. Prior to the nineteenth century, some visionaries may have professed nationalist ideals, but never the majority of people in any society. Still, the reasons for its modernity are far from clear.

On one view, nationalism's modernity derives from new ideas and conceptions that emerged in the nineteenth century. Some consider nationalism to have been an unintended consequence of the French Revolution (Kedourie 1960: 12–13). In the course of the Revolution, so the story goes, the nation came to be understood as that body of persons who could claim to represent a particular territory at councils, diets, or estates. In contrast, others discern its roots not in revolutionary France, but in German romanticism of the 1820s (Berlin 1992: 175–206). Prior to this period the idea of universal values held sway, but romanticism fostered the novel conception that values were multiple and incommensurable. Such a conception was needed to legitimate the assertion of parochial, national values. If nationalism is modern, then no doubt it was associated with new ideas, but the popularity of these ideas requires its own explanation.

The modernity of nationalism has also been explained as a consequence of the rise of new social structures in the wake of industrialization (Gellner 1983). On this view, preindustrial societies had no nationalism because their élites and masses were always separated along class lines. The high culture of the élites clashed with the low culture of the masses and precluded the development of an ideology that could overcome this class divide. Industrialization erodes this cultural dualism, however, because it requires a mobile, literate, technologically sophisticated labour force. The modern state is the only agency capable of producing such a labour force. It does so principally by establishing mass public education systems. As industrialization spreads unevenly from its regions of origin, it uproots traditional ways of life, throwing many people out of familiar small-scale social structures into anonymous urban settings. If newcomers to the cities are not assimilated into the dominant culture, then nationalism (somehow) will come about.

It is easy to think of counter-examples, however. Nationalism often arises in non-industrial settings: on the Indian subcontinent, in sub-Saharan Africa, and in the heart of Central Asia. In some places (as in Catalonia) it unites different classes, while in others (the Basque Country) it divides them (Diez-Medrano 1995; Evans and Duffy 1997).

This book proposes an alternative explanation. If nationalism is collective action designed to make the boundaries of the nation and governance unit congruent, then it can only emerge when there is a disjuncture between the boundaries of the nation and those of the governance unit. For the great bulk of human history no such disjuncture existed, however.

The first groups to evolve—families, camps, hamlets—had less than fifty members and no specialized governance institutions (Johnson and Earle 1987). Local groups evolved next; they numbered several hundreds of members and constituted loose alliances of smaller solidary groups (Earle 1997). Nationalism cannot arise in such societies, if only because they have no separate governance units.

Nationalism requires some kind of state—a specialized institution responsible for protection, dispute resolution, and redistribution. Although the first states were very small, some ancient ones—like those in China and Java—came to rule over millions of people. Since they had both separate governance structures and culturally and spatially concentrated populations, these premodern states should have been ripe for nationalism.[1] Yet little nationalism, if any, emerged in them.

What inhibited nationalism in the premodern state? The answer is indirect rule. It thwarted nationalism because it often made the nation congruent with its governance unit. The disjuncture between these two elements that is required for nationalism only arose with direct rule. Since direct rule did not make its initial appearance until the nineteenth century, this is principally why nationalism is a modern phenomenon.

The first part of this chapter therefore sets out to understand reasons for the ubiquity of indirect rule previous to the nineteenth century. It argues that indirect rule becomes the dominant state form because it reduces the cost of governance in large societies. The second part of the chapter discusses why indirect rule inhibits nationalism.

The Rise of Indirect Rule: A Theory of Primary State Formation

If nationalism cannot arise without the state, then how does the state emerge? Primary states emerge spontaneously among individuals and groups having had no previous concept of the state (Fried 1967; Cohen and Service 1978).[2] In contrast, secondary states arise when already-extant state forms are introduced into a given territory from without, usually as a result of conquest. The analysis of group formation in the previous chapter holds an important clue for the development of primary states.

Consider a number of highly solidary groups rubbing shoulders, so to speak, in the same territory.[3] Although they will tend to routinely interact with neighbouring groups for the purpose of marriage and exchange, there is no reason to expect that these groups will always coexist peacefully (Gamble 1986: 41–7). Instead, on occasion some may use force to appropriate resources from others.[4] To the degree that the respective groups have different cultures and modes of production, then subjugation is likely to replace theft as a motive for the use of force. This predation represents the greatest continual threat to a group's welfare. Thus, when a group of Scots encountered a group of English in the borderland in 1138, 'The [English] men were all killed, the maids and widows, naked, bound with ropes, were driven off to Scotland in crowds to the yoke of slavery' (Bartlett 1994: 80).[5] One can be sure that, soon after, the English returned the favour. Similarly gruesome stories can be found from all parts of the globe.[6]

The members of all such groups would be better off if they could be protected from predation. Hence there will be a demand for social order in the territory (cf. Johnson 1982, who suggests this demand is likely to be triggered by population growth alone). To the degree that subjugation is a threat, this demand will increase. As Hobbes argued, protection could be provided if everyone could agree to erect a state endowed with police powers. But how can such a state ever be established voluntarily?[7] Social order is a collective good that is notoriously vulnerable to free riding.

To forestall intergroup violence, the groups must remain internally solidary and at the same time establish an institution that binds them together externally. In Chapter 2, I explained how individuals could form insurance groups to provide themselves with desired goods like protection. The present situation is in many respects analogous. But there is one significant difference. Whereas the previous problem concerned individual collective action, this one concerns collective action among groups. Does this difference rule out the analogy? Not necessarily. The group-formation mechanism encountered in the previous chapter can be extended to include *supergroups* whose individual members consist not of persons, but of groups. This extension makes it possible to attain order in progressively larger groups without fundamentally altering the mechanism.

By what sleight of hand can groups suddenly be considered to be unitary actors? By no sleight of hand: groups can be treated as unitary actors if and only if they can maintain a high level of solidarity. To the degree that groups can control their own members, they can be considered as unitary members of higher level groups. The rationale behind this assumption is straightforward: if groups can maintain internal solidarity, then they can guarantee that their members will not violate obligations enacted at a higher level of aggregation.

Each of the types in the evolution of governance units—the local group, the chiefdom, and ultimately the state—consists of super-groups made up of the various lower level highly solidary groups in a given territory. Further, group solidarity can occur at more than one layer below the level of the state. The state can be regarded as the top level of a hierarchy of nested groups extending down to the individual level. The attainment of order can be viewed analogously at each level of nesting, with the unit that is macro on one level becoming micro on the next highest level. Group members that are themselves groups will have to expend resources sufficient to maintain internal order for them to be treated as unitary corporate individuals at the next higher level of analysis (Coleman 1993). This holds true down to the level where group members are single individuals.

States are formed for the self-same reasons that groups are formed—either as a voluntary agreement among groups (as in primary state formation), or as a coercive structure used by one set of groups against another (as in secondary state formation: Levi 1988; Olson 1993; Tilly 1985). In the voluntary case, a state emerges in an anarchical environment when a number of smaller groups come together to form a single control structure that prevents them from acting as mutual predators and resolves inter-group conflicts.[8] In the coercive case, it emerges when a group with superior military technology imposes its will on more vulnerable groups.[9]

Up to a point, this explanation follows Hobbesian logic concerning the formation of the state, with the important proviso that in this theory highly solidary groups—not individuals—are the agents.[10] Just as people with a common interest in some joint good cannot obtain it without controlling individual members, so highly solidary groups with a common interest in order cannot realize it without a means of controlling groups.[11] This higher level control structure is the state.[12]

Hence, attaining solidarity in a group is like attaining order in a territory composed of multiple solidary groups; both are instances of the same mechanism.[13] Social order in a given territory is simply group solidarity writ large. The idea that state control is isomorphic to lower level group control raises several related questions, however. Why are pre-existing solidary groups necessary for the formation of state, and why do these groups persist even after the state has formed? Further, what prevents individuals who are not attached to groups from forming and maintaining a state? The answers hinge on the costs of maintaining a state, which are reduced when groups intervene between individuals and the state. In general, the more resources that must expended to maintain order, the less efficient the control structures are. Efficiency increases with the size of constituent social groups, even if the total population of the society remains constant and the costs borne by the groups increase proportionately with the number of individuals they encompass.

The existence of groups mediating between individuals and the state lowers the state's costs of maintaining order. Further, states in societies with fewer and larger intermediate groups are more efficient at maintaining order than states in societies containing several groups, because they require a smaller outlay of resources per individual for monitoring and sanctioning.

Does this analysis not bias the results by only considering the *state's* costs of maintaining order? The state's savings from group mediation are simply being passed down to the groups, which have to take responsibility for maintaining solidarity among their members. Hence, the cost to society as a whole may be affected differently by this group mediation than the cost to the state. The state's costs are particularly important because they are the final determinant of the existence of social order in a given territory. In addition, highly solidary groups are more capable of demanding contributions from their members than the state—particularly when this state is a new entity on which individuals are not highly dependent (Stinchcombe 1965: 148)—because it costs them less. Likewise, due to their scale, groups are much more capable of monitoring and sanctioning than the state can ever be because it costs them less (Hechter *et al.* 1992; Hechter and Kanazawa 1993; Kanazawa 1997). None the less, the total social costs at all levels are important since they determine the overall burden borne by individuals, who typically seek to minimize these costs. Even when total social costs are taken into consideration, however, group mediation—that is, some type of indirect rule—reduces the costs of maintaining order.

The total resources necessary to maintain order in a given society consist of those resources needed to maintain order between the various groups in society plus those needed to maintain solidarity within each group. As the number of groups decreases in a society of fixed population, the average size of groups increases, and the cost of maintaining group solidarity rises as the cost of maintaining order between them falls. By this logic, incorporation into a few large groups raises the amount of resources devoted to maintaining solidarity at the group level, although it lowers the amount of resources devoted to maintaining order at the societal level.

Which scale of nested control structures is most conducive to the maintenance of social order at the lowest overall cost? The issue is complex, since no arrangement is most efficient at all levels of organization. Consider the simplest case, where hierarchies are structured such that all groups at each level contain some uniform number of members. This number can be seen as some measure of the shallowness of the chains of control in a society. At one pole, there is a mass society having only a single level of control between the state and atomized individuals. At the other extreme, the deepest hierarchy will be one in which no group has more than a few subgroup members. The total cost of maintaining order is simply equal to the number of layers multiplied by the cost at each layer.

The steepness of the relationship between group size and the cost of monitoring and sanctioning reduces the optimal number of members in groups at each layer. When monitoring becomes difficult as group size increases, order can be maintained at the lowest cost through narrow and deep chains of control. Multicultural societies lacking advanced communications tend to have this kind of organizational structure.[14] When monitoring is less difficult, however, broad and shallow chains of control become less costly. This helps explain why some societies are organized into a few groups just below the state level having long, narrow lines of control (as in feudalism), while others are divided into more numerous groups with broader control (as in modern unitary bureaucratic states).

The upshot of this analysis is that *some* sort of group mediation between states and individuals—or indirect rule—is necessary to minimize the cost of maintaining order in large societies.[15] Yet mediating groups that are too large, given the constraints of the environment, actually may decrease social order since they must expend considerable resources to establish and maintain internal solidarity.

Although the preceding story may sound complex, it is based on the simplest of notions, that primary state formation could only proceed by the progressive confederation of highly solidary groups. The idea is intuitive. It is also venerable, dating from Johannes Althusius (born in Westphalia in 1557), who developed a federalist theory of the state to compete with the centralized notions of sovereignty popularized by Bodin (Althusius [1614] 1964).[16]

Neither Plato nor Aristotle, nor writers following in their footsteps in classical antiquity, developed a concept of federalism. The idea developed only in the Middle Ages, as the politics of the great city leagues—especially in Germany—caught the attention of theorists. Althusius developed the position implied in the political views of Calvin—a defensive federalism protected by guardians of a constitutional order, such as the *ephors* of Sparta to whom Calvin had referred. Examples of this kind of federal order were evident to Althusius in the form of the Calvinist church, as well as the Swiss Confederation and the federal union of the Netherlands. (The development of the University of Oxford from a number of autonomous colleges also illustrates this principle well.) Beginning with the family, Althusius suggested that on successive levels of political community those who live together in order are united by an explicit or implicit pact to share things in pursuit of common interests and utility. For him, the village was a federal union of families, as was the guild; the town was a union of guilds; the province a union of towns and villages; the kingdom or state a union of provinces; the empire a union of states and free cities. This concept transformed the feudal hierarchy of successive levels of lord and vassal into a cooperative constitutional order.[17]

The key to this theory of primary state formation is that on all levels the union is composed of the units of the preceding lower level. Thus, at the top, the members of a state are neither individual persons nor families, but rather politically organized collectivities—provinces and cities. Further, all of these social units share common problems of political organization. As the nineteenth-century German historian Jacob Burckhardt ([1860] 1958) put it, the state is far from an organic entity; it is, on the contrary, a work of art. For present purposes, the theory's main implication is that states faced with high monitoring costs are compelled to rely on some form of indirect rule.[18]

If indirect rule has been instituted to control culturally distinctive territories, it is important to understand that these territories may be more or less culturally homogeneous.[19] To simplify matters, assume that indirect rule has been installed in four possible situations (Figure 3.1). What are the implications of these situational variations in indirect rule for the emergence of nationalism?

Situation I: Here there can be no nationalism because, despite the fact that the territory may be only a small part of a larger empire, the boundaries of the nation and the governance unit are congruent. This attenuates the demand for national self-determination, if not rendering it superfluous.

Situation II: This is unstable. By definition, culturally mixed groups cannot have traditional authorities. Traditional authorities emerge from culturally homogeneous groups—this is the meaning of 'traditional rule'.[20] If the territory is divided between two cultural groups, then either one will be governed by a traditional ruler (as in Situation I), and the other by a non-traditional one (as in Situation III), or both will be governed by a non-traditional ruler. Thus Situation II devolves either into Situation I or into Situation III.

Situation III: Here the central ruler either installs a culturally alien non-traditional authority in the agent's role (as in the Norman invasion of England), or an alien force conquers a culturally homogeneous territory (as in the late medieval Germanic colonization of Eastern Europe). Conflict between the alien indirect ruler and his subjects often takes on a cultural cast. Despite this, however, nationalism is unlikely to develop for at least three

Degree of Cultural Homogeneity of the Peripheral Territory

Type of Agent

	High	Low
Traditional	**I** Traditional Authorities Governing National Groups *the modal case* Poland and Hungary, from 19th c. to 1945; Ottoman millets; Soviet Republics; Native American tribes	**II** Traditional Authorities Governing Mixed Groups *unstable—evolves into Situations I and III*
Non-traditional	**III** Non-traditional Authorities Governing National Groups *a frequent consequence of invasion* 19th c. Czechoslovakia; Serbia and Bulgaria the Baltic states; 1940s Quebec; colonial Ireland	**IV** Non-traditional Authorities Governing Mixed Groups *parts of Eastern Europe; the colonial situation in Africa* Romania, the Balkans; colonial Nigeria, etc.

FIG. 3.1. Situations of Indirect Rule

different reasons. In the first place, in traditional polities subjects' expectations about their individual outcomes are determined by custom (Weber [1922] 1978). So long as the alien agent governs according to custom, therefore, political conflict ought to be held in check. This inhibits the development of nationalism. In the second place, after several generations the alien agent is likely to become culturally assimilated to his subjects, if for no reason than the need to produce heirs. The Old English in Ireland provide an apt example: unlike more recent British immigrants to Northern Ireland, they were among the strongest supporters of Irish nationalism. Once assimilation has occurred, the situation reverts to Situation I, in which the boundaries between nation and governance unit are congruent. Hence, no nationalism.

In the third place, even if the agent remains culturally alien in the long run (as occurred in some cities in Eastern Europe), and even if he squeezes his subjects more than custom permits, he still retains considerable control capacity over them because his territory is relatively small. Thus the alien agent is likely to be able to repress discontented subjects. After all, if the agent lacked high control capacity, the central ruler would have had nothing to gain by delegating authority to him. Once again, therefore, nationalism is precluded.

Situation IV. Although this situation intuitively seems unstable, the agent may profit from employing a strategy of divide and rule. This too limits nationalism. To the extent the ruled are culturally divided, they are unable to form a nationalist coalition. The conclusion is inescapable: indirect rule inhibits nationalism.

Indirect Rule in European History

It has often been noted that the number of autonomous territorial units has declined enormously since prehistoric times, and that the resulting size of the surviving autonomous units has increased. Less well-appreciated is the fact that these fewer and larger units have become increasingly subdivided into varied territorial sub-units (Sack 1986: 53). Whereas small polities in early modern Europe (city-states, autonomous bishoprics, and petty principalities) could be ruled in a relatively direct way, larger states had to rely on some form of indirect rule. Prior to the seventeenth century, every large European state ruled its subjects through powerful agents who enjoyed significant autonomy, hindered state demands that were not to their own interest, and profited on their own accounts from the delegated exercise of state power:[21]

The emperors, kings, princes, dukes, caliphs, sultans, and other potentates ... prevailed as conquerors, tribute-takers, and rentiers, not as heads of state that durably and densely regulated life within their realms. Inside their jurisdictions, furthermore, rivals and ostensible subordinates commonly used armed force on behalf of their own interests while paying little attention to the interests of their nominal sovereigns. Private armies proliferated through much of the continent. Nothing like a centralized national state existed any-where in Europe. Within the ring formed by these sprawling, ephemeral states, sovereignty fragmented even more, as hundreds of principalities, bish-oprics, city-states, and other authorities exercised overlapping control in the small hinterlands of their capitals (Tilly 1990: 39–40).

Consider England, one of the first polities to attain a strongly defined identity as a separate, autonomous state (Elton 1982: 353). This common identity depended, first and foremost, on regular communication linking London to peripheral regions. One indic-ator of England's communication capacity is provided by the increasing circulation of inexpensively printed material, such as pamphlets, 'chapbooks', and broadsides that enabled the centre to influence readers on questions of politics and religion, and to legit-imize its rule. Such printed material was distributed by individu-als who often travelled long distances, selling their wares in alehouses located on major highways (Watt 1991: 33, 131–43). By the end of Elizabeth's reign, these pamphlets were widely distrib-uted even in the humblest of dwellings. The establishment of a state church, and the growth of inland trade and of a national educa-tional system (albeit one that was limited to the élite), contributed to the sense of English statehood, and emphasized the power and importance of the central government. This central government promoted state-wide legislation on education, taxation, religious worship, taxation, conscription, and law and order. Local author-ities, such as Justices of the Peace, were all made accountable to the Privy Council for their actions:

The Council's intricate network of informants, coupled with close personal relationships which existed between its members and the county elites, kept it in close touch with ecclesiastical and secular issues in the localities. By these and other means, the 'infrastructural reach' of the state became ever more powerful and its policies were more effectively implemented on the ground (Brayshay *et al.* 1998: 267).

Even so, central control over peripheral regions ultimately depended on the cooperation of local authorities (Griffiths *et al.* 1996). Indirect rule persisted in centralizing England because com-munication capacity was uneven and highly limited. This is not to say that no progress had been made. In the late fifteenth century, it took at least six days to bring news from York to London. Travel times were rapidly reduced after the introduction of the Treasury-funded post system: in 1570–1620 official correspondence between these two cities took a mere fifty-five hours (Brayshay *et al.* 1998: 273). However, communication from the centre to localities not on the major roads remained poor (see Figure 3.2). If central control spread along the major English roads, it was sharply attenuated in the remainder of the country. This mandated the centre's considerable reliance on indirect rule.

Indirect rule implies the existence of separate governance units for different groups within the state. In feudal Europe, for example, militarily self-sufficient manors provided protection from invaders and dispensed justice and other joint goods to their dependants. Save for matters of religion, the manor was an autonomous governing unit that owed tribute and various services to the king.

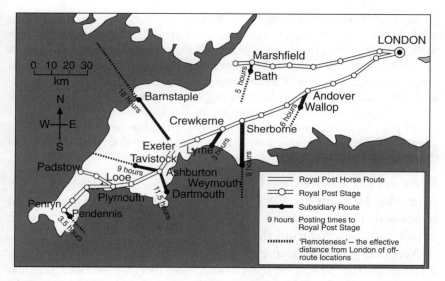

FIG. 3.2. The Remoteness of Places in South-West England Located Off the Main Highway from London, 1570–1620. Dotted lines show distances royal postboys would have travelled (at 5.5 miles per hour) during the average length of time *actually* required to convey letters from various 'off-route' locations to the nearest main highway post-room
Source: Brayshay et al. (1998: fig. 7, p. 283)

In more peripheral parts of Europe, however, indirect rule was carried out by a culturally alien ruling élite imposed by a superior coercive power over an indigenous population. There was a kind of colonial expansion from the Carolingian core in Europe to the Anglo-Saxon and Celtic peripheries of the west, the Slavic peripheries of the east, and the Moorish peripheries of the south. The roots of this colonization probably were to be found in the primogeniture of the Carolingian core combined with an expanding European economy: 'He who was "of Rheims" or "of Chartres" is now "of Tyre" or "of Antioch," wrote one new settler, "we have already forgotten the places of our birth." The knights settled in Sicily took surnames from their new fiefs, while in Frankish Greece the new lords dropped their old names and adopted new, like snakes shedding skin (Bartlett 1994: 56).' In these non-feudal regions, evidence of indirect rule comes from the existence of separate systems of law for distinct groups within the multinational state:

In the High Middle Ages most parts of Latin Europe included at least one minority, the Jews, marked out by their own legal regime. Special provisions were made regarding the rights of Jews to bring suit or bear witness, the exact nature of the testimony needed to prove their charges or to convict them and the form of oath they would be required to swear. Such rules were . . . predicated upon the principle of different legal treatment for those of different ethnic-religious states. On the frontiers of the Latin world, where the different populations formed not enclosed minorities but large and ubiquitous groups, an even more highly charged ethnic-legal pluralism was to be found (Bartlett 1994: 205–6).

Consider the city of Toledo. It was captured by Christian forces from the Muslims in 1085. Thereafter, Toledo had separate but (ostensibly) equal judicial regimes for the three main Christian ethnic groups inhabiting the city.

According to the *Sachsenspiegal*, a compendium of Saxon law written in the 1220s, Saxons could not judge nor bear witness against Slavs, nor vice versa. Similarly in Castile and Aragon: 'if a Moor is suspected of theft or fornication or anything for which justice must be done, the only witnesses that will be admitted against him will be trustworthy Moors; Christians will not be admitted (Bartlett 1994: 210).' These various groups often lived together in a state of chronic mutual distrust; there was a pervasive fear of being framed in legal proceedings.

Still, this situation often resulted in a culturally homogeneous population in the colonized periphery, due either to extermination (as occurred in the Crusader states), or expulsion (as occurred to the Moors in Spain), or assimilation. Over the course of generations, the ruling élite often assimilated to the indigenous culture:

The solidarity of the new arrivals depended on the circumstances of their migration. Marriages between incomers and natives were sometimes common. Since there was almost always an imbalance in the immigrant population, with men preponderant by far, intermarriage was usually between immigrant men and native women. Marriage into powerful local families was indeed one way newcomers could establish their position, since they would immediately acquire kin, property and patrons . . . At the highest level there was little in the way of a barrier to intermarriage. Of the wives of the first margraves of Brandenburg, sixteen in number, half were of Slav descent. The long-term impact of aristocratic immigration was largely determined by issues of manpower. Where the immigrants were few in number it would prove impossible to pursue a policy of expropriation and expulsion. One sign of this assimilation is the adoption of toponymic surnames from the new rather than from the old home . . . Few landed families in the Crusader States had western European toponyms (Bartlett 1994: 55–6).

Similar institutional arrangements can be found outside of Europe.[22] A classic instance of indirect rule occurred in the Ottoman Empire, where the different cultural groups comprised self-governing *millets* that paid tribute to the emperor.[23]

Indirect rule is not constant, but variable. There were different varieties of indirect rule, even in the European states (Tilly 1990; te Brake 1998: 183–8). One type was the tribute-taking empire, which built a large military and extractive apparatus, but left most local administration to regional powerholders who retained great autonomy. When the emperor lost the ability to deploy massive coercion, the structure tended to disintegrate. Given communication costs and agency problems, all such rulers faced repeated challenges to their hegemony. Hence they sought to coopt local and regional powerholders without undermining their bases of power and to create royal agents dependent on the crown. Thus, Mamluk sultans maintained a whole caste of enslaved foreigners who became warriors and administrators. Except for fiefs directly supporting officials, the Mamluks left local magnates in place within their domains. Under just such a system, slaves ruled Egypt and adjacent territories from 1260 to 1517.

A second type of indirect rule existed in city-leagues and federations, such as the Hanseatic League of Northern Europe. Here temporary coalitions and consultative institutions played significant parts in war and extraction, but little in the way of a state apparatus emerged. In such polities, a relatively small coalition of nominal subjects could equal the ruler's forces, while individuals, groups, and whole populations had abundant opportunities for defection to competing jurisdictions. Rulers often attained tight control over a single city and its immediate hinterland. Beyond that, however, they had to bargain with the authorities of competing centres.

The more geographically peripheral the territory within a state, the greater the prevalence of indirect rule.[24] These arrangements left considerable power and discretion in the hands of local authorities, so long as they contained the monarch's enemies and kept the revenues flowing to the state capital:

All told, therefore, no European state (except, perhaps, Sweden) made a serious attempt to institute direct rule from top to bottom until the era of the French Revolution. Before then, all but the smallest states relied on some version of indirect rule, and thus ran serious risks of disloyalty, dissimulation, corruption and rebellion. But indirect rule made it possible to govern without erecting, financing, and feeding a bulky administrative apparatus (Tilly 1990: 25).

Indirect Rule in European Colonies

Indirect rule not only characterized early modern states in Western Europe and in the Ottoman Empire, but more modern colonial states in Asia and Africa. How else could colonial authorities manage to provide social order with limited staff in far-removed territories? British, Dutch, German, Belgian, and Japanese administrators all employed indirect rule. Dramatic economies of administration (that is, reduced civil and military budgets, as well as expenditures for manpower) were the principal benefit of indirect rule to the colonial authorities. For example, the ratio of European officials to the local population during the 1930s in British Kenya, which had direct rule, was 1:18,900. In 1872 Hyderabad, which was ruled indirectly, this ratio was about 1:5.3 million (see Table 3.1). Indirect rule offered a number of other benefits to the colonial authorities. It reduced frictions with the indigenous population and provided economies of information (since indigenous officials had more extensive knowledge of local conditions and languages than did colonial officials). For metropolitan politicians, indirect rule tended to have:

TABLE 3.1. *Ratio of European Officials to Estimated Local Population Direct and Indirect Rule in Africa and India*

Colony or Local State	Type of Rule	European Officials[a]	Estimated Population	Year	Ratio (nearest 100)
British Kenya	More Direct	164	3,100,000	1930s	1:18,900
French West Africa	Mixed	526	14,500,000	1921	1:27,600
Belgian Congo	Mixed	316	11,000,000	1936	1:34,800
British Nigeria and Cameroons	Mixed	386	20,000,000	1930s	1:51,800
India (all)	Mixed	c.950	253,900,000	1881	1:267,300
Awadh	More Direct	38	11,220,000	1872	1:295,300
Princely India	Indirect	107[b]	94,000,000	1947	1:878,500
Hyderabad	Indirect	2[c]	10,666,000	1872	1:5,333,000
Awadh	Indirect	2[c]	11,000,000	1856	1:5,500,000

Source: Adapted from Fisher (1991).

[a] For Africa, these figures include only officers in the Administrative Department and exclude those in Judicial, Military, Police, Health, Transportation, and all other Departments who would increase the total many fold. For India, these figures likewise include Europeans only in the covenanted civil service and exclude the Military and other branches of the British Government in India.

[b] This figure is the total for Europeans serving in the Indian Political Service.

[c] This figure represents the Resident and his assistant. On some occasions, the Resident was the only covenanted official present in a Residency. On other occasions, the Resident might have additional covenanted officials attached to his residency.

more positive and fewer adverse political implications than did direct rule. Indirect rule permitted more rapid expansion with fewer out-of-pocket costs and less recruiting at home, thus saving the imperial government from drawing too heavily on its home constituents. For instance, when seeking to create an empire rapidly and cheaply, Bismarck envisioned indirect patterns for German rule in Africa . . . [States] which recognized the legitimacy of indigenous political institutions, as the British tended to do, found indirect rule easier to defend in the European community on ethical grounds, as well. Indirect rule permitted *de facto* control without the political costs of controversy over extensions of *de jure* authority (Fisher 1991)[25].

Given that indirect rule provided colonial governments with such a litany of benefits, it comes as a surprise to learn that Spain, Portugal, and France forsook its control economies and employed more direct forms of rule later in the nineteenth century. Perhaps Spanish and Portuguese reliance on more direct rule contributed to the relatively rapid demise of their overseas empires, although the French Empire had much longer staying power.

What accounts for this forsaking of indirect rule? One possible factor is historical. Colonial indirect rule was invented by joint-stock companies—especially the (English) East India Company in India, and the Netherlands East India Company in Java—rather than by the British and Dutch crowns.[26] It is not difficult to understand why indirect rule appealed to company directors and stockholders. Presumably, the adoption of cost-effective governance procedures maximized both the likelihood of private investment and the expected return on that investment. After taking over the reins of colonial administration from the trading companies, the British and Dutch states simply adopted indirect rule as their own. Spanish and Portuguese colonization, in contrast, was initiated by these countries' crowns. Why the crown should be less vigilant than joint-stock companies concerning the loss of revenue is not clear, however.

In any case, the argument linking private investment and indirect rule does not account for the French case. Before 1789, the French, whose colonial adventures also emanated from joint-stock companies, relied heavily on indirect rule. Following the Revolution and the subsequent abolition of slavery in 1848, the French reconsidered their strategy of colonial rule (Mamdani 1996: 82–4).

As a result of its *mission civilisatrice*, citizenship was conferred on all the inhabitants of French colonies. Between 1890 and 1914, the French called their administration of African colonies 'direct administration'. To make up for the shortage of European administrators, the French relied on an educated native stratum as mediators between them and newly conquered subjects in the interior. A decade later, however, both direct administration and the role of Black citizens came under fire. The policy of native cultural assimilation, which underlay direct administration, stimulated native political demands rather than inhibiting them. Subsequently, the French reverted back to indirect rule.

Conclusion

One of the few non-contentious conclusions about nationalism is that it is a modern phenomenon. This chapter aims to explain why nationalism did not tend to emerge prior to the nineteenth century. It does so by discussing the evolution of polities in history. Although state formation has occurred at different times and in different historical eras from one part of the globe to another— hence under quite different conditions—it can also be seen as the unfolding of a universal process. The same mechanism responsible for the formation of small insurance groups can come into play at a higher level of aggregation in the formation of the state.

The theory of primary state formation introduced above explains why the preindustrial state was compelled to rely on indirect rule to provide order in extensive populations and territories. Previous to the nineteenth century, all large states adopted indirect rule because of technical limits to central control. Since states based on indirect rule were either disinclined or unable to intervene in the affairs and governance of constituent lower level groups, these groups usually constituted their own governance units. States based on indirect rule provided little or no threat to the prerogatives of local authorities. Nor were they a tempting target for political capture. Although the great agrarian empires—the Roman, the Chinese, the Ottoman, and the Habsburg among them—cer-

tainly did possess institutions of central governance, and although
they encompassed populations having highly diverse cultural practices and beliefs, so long as they relied on indirect rule they generally did not face nationalist challenges.[27]

Indirect rule thwarted nationalism in two different ways.[28] It
often provided existing nations with their own governing units,
thus precluding the demand for national sovereignty. Even when
governance was in the hands of culturally alien rulers, cultural
conflict was often short-lived. This is because indirect rule encouraged the cultural assimilation of alien rulers by the rural population. Thus, over the course of several generations the Norman
conquerors became culturally English; the Anglo-Irish culturally
Irish, and so forth. The pressures for assimilation were caused
by the search for marriage partners, the desire to communicate,
the gains from trade, and many other factors. But once the governance unit became culturally homogeneous, national sovereignty had already been achieved. This allowed no scope for
nationalism.

In some places (such as the Baltics and parts of Europe east of
the Elbe), the aristocracy tended to resist assimilation, however.
Often it resided apart from rural cultivators in culturally alien
cities. As a result, these governance units were liable to cultural
conflicts. In such systems, the political salience of culture tends
to increase, encouraging the development of nationalist ideals.
Despite this, there was little opportunity for the rural workers to
engage in collective action crystallized around their cultural distinctiveness because the alien aristocracy was in a position to
repress it. In fact, the control capacity of the aristocracy was
responsible for the emergence of the indirect-rule state in the first
place. Without it, the state would have come crashing down.

Finally, the theory implies that the disintegration of *any* state
will lead to conflict among highly solidary groups, whatever the
basis of their formation. This implication follows simply because
the cooperation of these solidary groups is what makes the establishment of the central state possible in the first place. Thus the
failure of the central state means that all responsibility for order in
the society reverts to lower level groups, however they may be
constituted. When the centre of a state whose lower level groups

are constituted nationally disintegrates, then nationalism ought to come to the fore. The renascence of nationalism in the republics of the former Soviet and Yugoslav federations is consistent with this expectation.[29]

If nationalism is defined by the non-congruence of nation and governance unit, then it could not make an appearance until nation and governance unit were somehow severed. This severance did not tend to occur until the advent of direct rule in large, culturally heterogeneous polities. The consequences of this process for nationalism are outlined in the next chapter.

CHAPTER 4

State-Building Nationalism

O NE of the hallmarks of the modern state is that it is the master of its own domain. This mastery presupposes the centralization of control, for without this the state is unable to enforce its will throughout its realm (Migdal 1988: 32–3).[1] Unlike wealth, authority is a zero-sum commodity. The centre can only gain control by wresting it away from the local authorities encountered in the previous chapter. In this way, the modern state substitutes its own direct rule for what had been indirect rule. Whereas direct rule does not necessarily do away with these local authorities, by subjecting them to central control it does do away with much of their autonomy.

While the pace of political centralization varies widely according to local circumstances, this chapter briefly discusses the rise of direct rule, and then concentrates on its effects for the development of nationalism. Its principal argument is that in multinational polities the growth of direct rule usually leads to efforts at cultural homogenization. These efforts constitute state-building nationalism. Yet this process tends to be beset by unintended consequences. When it succeeds, state-building nationalism can stimulate nationalism in other countries; when it fails, it can generate peripheral nationalism within state borders (Chapter 5). Since direct rule plays such a large part in the development of nationalism, it is essential to understand its genesis.

The Rise of Direct Rule

Although it was not the first to adopt it, France offers perhaps the most dramatic example of direct rule.[2] Unlike Japan and some of the Scandinavian states, France had once been multinational. In the course of centuries, the Île de France gradually extended its control over rival states, such as Burgundy, as well as over the culturally distinct territories of Brittany, Occitania, and Alsace. Direct rule enabled France to transform itself into something approaching a full-fledged nation state by the latter part of the nineteenth century.

Like nearly all other states, before 1789 France employed indirect rule.[3] Although the King used *intendants,* royal agents, to collect taxes, the bulk of governance in the countryside was carried out by local authorities, primarily nobles and priests. These notables jealously guarded their prerogatives from incursions by the centre. So long as the terms of trade between the centre and the localities were stable, there was little problem. However, central demands for increased rights and resources provoked reactions in the countryside among notables and peasants. In fact, one such demand for increased taxes in the late eighteenth century ultimately led to the Revolution (Tilly 1990: 108).

Following the Revolution, the positions that local notables filled were taken over by militias and committees made up of members of the victorious bourgeoisie. Yet once they attained their positions, these new local authorities also resisted central control. In time, the centre devised a strategy to increase its power. It divided the country into new administrative units—departments, districts, cantons, and communes—and enacted innovations in taxation, justice, public works, and policing. For example, national police forces penetrated local communities. The centre also asserted its control over the military, bringing it more firmly under the government's wing.

All told, over time these innovations greatly concentrated resources in Paris, and gradually loosened the dependence of citizens on local authorities. Thus was direct rule born. The French central government used its new-found powers to create more efficient markets, stimulating economic growth. This helped fund modernization of the military. The net result was that France developed into a highly efficacious state.

This new kind of state became the bull in continental Europe's china shop. Due to French aggressiveness, direct rule was either imposed on neighbouring states, or adopted in them for reasons of defence. On the one hand, France usually imposed variants of direct rule in the vast territories that it had succeeded in conquering. On the other, France provided a model of centralized government that other states could only ignore at their peril. The triumph of Napoleonic France (1804–15) is a testament to the geopolitical advantages of direct rule, and the sad fate of nineteenth-century Poland is a cautionary tale about the failure to enact it.

If direct rule was so efficacious, then why was it instituted so late in European history? The reasons for the rise of direct rule are the subject of an ongoing debate.[4] Leading explanations tend to stress factors of supply or demand. Supply explanations assume that central rulers always wished to rule directly, but simply were unable to do so. On this view, indirect rule was very much a second-best governance strategy, for the agency problems and corruption that it spawned invariably sapped central authority (Kiser and Schneider 1994). Once the technical preconditions for direct rule existed—a monetized economy, modern communication and transportation technology, and a supply of trained officials—central rulers were free to institute direct rule.

In contrast, demand explanations suggest that direct rule is a result of a shift not in technology, but in rulers' incentives. On this view, increasing geopolitical pressure rewards those rulers who can successfully wage war.[5] Going to war is not only risky, but it is also extremely costly. Due to its inefficiencies, indirect rule severely limits the quantity of resources rulers can extract from the ambient economy (Barkey and von Hagen 1997). As a result, revenue-hungry rulers seize on direct rule as their best means of funding their military ambitions. Direct rule emerges as an unintended consequence of rapidly increasing military expenditure. The centre assumes organizational burdens to solve agency problems. What is key in demand explanations, therefore, is not so much the technical preconditions that reduce control costs, but increasing geopolitical competition, which heightens the centre's demand for tax revenues. To meet this demand, central rulers adopt direct rule and the greater revenue enables them to increase their military investment.

Neither supply nor demand perspectives do justice to the historical record, however. If monetization, technology, and trained personnel were a sufficient cause of direct rule, then countries like Switzerland and the Netherlands would have adopted it about the same time that France and England did. Their failure to institute direct rule provides compelling evidence against this view. And if geopolitical competition were a sufficient cause of direct rule, then Switzerland and the Netherlands would have been compelled to institute direct rule to defend their territories against their more powerful neighbours. Cultural heterogeneity in both countries played an important role in limiting the adoption of direct rule (Chapter 8).[6]

Demand and supply perspectives are better conceived as complementary views that emphasize different causal mechanisms.[7] Geopolitical threat—itself a creature of the rise of direct rule—probably encouraged lords in indirect-rule states to increase their contributions to the centre as a form of insurance against subjugation. As Napoleon's military successes illustrated, this kind of loss became all too tangible after the emergence of direct rule.

The precise causes of direct rule vary from country to country. Perhaps the earliest onset of direct rule came in Denmark, Sweden, and England. In these relatively small and compact domains, ambitious princes gained important political support by aligning themselves with zealous proponents of the Protestant Reformation (te Brake 1998: 181). In general, any change that disproportionately aids the central ruler *vis-à-vis* local authorities will tend to foster direct rule. The development of transportation and communications technology was one such shift: new road, rail, and telegraph systems extended the centre's ability to respond to distant challengers. Advances in military technology was another: capital-intensive military technology favoured central rulers because they generally had greater access to capital than local authorities. The growth in international trade may have been a third, for it is often less costly for the centre extract revenues from international than from local trade.[8]

The Effects of Direct Rule

Direct rule permits the state to become the governance unit in geographically extensive and populous territories. This means that the centre assumes rights, resources, and obligations formerly held by local authorities. As direct rule proceeds, therefore, individuals become increasingly dependent on the centre for their access to protection, dispute resolution, education, and other goods promoting individual welfare.[9] By providing these goods, central rulers increase the dependence of their subjects at the expense of local authorities.[10]

We are so accustomed to the power of the central government in the modern world that it is easy to forget just how novel a situation this is. Instituting direct rule poses a daunting challenge to central authorities. This is because *it can only be attained by destroying the previous basis of social order*—namely, that social order that was built upon indirect rule (Hobsbawm 1992: ch. 3). As Chapter 3 reveals, central rulers traditionally attained order by delegating much of the responsibility for social control to local authorities. The advent of direct rule weakens the power and prerogatives of these local authorities, many of whom do not go gently into that good night. Political centralization thus entails fearsome conflict.[11]

How could central rulers secure the compliance and loyalty of large numbers of geographically dispersed and culturally heterogeneous subjects whose traditional allegiance was owed to local authorities? As indirect rule eroded, the allegiance of hitherto controlled subjects increasingly was up for grabs. Central rulers were faced with two kinds of competitors in the ensuing struggles for control and legitimation. On the one hand, local authorities (mainly nobles and priests) could be relied on to mobilize their dependants to resist growing central control, thus planting the seeds of what would later become peripheral nationalism. On the other, a variety of workers' movements sought to mobilize the rapidly growing ranks of factory labourers against the established order.

Faced with challenges to their authority from both territorial and class-based social movements, central rulers responded in several ways. In the first place, they sought to increase their domestic military capacity and to disarm the population. The spread of state-wide police forces in European states occurred roughly at the same period of time, beginning in the early nineteenth century (Bayley 1975; Dandeker 1990; Emsley 1993). The model for many of these police forces was the French *gendarmerie*, which had developed from the old regime's *maréchausée*. Whereas the police tended to develop in urban areas, policing *à la gendarmerie* differed from that which arose in more culturally homogeneous states, for *gendarmeries* were involved in turning indigenous peoples into loyal subjects of their respective crowns:

Nobles, like the East Prussian Junkers, might owe allegiance to their king but resent the emerging nation state and insist on the maintenance of their traditional courts and system of control. Peasants were often notorious for their stubborn inability, or refusal, to recognize the existence of a polity beyond their *pays natal* ... Members of the *gendarmerie nationale*, the *Carabinieri*, the *Guardia Civil*, the Third Section were as much involved in turning peasants into Frenchmen, Italians, Spaniards and Russians and marking out 'national' territory, as members of the Northwest Mounted Police or the Royal Irish Constabulary were involved in turning indigenous peoples into loyal subjects of the British Crown and marking out imperial territory (Emsley 1993: 87).

In the second place, the centre attempted to monopolize judicial authority and create a uniform civil law. In the place of a patchwork of customary legal systems, the Code Napoléon (1804) stipulated property rights and regulated relations between individuals throughout French territory. It soon spread to the remainder of the continent and across the Atlantic.

In the third place, the centre intervened in the economy. Assuming these new responsibilities was very expensive, and the centre was compelled to raise more revenue to defray the additional burden. The centre began to collect revenue directly rather than relying on agents to engage in tax farming. It promoted uniform systems of coinage, weights and measures, and standards (Heckscher 1955). It eliminated internal tolls and customs barriers, spurring technological and economic growth. The resulting increase in revenues and new technologies (like the railway and electric telegraph) acted, in turn, to further strengthen direct rule (Dandeker 1990: ch. 3).[12]

If these are the effects of direct rule, just what implications do they have for the development of state-building nationalism?

Direct Rule and State-Building Nationalism

Prior to direct rule, the groups most capable of engaging in collective action are local governance units, manors, *millets*, and provinces that are effectively controlled by local authorities. When these governance units are spatially concentrated, culturally distinctive, and of sufficient size, cultural entrepreneurs can guide their inhabitants to the view that they share a common history, culture, and homeland. In this fashion are nations built. Whereas indirect rule may promote this kind of nation-building, it is generally immune to national*ism* because it provides few incentives for the authorities, or the other residents of culturally distinctive territories, to demand sovereignty—save when the imperial centre collapses.

The central argument of this and the following chapter is that the expansion of direct rule in multinational polities spurs at least three different kinds of nationalism. The present chapter discusses its effects on state-building nationalism, the nationalism of the aspiring nation state. This kind of nationalism aims to render the boundaries of the nation and governance unit congruent by transforming a multinational state into a national one. Whereas indirect rule tolerates cultural heterogeneity as a means of governance, cultural uniformity helps to facilitate, and to legitimize, direct rule.[13]

Cultural homogeneity in a polity can be fostered by either inclusive or exclusive strategies (Brubaker 1992; Linz and Stepan 1996: 428–33). Central authorities adopt *inclusive* strategies when they enact policies designed either to assimilate culturally distinctive individuals to the dominant culture (as in France), or to promote the conception of a multinational polity (as in the United States). Central authorities adopt *exclusive* strategies when they enact policies to limit political and civil rights to members of the dominant culture (as in Germany), or to expel such individuals from the polity altogether (as in ethnic cleansing or genocide). Of course, any given regime can employ each strategy seriatim, or even both simultaneously.[14]

The initial strategies of cultural homogenization in Western Europe—such as the expulsion of foreign merchants and religious minorities beginning in late thirteenth-century England and moving to Spain by the sixteenth century (Wallerstein 1974: ch. 3)—were exclusive, but they long antedated direct rule. Since the purpose of state-building nationalism is to legitimize the new order of direct rule, it is counterproductive to adopt exclusive strategies—at least in the case of relatively large groups. Hence the logic of state-building nationalism inexorably favours the use of inclusive strategies.[15]

The usual means of legitimizing direct rule is by encouraging peripheral nations to assimilate to the culture of the centre. Under indirect rule cultural diversity had been irrelevant to social order. But when the responsibility for order shifted from local to central authorities, cultural distinctiveness was perceived as a threat. Here, Sweden led the way. The Swedish state managed to convert the Danish-speaking population of the southern provinces of Scania, Halland, and Blekinge into Swedish speakers between 1660 and 1700 (Østergård 1992). After the Revolution, France followed in its footsteps:

All French citizens had to understand what the interests of the Republic were and what the Republic was up to, Barthélémy de Lanthemas told the Convention in December 1792. Otherwise, they could not participate, were not equipped to participate in it. A didactic and integrative regime needed an effective vehicle for information and propaganda; but it could hardly have one if the population did not know French. In November 1792, just a month before Lanthemas's speech, the Minister of Justice had set up an office to translate laws and decrees into the German, Italian, Catalan, Basque, and Lower Breton languages (Weber 1976: 72).

Similar state-building linguistic policies were adopted in Spain and Japan (Laitin 1992: 13–14), among other countries.

Even so, the pace of linguistic homogenization in France was slow. As late as 1863, at least 20 per cent of the population of

France did not speak French (Weber 1976: 310). Cultural practices are like addictions: people become heavily invested in them and the substitutes are unappealing. Changes in hearts and minds are required to shift cultural practices, but the top-down means that central authorities adopted to this end could prove inappropriate. To foster a common language in France, for example:

Breton was hunted out of the schools. Children caught using it were systematically punished—put on dry bread and water or sent to clean out the school latrine . . . A favorite punishment . . . was the token of shame to be displayed by the child caught using his native tongue. The token varied . . . A child saddled with such a 'symbol' kept it until he caught another child not speaking French, denounced him and passed it on. The pupil left with the token at the end of the day received a punishment (Weber 1976: 313).

Such policies are liable to be counterproductive (Ford 1993: 227). The French language spread more readily as a by-product of other policies concerning universal military service, the education of girls, and the rise of free schooling.

Language is only one element of the cultural mix, however. Whereas loyalty to the indirect-rule state was expected to be transferable merely by dint of dynastic marriages, state-building nationalists ultimately seek to build loyalty to the centre throughout the realm. To that end, states actively promote new traditions, such as national anthems, flags, monuments, and public ceremonies (Spillman 1997). Whereas national anthems and flags might seem to have existed from time immemorial, all of them, in fact, are of recent vintage. The oldest national anthem, the British, dates from 1740, the first national flag, the French, evolved in 1790–4 (Hobsbawm 1983a: 7, 13–14).[16] These invented traditions, often deliberate exercises of social engineering, were designed to impart a sense of national history that might supplant long-held popular attachments to local territories and authorities (Hobsbawm 1983b; Lewis 1977).[17] The daily recital of the pledge of allegiance by American schoolchildren has its analogues in every direct-rule state.

Some symbols of nationhood are eagerly embraced by target populations. Many Americans, for example, regard their flag as a quasi-sacred object (Welch and Bryan 1996–7). Often national symbols become the flash-points of intergroup conflict: the decision to fly the provincial flag above the Canadian maple leaf at City Hall in Quebec angers federalists. When the Montreal Expos play at home on the separatist holiday of St Jean Baptiste in late June, the Canadian national anthem has to be sung at least half an hour before the game begins to avoid trouble (De Palma 1997). Northern Irish Catholics and Protestants fight over the proper name of the city of Londonderry (Catholics refer to it as Derry). And the name of the former Yugoslavian territory of Macedonia is unacceptable to Greeks.

The idea that cultural uniformity fosters political loyalty to the centre is a sound one. For example, Sweden's success in converting the language spoken in its southern provinces from Danish to Swedish was accompanied by a corresponding shift in political loyalty.[18] Many believe that cultural homogeneity increases the state's military power, as well (Posen 1993*b*: 30). Prior to the nineteenth century, from one-third to one-half of any state's soldiers were foreigners (Finer 1975: 102). Much of Napoleon's military success has been understood, both by military experts and civilian scholars, as a by-product of a strong French national identity that was forged during the Revolution (Clausewitz [1827] 1984: 591–2). By employing stand-alone musketeers known as skirmishers, the French Revolution led to a change in the prevalent European military strategy. A few skirmishers could easily terrorize immobile continental armies. The isolation of the individual skirmishers meant, however, that they were beyond the supervisory control of their officers. The preferred solution was to socialize the skirmishers to comply with their orders out of a commitment to the national interest. As a result, European armies came to promote nationalist ideology to induce greater compliance of these troops (Posen 1993*a*: 95). Further developments in military technology, such as the deployment of the muzzle-loading percussion rifle and the breech-loader (after 1866) posed greater challenges to the maintenance of order on the battlefield. In general:

developments in military technology that favor dispersal on the battlefield prompt a constant concern for the motivation of soldiers. These same developments may make it difficult to rely on lengthy training and lengthy terms to service to create this motivation, since improved weaponry kills these 'custom-made' soldiers too fast. Developments in military technology that increase the human costs of war increase the state's propensity to prepare people to pay these costs, and the sponsorship of [patriotism] is one solution to the problem (Posen 1993*a*: 120).

The institution of free public education also was designed, in part, to foster civic loyalty. The content of schooling placed a strong emphasis on patriotic socialization, which aimed to increase the state's legitimacy.[19] Thus, in 1881, eminent educators in France were saying that student teachers:

must above all be told . . . that their first duty is to make [their charges] love and understand the fatherland. Another ten years, and the high aim is again repeated, that a 'national pedagogy' might yet become the soul of popular education. The school is 'an instrument of unity,' an 'answer to dangerous centrifugal tendencies,' and of course the 'keystone of national defense' (Paret 1970: 5).

Children were compelled to recite a mantra,

a sort of catechism designed to teach the child that it was his duty to defend the fatherland, to shed his blood or die for the commonweal ('When France is threatened, your duty is to take up arms and fly to her rescue.'), to obey the government, to perform military service, to work, learn pay taxes, and so on. At the very start of school, children were taught that their first duty was to defend the country as soldiers. The army . . . 'is composed of our brothers and parents' or relatives . . . There were no better instruments of indoctrination and patriotic conditioning than French history and geography, especially history, which 'when properly taught [is] the only means of maintaining patriotism in the generations we are bringing up' (Weber 1976: 333).

That the rise of direct rule spurred the centre's interest in state-building policies aiming to increase cultural homogeneity cannot be doubted. What can be questioned is the efficacy of these policies. For one thing, not all state-instigated invented traditions take root. Little is known about the circumstances under which they become institutionalized and contribute to the establishment of something akin to civic religions (the term is borrowed from Rousseau; see Bellah 1988) or merely disappear, like hula hoops and lava lamps, into the mists of time.[20] For another, some cultural homogenization in direct-rule states may be an unintended by-product of economic and technological development, or military policy,[21] rather than the result of any self-conscious state-building agenda. To the degree that cultural homogenization comes about in such a bottom–up fashion, it is less likely to engender political antipathy.

Conclusion

Direct-rule states are not voluntary associations to be joined and exited at will. On the contrary: their citizens tend to face very high exit costs. In this sense, citizens are highly dependent on their states. This dependence, in turn, justifies expenditures for nation-building. Groups with less dependent members, like firms and country clubs, do not tend to have flags and anthems.[22]

It is obvious that considerable amounts of resources were allocated—and continue to be allocated—to projects that attempt to increase the loyalty of citizens to their states. How successful have these investments been? Even in France, the first country to embark on state-building nationalism and the one that has carried the process further than any other, success has been mixed.[23] The attempt to impose linguistic homogenization engendered political conflict in France and elsewhere.[24] It was resisted by bilingual peripheral élites, whose linguistic monopoly in the standard language afforded them monopoly rents and perpetuated their local influence. As a result, there were significant struggles over the development of universal free elementary education in Germany, France, Britain, and the Netherlands; in France, in particular, state policy on education oscillated wildly from the Revolution onward (de Swaan 1988: ch. 3). These conflicts were not merely replays of earlier court versus country struggles. The Roman Catholic Church also played a key role in resisting state initiatives in public education for fear that it would lose its monopoly position. Where the Church thought it could maintain its monopoly, it favoured state educational institutions; where it did not, the Church tended to support local notables.

Resistance to assimilation was greatest in those territories (as in Brittany; see Brustein and Levi 1987) where strong patron–client ties and organized community relations allowed local notables to mobilize a dependent peasantry.[25] Patterns of draft evasion and self-mutilation (to avoid conscription) indicate something about the distribution of patriotic sentiments in nineteenth-century France (Weber 1976: 106–7).[26] The picture that emerges, not surprisingly, shows low patriotism in the Midi and, to some extent, in Brittany, both regions that are far removed in space and culture from the Île de France.

Other states had much greater difficulties imposing state-building nationalism. The Habsburg Empire, perhaps the quintessential nineteenth-century multinational state, had relied on indirect rule to cobble together its vast holdings.[27] As part and parcel of this control strategy, education was carried out in the vernacular languages. After the revolutions of 1848, however, the Empire began to impose cultural homogeneity in hopes of unifying these wayward territories. The Austro-Hungarian compromise of 1867 reinstalled Magyar cultural hegemony in the Hungarian territories of the Empire with a vengeance. The number of elementary schools using Slovak as a language of instruction fell from a peak of 1,971 in 1874 to 510 in 1900. After 1874 all higher education was in Magyar. 'In a backward and impoverished area like Subcarpathian Rus, this process virtually wiped out the native intelligentsia, leaving only the church or emigration as realistic alternatives to some form of assimilation' (Eley and Suny 1996*b*: 15–17). Intellectual élites tend to respond to threats to their livelihood and influence much as other élites do, but they have different kinds of resources to call upon in their defence. As a result, peripheral nationalism often emanated from the ranks of teachers and other élites who promulgated distinctive cultural practices (see Chapter 6).

The recent history of the Soviet Union provides another example of just how difficult it can be to implement direct rule in a multinational state, even when central authorities have relatively modern technology at their disposal. As had the Habsburgs before them, Soviet rulers initially resorted to indirect rule (in this case, a formal federation of national republics) to weld their vast multinational territories into a unified state. Although fitful attempts were made to promote Russian culture, as late as 1989 very little linguistic standardization and intermarriage had occurred, save among local (republican) élites (Kaiser 1994: 323). It stands to reason that former colonies like India and most African states that lack modern industrial and communications technology are unlikely candidates to implement direct rule.[28]

Let there be no misunderstanding: the distinction between direct and indirect rule is quantitative, not qualitative, and full direct rule remains beyond the state's capacity in large societies even today. Due to the costs of attaining control over large populations and territories, the attainment of social order in large societies—and even formal organizations (Ahrne 1994)—still requires a healthy leavening of indirect rule (Chai and Hechter 1998; Hechter *et al.* 1992; Hechter and Kanazawa 1993; Putnam 1994). Hence, direct rule is never absolute: the more authority a central government has over economic, judicial, military (including policing), and cultural policies throughout its territory, the more direct its rule. The rise of direct rule has been temporally and geographically variable. The next chapter explains how the initial emergence of direct rule in Western Europe bred other types of nationalism there and elsewhere.

CHAPTER 5

Other Types of Nationalism

SINCE state-building nationalism arises to fill the gap left by the erosion of indirect rule, it is the first type of nationalism to emerge. The other types of nationalism are reactions to, or by-products of, direct rule. If so, then the onset of direct rule in multi-national polities should account for temporal variations in these types of nationalism. To that end, this chapter first discusses the timing and the (rather limited) success of the most prevalent type of nationalism, the peripheral variety. Then it discusses the conditions under which irredentist and unification nationalism occur. The chapter concludes by suggesting that the present analysis also sheds some light on reasons for the varying inclusiveness of nationalist strategies.

Peripheral Nationalism

Peripheral nationalism seeks to bring about national self-determination by separating the nation from its host state. As Chapter 3 argues, previous to the late eighteenth century culturally distinct territories located in imperial states were ruled indirectly. This provided a local rather than a central target for political demands. The growth of direct rule fundamentally changes this situation, however. By wresting power and responsibility from local authorities, direct rule increases the population's dependence on the centre. Subsequently, decisions about the administration of the periphery are decided in a larger political arena, one in which the interests of peripheral residents are destined to play a minor role. As a result, the centre increasingly becomes the focus of collective action by the periphery. Local authorities have no intention of standing idly by while their prerogatives are stripped from them. Often they instigate peripheral nationalism, or at least lend their support to it. If the growth of direct rule motivates peripheral élites to embrace nationalism, the emergence of a cultural division of labour—often a concomitant of direct rule—does likewise for peripheral masses (Chapter 6).

As there are far more peripheral regions within states than states themselves, peripheral nationalism is by far the most prevalent form of nationalism. Although the bulk of scholarly attention devoted to peripheral nationalism has focused on highly developed societies, such as Britain, Canada, Belgium, and Spain (Tiryakian and Rogowski 1985), it is found in societies at all levels of development, and in the East as well as the West.[1]

In a previous book, I analysed the sources of peripheral nationalism in the British Isles from 1536 to 1966 (Hechter 1999; see also Canny 1998; Ohlmeyer 1998). Here, the analysis is extended in two directions. First, I explore whether, as the present theory contends, peripheral nationalism follows from the imposition of direct rule in multinational states. Then I discuss some of the factors responsible for the infrequent success of these movements.

The Timing of Peripheral Nationalism in the Ottoman Empire

The Ottoman Empire ranks among the greatest multinational states of all time, reigning over much of Eastern Europe, the Middle East, and parts of North Africa from the fourteenth to the early twentieth century. Like its counterparts, the Empire was a virtual tower of Babel, composed of a bewildering array of linguistic, religious, and ethnic groups. Despite its extreme multinationality, however, the Empire experienced little if any peripheral nationalism prior to the nineteenth century. This absence of peripheral nationalism was the accomplishment of a governance structure based on the *timar* and *millet* systems that the Ottomans had devised beginning in the fifteenth century.

The *timar* system was designed to acquire and control territory. Under it, conquered lands were divided into estates (*timars*) and distributed as fiefs to military officers who had served the state well. The *timar* system provided both the impetus and the reward for territorial expansion. Once in place, the *timar*-holders were obligated to raise a military retinue for service to the centre. The system also provided the economic foundation of the Empire: *timar*-holders supervised agrarian cultivation, levied taxes, and passed revenue to the centre. Although the *timar* system relied on indirect rule, the centre attempted to control the *timar*-holders by regularly rotating them from one territory to another, thereby undermining their capacity to develop an independent power base among the local peasantry (Barkey 1994; Barkey and Parikh 1991).

The *millet* system was a non-territorial form of indirect rule that was designed to cope with the Empire's cultural diversity.[2] It allowed subject peoples to retain governance over their cultural practices and local administration. *Millets* kept the records of birth, death, marriage, and wills, and were also responsible for education. They had the right to levy taxes on their members and adjudicated disputes between them. These members, in turn, had no direct relations with the Ottoman administration. The head of the *millet*, the *millet-bashy*, was chosen by his community and confirmed by the sultan; his role resembled that of an ambassador (Laponce 1960). In return, the *millets* had to declare their allegiance to the state and pay annual tribute to it (Karpat 1973).

This two-tiered form of governance functioned well only as long as the centre could maintain control over the *timar*-holders (central control over the leaders of the *millets* had always been tenuous). For a variety of reasons, its ability to do so began to diminish in the sixteenth century. Increasing provincial autonomy sapped the centre's resources. To attain greater control over its wayward provinces, the centre instituted direct rule. At this point peripheral nationalism made its appearance in many parts of the Ottoman Empire. It is the timing of these nationalist movements that is of concern here. Peripheral nationalism arose first in Serbia, then Greece, Rumelia, Bulgaria, Albania, and, last, in the Arab provinces. Does the imposition of direct rule account for this temporal sequence?

Beginning in the late sixteenth century, many areas of the Empire experienced rapid demographic growth with only a small corresponding increase in cultivated land (Goldstone 1991; Inalcik 1970; Shaw 1976). The resulting population pressures pushed many peasants into cities in search of work. An influx of cheap American silver destabilized the Ottoman economy by causing high inflation (Tachau 1984). After the development of modern artillery, the centre replaced the *timar* cavalrymen and invested in a more modernized army employing janissaries, an élite corps of soldiers known for their military prowess. This shift in military technology imposed greater costs on the centre.

Soon new social groups eclipsed the *timar*-holders. In regions of the Empire closest to Western Europe, local commercial and intellectual notables came to the fore. Elsewhere *ayans*, a new semi-feudal aristocracy of landed élites, arose. The *ayans* became the primary holders of tax farms and arrogated to themselves much local political authority (Davison 1963: 17; Karpat 1968: 71–8; Inalcik 1995: 126; Heper 1985: 30–2; Keyder 1997: 31). The upshot is that both groups were far less dependent on the centre than the *timar*-holders had been.

The centre attempted to redress provincial autonomy by instituting direct rule in the late eighteenth century. The road was a rocky one, however. A coalition of janissaries and local authorities revolted in 1807, successfully deposing Sultan Selim III (Inalcik 1995: 130). Further, the leaders of the *millets*, which had remained intact during the centuries of state decline, became more autonomous as they participated in commerce. They began to organize to resist the increasing incursions by the centre.

The centre first attempted to impose direct rule in its western provinces. This, I argue, is why the Balkan regions were first to develop peripheral nationalism.[3] Serbia and Greece were the territories most closely tied to the developing world economy. The opportunity to exchange with the rapidly developing societies in the West enabled local Serbian and Greek authorities to be more autonomous of Constantinople—thus more capable of resisting direct rule—than any others in the Empire. Their autonomy was also fostered by the Western powers' sympathy for the rights of Christian subjects living in what, after all, was a Muslim empire.

Serbia was the first Balkan province to develop a strong national identity.[4] After enjoying considerable autonomy under a benevolent governor of Belgrade, it was besieged by the centre's crack troops, the janissaries, who killed the governor and many village chiefs. Local notables fought back in the first Serbian insurrection in 1804 (MacKenzie 1996: 210). What began as a series of revolts by local leaders against the janissaries soon acquired the larger goal of national independence as local notables sought to secede from the Empire. In 1813 Turkish armies invaded Serbia in an attempt bring it to heel once more. Nationalist insurrections followed and in 1833, at the behest of Russia, Serbia was granted its autonomy, but it remained within the Empire. Independence was only acquired following the defeat of the Ottomans in the Russo-Turkish War (1878).

Although it was the most economically developed—hence, economically autonomous—province in the Empire, Greece was the second Balkan province to become nationalist. The Greeks possessed their own administrative, political, and even military institutions (Braude and Lewis 1982: 19). Preserved by the *millet* system, Greek culture had remained vibrant through the years of Ottoman rule. Had Serbia not faced the wrath of the janissaries, Greece probably would have been the first province to develop peripheral nationalism (Gewehr 1967: 16). The immediate cause of the Greek war of independence (1821–7) was Mahmud II's attempt to impose direct rule.

The central government undertook the *Tanzimat* reforms (1839–76), an unprecedented attempt to institute direct rule, to respond to events in Serbia and Greece, and to halt the Empire's decline (Davison 1963; Hale 1994; Karpat 1972; Shaw 1968, 1976). These were designed to achieve political centralization, the improvement of social and economic conditions, and the promotion of a sense of 'Ottomanism' among all the peoples of the Empire. Naturally, these goals could only be attained by doing away with many of the privileges of local notables and leaders of the *millets*.

Thus began the next round of peripheral nationalism in the remaining Balkan provinces under central control. Uprisings in Nish and Vidin, two Rumelian territories near Serbia, occurred in

1841 and 1850 respectively, the result of upheavals brought about by *Tanzimat* tax reforms (Inalcik 1976: 18–33). Hostilities in Rumelia took on a religio-national form as Christians attacked Muslims, attempting to drive them out of the province. Bulgaria also witnessed the birth of peripheral nationalism in this period: anti-centre revolts occurred in 1835, 1841–2, and 1850.

The tardiness of Bulgarian nationalism, relative to that of Serbia and Greece, was due to a number of factors. Since Bulgaria was the nearest of all the Balkan provinces to Constantinople, it was more remote from Western third parties. Further, the province was more religiously heterogeneous than Serbia and Greece: Muslims constituted a large proportion of the population. Religious heterogeneity impeded territorial solidarity. Like many other provinces, Bulgaria did not manage to secede from the Empire on its own steam. Independence for Bulgaria, Serbia, and Romania only came with the defeat of the Ottomans in the Russo-Turkish War (1877–8) and the ensuing Treaty of Berlin (1878).

Albania was the last of the Balkan provinces to develop nationalism and the last to secede. It lacked many of the conditions that fostered peripheral nationalism elsewhere (White 1937: 106). Most of its tribes enjoyed almost complete autonomy from central influence and its population was very culturally heterogeneous. Although the Albanian League was established in 1878 to spread Albanian language and literature and raise a national militia, it was banned in 1886. Only after the rise to power of the Young Turks in 1908 was direct rule imposed on Albania in earnest. Attempts to disarm the population in the north in 1910 led to nationalist insurrections. Albania declared independence in 1912.[5]

Although the Arab provinces were least affected by the centralizing policies of Selim III and Mahmud II,[6] they did not escape the *Tanzimat* reforms altogether. Syria and Lebanon were specifically targeted for conscription, disarmament, and direct taxation. Yet far from producing peripheral nationalism, these reforms instead led to conflict between Christian Maronites and Muslim Druzes (Maoz 1982: 91–2). During the nearly two decades of Ottoman direct rule, civil and cultural unrest escalated, resulting in the widespread massacres of 1861. Sultan Abdülhamid (1876–1908) took care to advance the political and economic interests of local Arab notables, who were given important positions in the imperial civil service and military.

The rise of the Young Turks—the Committee of Union and Progress (1908–18)—turned the Arabs' attention toward Istanbul by replacing local notables in key provincial posts, and imposing the Turkish language in government schools, the judicial system, and local administration. Not surprisingly, this met with strong resistance among local Arab notables. Although many of the reforms instituted by the Young Turks were strongly centralist, some—such as the introduction of mass politics, the expansion of educational opportunity, and the development of a more liberal press—facilitated the expression of nationalism (Kayali 1997: ch. 2). Consequently, the seeds of Arab nationalism developed from 1909 through 1918 (Karpat 1972; Keyder 1997; Safi 1992: 347). Ottoman territorial losses during the Balkan Wars and the First World War convinced Arab notables (most notably, Sharif Husayn of the Hijaz) to 'pursue opportunities other than those emanating from a close indentitifaction with Istanbul that would enhance [their] personal power and prestige' (Kayali 1997: 172).

All told, the sequence of peripheral nationalism in the Ottoman Empire follows the timing of the imposition of direct rule. Direct rule was first imposed in the western provinces, and last in the eastern ones. Wherever there was sufficient cultural homogeneity to foster territorial solidarity, peripheral nationalism often followed suit.

Yet the relationship between direct rule and peripheral nationalism is not instantaneous. This is well illustrated by the development of Kosovar nationalism in the 1990s. A resource-rich mountainous region settled by the Slavs, Kosovo became part of Serbia in the twelfth century. Following Serbia's defeat at the hands of the Ottomans in 1389, Kosovo remained under Ottoman rule until 1913. After the First World War, it was incorporated in Yugoslavia. The predominantly Muslim and Albanian-speaking region became an autonomous region within Serbia in 1945.

During all this time Kosovo was ruled indirectly. Although it remained formally part of Serbia, for all practical purposes Kosovo became self-governing after 1974. It even had its own representatives in the federal parliament (Hayden 1998). In 1989, however,

Serbia imposed direct rule on Kosovo. This immediately led to the establishment of a non-violent opposition (The Albanian Democratic League of Kosovo, the LDK). In 1992, the Kosovo Liberation Army (UCK) was formed to fight for independence and closer affiliation with Albania. It carried out its first armed attack in 1993, but regular and sustained attacks against the centre were not mounted until mid-1997. By March 1998, the Kosovar nationalists had overrun more than a dozen police stations, looting them of scores of automatic weapons. Serbian police patrols and checkpoints were targeted, and more than fifty Serbian policemen and officials were assassinated. In the most brazen attack to date, the nationalists brazenly stepped into the road near the village of Srbica at midday and killed a local Serbian official on 23 January 1998. The central government response was to conduct brutal military sweeps in territories of nationalist strength. In March 1998, for example, Serbian police, armed with helicopter gunships and armoured personnel carriers, tortured and killed twenty-four people in the village of Likosane. A mass funeral held near the village was attended by 40,000 mourners. As the spiral of violence escalated, the Serbian government responded by instituting a new round of ethnic cleansing against the Kosovar Albanians. At the present time (May 1999), the North Atlantic Treaty Organization is waging an air war on Serbia to reinstitute autonomy (read: indirect rule)—but not sovereignty—in Kosovo.

The story is familiar.[7] As the present analysis suggests, Kosovar nationalism arose just after the imposition of direct rule. Why then did it take eight years to become noticeable to the world at large? The collective action exemplified by the establishment of Kosovar nationalist groups is never instantaneous. A certain amount of time must pass to persuade recruits that the new regime is here to stay. Beyond this, both resources and time must be invested to build effective political organizations. The nationalists have erected their own parallel government, which levies taxes, as well as having shadow institutions—like a school system—that operate from private homes (Hedges 1998*b*). Beyond this, establishing the underground paramilitary organization required to carry out violent attacks is particularly costly and time-consuming. Under conditions of secrecy, recruits have to be attracted, trained, and provisioned. Weapons have to be acquired—usually from abroad —before paramilitary campaigns can be undertaken to steal more weapons from central authorities.[8] The temporal lag between the imposition of direct rule and the emergence of visible nationalism therefore is due, at least in part, to the time intensity that is inherent in organizing militant collective action. Of course, if free riding cannot be prevented, then collective action may never arise at all.

Pure Secession in Norway and Ireland

The distinguishing characteristic of peripheral nationalism is the demand for secession. Secession is the formal withdrawal from a central political authority by a member unit on the basis of a claim to independent sovereign status.[9] Many such demands come to nothing: during the summer of 1997, for example, quixotic secessionist actions were mounted in two self-conscious regions—Texas in the United States, and Veneto in Italy.

If there is one constant in history apart from the imposition of taxes, it is the reluctance of states to part with contiguous territory. Land is the pillar of the state; it provides tax revenue, a labour force, mineral and other geographically based resources, and it is vital for defence. Beyond this, the permanence of state borders is among the most tenaciously held givens in political culture (Lustick 1993: 57–80). For these reasons, it is axiomatic that when rulers contemplate changing state borders, their fantasies are expansionist rather than contractionist. This is why most secessions are the result of *fragmentation*: they are either imposed on unwilling rulers who are defeated in war, or are the by-product of endemic imperial weakness or collapse (Posen 1993*b*).[10] Ottoman peripheral nationalisms are all of this type.

Fragmentation is qualitatively different from *pure secession*, which only occurs when a *highly effective* state permits a secessionist territory to withdraw from its embrace. The members of nationalist groups located in highly effective states are not likely to regard secession is a realizable political goal. Their perception is, however, extremely sensitive to signs of disarray in the centre. If central authorities signal their willingness to renegotiate the terms of exchange with its peripheries—as the Soviet Union did in its waning days by adopting *glasnost'*—then secession suddenly enters the realm of the feasible.[11] Pure secession is among the rarest of political outcomes. It has only occurred twice in the twentieth century: when Norway left Sweden in 1905, and when Ireland left the United Kingdom in 1922.[12]

Why, then, does pure secession ever occur? To say that rulers will cede territory only when the net benefit of doing so is positive is a truism.[13] An answer to this question requires the specification of factors that are most likely to enter into the rulers' political calculations. Even if they are faced with a highly mobilized secessionist movement, central rulers still have a variety of possible reactions that stop short of secession.

They can offer secessionist leaders *incentives* by rewarding them with good jobs contingent on abandoning their support of secession. The regime also may promise, and perhaps even provide, other kinds of resources (such as development projects) to the region so as to persuade rank-and-file members of the secessionist movement that their core interests lie with maintaining a tie to the host state. In similar fashion, they can threaten economic non-cooperation in the event that secession occurs. Although such a threat is not likely to be regarded as highly credible, it nevertheless increases the costs of secession to potential supporters (Young 1994).

Constitutional reforms are a more costly response to secessionism. They can help forestall secession either by providing federation, devolution, and other institutional changes that effectively vest greater decision-making authority within the nation (as is ongoing with respect to Quebec), or by instituting administrative redistricting that inhibits the secessionists' potential for collective action, as occurred in Nigeria and India (Wood 1981).

If all else fails, *repression* is likely to be the state's last resort. Its efficacy, however, depends on at least three kinds of factors. First, geographic: the larger and more mountainous the secessionists' territory, the more difficult it is for the centre to control it militarily. Second, military: the military capacity of the host state relative to that of the secessionist territory depends not only on the secessionists' *matériel* and training (Do they have an army? If so, how effective is it?), but also on each population's morale, which directly affects conscription rates and soldiers' combat performance. For example, it is far more difficult to conscript an army in a population that has recently experienced high rates of military casualties than one that has enjoyed an extended period of peace. Last, geopolitical: how are third parties in the international system likely to react to the host state's repressive moves?[14]

For the most part, geopolitical factors tend to militate against secession. In the first place, as the origins of most current states are multinational, almost all central rulers can imagine that they too may some day face potential secessionist movements. Supporting secessionist movements elsewhere therefore might help stir up unpleasant problems at home. This provides most central rulers with a reason to collude by universally discouraging secession. Further, support for a secessionist movement necessarily comes at the expense of relations with its host state.[15] Given geopolitical realities, the net benefit to be gained by courting secessionists tends to be negative.[16] Sometimes international support helps sustain a state built on shaky foundations (as has been argued with respect to Tito's Yugoslavia (Omrĉanin 1976).

Several of these factors come into play in accounting for the unusual success of Norwegian and Irish secession. Norway initially became subject to Swedish rule as the result of an 1813 agreement among the United Kingdom, Russia, and Sweden. Sweden was promised Norway as compensation for its loss of Finland to Russia if it helped the allies defeat Napoleon. Pursuant to the agreement, Denmark handed over the governance to Sweden one year later. Sweden's interest in Norway initially was based on its fear of Russian expansion and was stimulated by Russia's aggressiveness in Finland (Derry 1979: 272). Separatist sentiment in Norway grew during Swedish rule, however, and by 1905 it had become almost universal: a referendum on Norwegian secession passed by 368,208 to 184, with a turnout of 84 per cent of the electorate (Omrĉanin 1976: 10). The referendum results left Swedish rulers with a quandary. Owing to Norway's physical size and topography and to Sweden's small population, military repression was an unattractive option. Swedish defences would be more vulnerable if most of its military resources were expended occupying a hostile Norway than if Sweden had a friendly Norway that was responsible for its own security. Occupying Norway would be difficult, not least because, during the years immediately prior to independence, Norway had strengthened its military by buying new field artillery and building forts on the Swedish frontier (Derry 1979: 270).

Further, Sweden's domination of a hostile Norway was an obstacle to Scandinavian regional cooperation. By consenting to Norway's independence, this obstacle was removed and Scandinavian leaders then were able to cooperate as equal partners in establishing the Nordic Interparliamentary Union (1907) and subsequent international institutions that benefited the entire Nordic region (Hancock 1972: 255–6). Last, Sweden's decision may have been influenced by international pressure. Norway had made successful efforts to attain foreign support, and its decision to establish a monarchy may have allayed fears about its future instability (Larsen 1948: 273).

Ireland's incorporation in Great Britain lasted from 1801 to 1922. As in Norway, Irish support for nationalism grew during this period—especially after the Easter Rebellion in 1916—and the nationalists also developed a military capacity. The British state had many military advantages in Ireland relative to that of Sweden in Norway, however. The size and geography of Ireland made occupation feasible, and the British already had been engaged in the occupation of Ireland during much of the late nineteenth century. In addition, British military resources far exceeded Sweden's. Why then did Britain accede to the secessionists' demands?

After the end of the First World War, British public opinion did not support a war in Ireland (Hachey 1973: 23–5). Continuing violence there was undermining the war-weary public's support for the Liberal government (MacDonagh 1968: 88). The government recognized that an utter lack of public support precluded an all-out offensive or a prolonged occupation (Beckett 1966).[17] In addition, many prominent people—including the king of England and the archbishop of Canterbury—objected to the government's Irish policy and this helped set the stage for negotiations in June 1921. International opinion, particularly in the United States, also inclined the government to concession.

Finally, Britain retained some control over the new Irish state and kept total control over Northern Ireland. Although the Irish nationalists sought an independent unpartitioned republic, they were forced to accept a compromise. Ireland was given status as a dominion in the British Empire, rather than outright independence. And Ireland had to give up Ulster, the six counties of Northern Ireland. Ireland remained subject to Britain in many ways: Britain kept control of certain Irish harbours that had been essential to its survival during the war (Beckett 1966: 453; MacDonagh 1968: 91). Britain retained ultimate appellate jurisdiction of court cases (MacDonagh 1968: 91), and also reserved the right to approve the new Irish constitution (Macardle 1965: 818).

Thus the ultimate settlement between Britain and Ireland was a compromise. Britain protected itself from the costs of Irish secession by maintaining close ties. The significance of those ties is revealed by the events that followed the signing of the treaty. Violence broke out in Ireland between those who still wanted a fully independent republic and those who accepted the treaty's terms. To some Irish, the treaty perpetuated Ireland's colonial subjection. Of course, the ties between Ireland and Britain—like those involving other Commonwealth countries—have changed dramatically over time.

Recent events in the Balkans and Eastern Europe have underscored the historical contingency of the role of geopolitical factors in state formation (Heraclides 1990). Geopolitical forces often conspire to promote the fragmentation of states (Lapidus and Zaslavsky 1992). During the post-Yalta *détente* between the United States and the Soviet Union, non-intervention in internal politics was a guiding principle of international relations (for reasons spelt out by Wallerstein 1991). This principle tended to deny secessionists any hope of third-party intervention on their behalf. Now that the American–Soviet *détente* is no longer operational, third-party intervention has been on the rise. The most important contemporary instance was Germany's decision to recognize the sovereignty of Slovenia and Croatia. This move, which was ultimately responsible for recognition of these new states by the European Union and a reluctant United States, would have been unthinkable during the cold war.

Most of the new states formed since the break-up of the Soviet Union and the Warsaw Pact have been the product of fragmentation rather than secession. It has long been appreciated that secession is a highly improbable outcome (Young 1976: 460–504). Why is it so improbable and why it will continue to be so in the future? Since many states are multinational, and many of these contain territorially concentrated national groups, on statistical grounds alone secession should be relatively common. Yet few regions have the structural requirements for the development of a secessionist movement. Not only do these include a national population disproportionately clustered in its 'own' territory which has ample intragroup communications capacity—for this requirement is met by many multinational states in the world. Beyond this, the nation must be located in a state that allows considerable freedom of association. Given a demand for sovereignty, the nation must develop political organizations capable of mobilizing the nationals.[18] This problem is far more severe in the case of secession than in the case of many other political agendas, because even in the best of circumstances, most people appreciate that host states will tenaciously hold on to their territory. Further, even when mobilization solutions are at hand, it is not even clear that secession is an outcome that most self-identified secessionists themselves sincerely desire.

The final reason for the improbability of secession is that the host state is far from powerless to protect its territorial integrity. If the secessionist territory is large and/or mountainous, if the regime has too few resources to provide the necessary incentives to coopt secessionist leaders, and if potential constitutional reforms are either too difficult to enact or likely to be regarded as insufficient by the territorial population, then and only then is the host state forced to contemplate acceding to secessionist demands.

Irredentist Nationalism

Irredentism—derived from the Italian *irredenta*, unredeemed— was first used to describe nineteenth-century Italian movements to annex Italian-speaking areas under Austrian and Swiss rule. It now refers to any effort to unite national segments of a population in adjacent countries within a common polity (Chazan 1991*a*). Irredentist nationalism is the least prevalent form of nationalism; for that reason it can dealt with briefly. If secession involves subtracting a national territory from a state, irredentism involves subtracting the territory from one state and adding it to another. Given the obvious difficulties of this, irredentist movements most often are initiated by states interested in annexing territories having a large proportion of their co-nationals. Nineteenth-century Romania and Greece relied on irredentist nationalism advocated by the respective governments (Sugar 1969: 50–1). Hitler's annexation of the Sudetenland is perhaps the most transparent recent example.

Unlikely as pure secession is, successful irredentist nationalism is far less likely, even though many nations—especially in postcolonial Asia, Africa, and the Middle East—are divided by state boundaries (Chazan 1991*b*; Horowitz 1992). In the last analysis, successful secessionist movements merely require the host state's consent to forego the given territory. Successful irredentist movements require not only that, but the consent of the putative beneficiary state as well. If host states are extremely reluctant to part with their territory, potential beneficiary states may also be leery to accept new territories.

The emergence of an irredentist cause in a given nation is directly related to the receptiveness of the beneficiary state to the prospect (Horowitz 1992: 122–3). Potential beneficiary states tend to waver in their support of irredentist movements. Thus, in 1975 Iran abruptly halted its military assistance to the Iraqi Kurds and eventually closed their borders to them, effectively dooming the movement. In 1987, India ceased its support for the Tamil secessionists in Sri Lanka, reaching an agreement with the Sri Lankan government for Tamil regional autonomy instead, and proceeded to join the Sri Lankan government in suppressing its armed rebels. Moreover, it is by no means certain that the national minority in the donor state will be recognized as kindred by members of the beneficiary state.[19] Perhaps the key reason for the improbability of irredentism is that it is seldom in the interest of the nationalist movement's leadership. Whereas successful secession affords them the prospect of gaining the reins of power in the government of the new state, irredentism merely provides them with the added competition of the established leadership pool in the beneficiary state. For all these reasons, nationalist groups are far more likely to espouse secession than irredentism.

Unification Nationalism

Unification nationalism is the obverse of state-building nationalism. Whereas the latter seeks to create cultural homogeneity within the borders of an existing multinational state, the former aims to create an overarching state that supplants a number of smaller sovereign units in a (relatively) culturally homogeneous territory.[20] What induces petty sovereigns to undertake collective action that results in a loss of their sovereignty? In general, they are only likely to do so when they perceive a threat to their rule.[21] The principal historical examples are the unification of Germany and Italy, whereas Poland offers an instructive counterexample.[22]

Before 1860, Great Britain and France were the only two prominent countries in Europe to undertake state-building nationalism.[23] Although Spain may have looked like a nation state on the map, in reality it was a multinational empire. Portugal, the Netherlands, and the Scandinavian countries were the closest to being nation states, but they were small and had less geopolitical influence. The characteristic European polities of this era were of two kinds. They were either small states comprising fragments of a nation, like Hanover, Baden, Sardinia, Tuscany, the Two Sicilies, or they were vast multinational states like the Romanov, Habsburg, and Ottoman Empires. For example, the Holy Roman Empire (controlled by the Habsburg dynasty) was split up into 314 territories and towns and into 1,475 free lordships, all of which guarded the sovereign rights guaranteed to them by the European powers after the Peace of Westphalia. The Germans, according to the Imperial Privy Councillor Friedrich Carl von Moser *(Von dem Deutschen Nationalgeist)* writing in the year 1766:

are a puzzle of a political constitution, a prey of our neighbours, an object of their scorns outstanding in the history of the world, disunited among our-selves, weak from our divisions, strong enough to harm ourselves, power-less to save ourselves, insensitive to the honour of our name, indifferent to the glory of our laws, envious of our rulers, distrusting one another, incon-sistent about our principles, coercive about enforcing them, a great but also a despised people; a potentially happy but actually a very lamentable people (Schulze 1991: 43).

Whereas feudal restrictions on commercial activity and political participation had begun to crumble in Britain, the Netherlands, and France, these developments had hardly affected the territories of the Reich, save in a few northern trading towns. Much the same could be said for the situation in Italy (Riall 1994: 5). Accord-ing to Giuseppe Mazzini, the ideologist of Italian unification, 'The States into which Italy is divided today are not the creation of our own people; they are the result of the ambitions and calculations of princes or of local conquerors, and serve no purpose but to flatter the vanity of local aristocracies for which a narrower sphere than a great Country is necessary' (Mazzini [1858] 1995: 95).

The impetus toward unification nationalism in Germany and Italy was an exogenous shock—the Napoleonic conquest. This conquest, which seemed to demonstrate the economic and military superiority of direct rule over alternative forms of governance, had important effects on the conquered territories. It consolidated the German and Italian polities, sharply reducing their numbers. And it increased the efficiency of their governance by establish-ing modern bureaucratic administration and law. In both the (extended) French Empire and all the dependent territories (including all of Germany and Italy in 1810), feudal authority was extinguished. Central governments were given authority over their individual subjects. The nobility lost its privileges in taxation, office-holding, and military command. The Church was stripped of much of its power as well (Palmer and Colton 1965: ch. 10).

The Napoleonic reforms laid the groundwork for unification nationalism in Germany and Italy in two fundamental ways. In the first place, by threatening the social and political position of local authorities the reforms gave prominent political actors a strong incentive to oppose Napoleon, as the extension of direct rule always does. The Napoleonic state spurred opposition among its non-French subjects by raising taxes in dependent territories to subsidize taxpayers in France.[24] Resistance to Napoleon united conservatives, who wished to return to the *status quo ante*, with liberals who wanted to preserve the liberties introduced by Napoleonic reforms, but insisted on greater self-government. Such ideological heterogeneity is, of course, typical of nationalist movements. The basis of all nationalist movements is the desire for self-government, but since they are nearly always coalitions of people whose other interests differ widely, the type of government that particular nationalists envision (whether liberal, conservative, or radical) is likely to be a matter of some dispute (see Chapter 1).

In the second place, the Napoleonic reforms fostered unification nationalism in German and Italy by sharply reducing the number of separate states in each territory, thereby substantially reducing the costs of collective action among them. For most of the eighteenth century, Germans had been the least nationally minded of all the larger European peoples:

They prided themselves on their world-citizenship or cosmopolitan outlook. Looking out from the tiny states in which they lived, they were conscious of Europe, conscious of other countries, but hardly conscious of Germany. The Holy Roman Empire was a shadow. The German world had no tangible frontiers; the area of German speech simply faded out into Alsace or the Austrian Netherlands, or into Poland, Bohemia, or the upper Balkans. That 'Germany' ever did, thought, or hoped anything never crossed the German mind. There was scarcely even a developed language, for the speech habits of Berlin and Vienna were more different than those of London and New York today. The upper classes, becoming contemptuous of much that was German, took over French fashions, dress, etiquette, manners, ideas, and language, regarding them as an international norm of civilized living. Frederick the Great (of Prussia) hired French tax-collectors and wrote his own books in French (Palmer and Colton 1965: 403).

Napoleon turned all the German states but one, Prussia, into political dependencies in the Confederation of the Rhine (Austria allied itself with Napoleon by marriage in 1810). Even though it suffered military defeat resulting in the loss of its territory west of the Elbe, Prussia was the sole German state to hold out against Napoleon.[25] Fifty years later, with a highly effective military, Prussia took the lead in German unification. While the Napoleonic conquest greatly simplified the German state system, German romanticism—itself a reaction against the influence of the French Enlightenment, the French Revolution, and Napoleonic rule—spawned nationalist treatises, like those of Herder and Fichte (Greenfeld 1992).[26] The defeat of Napoleon and collapse of the continental system, however, reintroduced great political complexity in the German lands. From 1815 to 1866 there were thirty-nine separate states in Germany.

There were significant parallels in Italy.[27] Italy had long been divided into about six large states and a few very small ones. From 1796 to 1814, the French regime in Italy broke the back of the various duchies, oligarchic republics, papal states, and foreign dynasties by which Italy had long been ruled. In the end, a veritable patchwork of sovereignties had been reduced to only three parts. Thus French influence made the notion of a politically unified Italy a reasonable aspiration. And the nationalist ideology of Mazzini articulated this aspiration.[28]

Napoleon's simplification of the Italian political landscape was undone by the Congress of Vienna. And by 1859—the beginning of the Risorgimento—Italy was once more divided into a number of separate states. However, the actions of the Congress of Vienna had provided the German territory with a more effective overarching political institution—the German Confederation—than had previously existed in Italian territory.[29] In the aftermath of the revolutions of 1848, therefore, Germany and Italy were politically divided territories. Both of these territories boasted home-grown nationalist writings dating from the Napoleonic period. Yet the political impact of these ideals was marginal, for the advocates of nationalism had little effective political organization (Breuilly 1993: 98). Nationalist support was generally confined to gymnastic societies, student fraternities, and to a variety of groups devoted to singing and other cultural and literary pursuits (Düding 1987). Unification did not result from the activities of these groups.

The increased effectiveness of the German Confederation was a more important stimulus to the development of a national opposition than the intellectual concerns with romantic nationalism (Breuilly 1993: 100). In taking a firm stand against Napoleonic constitutional reforms, the Confederation alienated liberal businessmen and officials advocating economic and political development. Further, Prussian government support for a customs union among German states helped provide an institutional base for other kinds of cooperation. The Prussian-backed customs union created an economic 'Germany' in the eyes of the world and in itself encouraged a sense of economic nationalism.[30]

When Bismarck later rejected the idea of joint Prussian and Austrian sovereignty over Germany, he became committed to the idea of a territorially concentrated state to better compete with continental rivals. In a letter written in 1857 Bismarck wrote, 'Situated in the centre of Europe we cannot afford that kind of passive incompetence which is happy to be left in peace. It will endanger us tomorrow as it did in 1805, and we shall be the anvil if we do nothing to be the hammer' (cited in Stürmer 1987: 141). Further, Prussian-led national unification was not the result of obvious popular demand in other German states: most German states were on the Austrian side in the Austro-Prussian War of 1866. German national sentiment was more a by-product of German unification than a cause of it.

Much the same could be said of Italian unification. Piedmont played an analogous role to that of Prussia, Cavour was Bismarck's counterpart, and Austria was a common enemy. Although Cavour lacked an institution like the German Confederation, which could have provided an institutional framework to press for political unification, Piedmont benefited from French support against Austria in its bid to extend its control over Northern Italy. As in Germany, there was little popular support for Italian unification.[31] Garibaldi's successful invasion of Sicily was both unanticipated and unsupported by Cavour. Garibaldi's military success:

was due to the decrepit state of the Bourbon regime on the island. The speed of his invasion made it possible for both popular opposition and the propertied elements hostile to the regime to see in him an ally and a means of overthrowing the government. Only this general support could have enabled the pathetically weak military force under Garibaldi's command to take over the island. The support had nothing to do with the nationalist cause, which was weaker in the south, particularly in Sicily, than in any other part of Italy. It was purely to do with the domestic problems of the Bourbon regime. Indeed, it is reported that when the cry of *Viva Italia*! was raised during Victor Emmanuel's entry into Naples some natives thought it must refer to his wife (Breuilly 1993: 113).

Even so, Italian unification failed to lead to an effective central state due to a poor communications infrastructure (Riall 1994: 59–60). Rome lacked economic resources relative to those controlled by local élites. As a result, antagonism to the centre persists in peripheral areas (it is worst in Sicily, but seemingly a problem in other regions, as well).[32] The Italian example suggests that national unification is far from sufficient to produce effective direct rule.

In both Germany and Italy, various liberal élites pressed for national unification in order to create a modern state that would be recognized by the two European superpowers, Britain and France. As the story of nineteenth-century Poland attests, however, not all unification nationalist movements manage to win the day. Poland too was split into a variety of separate states, many of which were controlled by foreign powers. As in Germany and Italy, a unification nationalist movement was established among the nobility in order to reassert their political position (Breuilly 1993: 116–18). However, the Polish nobility did not manage to organize militarily to advance their common interests. As a result, Poland never established a unified state that was capable of protecting its territory from its avaricious neighbours.[33]

Unification nationalism is a by-product of direct rule, but it occurs via quite different mechanisms. It arises in territories subjected to the geopolitical threat represented by the emergence of direct-rule states. It has little popular support and is a movement of élites. Because the élites seeking national unity in Germany and Italy were fragmented and without political authority, they looked to existing states for support. Like peripheral nationalism, part of its motivation is defensive: it is difficult to believe that Bismarck or Cavour would have been successful in a Europe without the challenge represented by the existence of other national states.[34]

French state-building nationalism therefore begat German and Italian unification nationalism as unintended by-products. Instead of seeking autonomy by seceding from the modernizing state, unification nationalism aims to *create* a modern state by eradicating existing political boundaries and enlarging them to be congruent with the nation.[35] In all of these cases, the impetus to political unity is the perception of an external threat. Once unification occurs, however, the mechanisms of state-building nationalism encountered in Chapter 4 come into play. Foremost among these is indoctrination in the schools, particularly in the teaching of history.[36]

Inclusive Versus Exclusive Nationalisms

This discussion ignores many other differences among nationalist movements. Chief amongst these are variations in the content of nationalist ideals. Why are some forms of nationalism (like the French) culturally *inclusive*, and others (like German) culturally *exclusive*? Max Weber tantalizingly broached the subject of accounting for strategic differences between tactics of monopolization and closure in social groups, but since then little research has focused squarely on the problem (see, however, the suggestive analysis of the dynamics of closure in the context of unionization in Friedman 1990). Recent research explaining differences in the citizenship policies of states offers further insight into the question. State-building and unification nationalism differ in one important respect: the former is inherently *territorially* inclusive, whereas the latter is *culturally* inclusive.[37] Thus post-Revolutionary France—the pre-eminent example of state-building nationalism—has continually defined citizenship expansively and is assimilationist, whereas Germany—the *locus classicus* of unification nationalism—has defined citizenship as a community of descent based on cultural factors (Brubaker 1992).[38]

Part of this difference is accounted for by the timing of these two forms of nationalism. Historically, state-building nationalism preceded unification nationalism. Unlike unification nationalism, the initial impetus for state-building nationalism was largely endogenous. Further, the process occurred in the absence of well-articulated nationalist ideals: it is no accident that nationalist ideologues like Mazzini, Herder, and Fichte were neither British nor French. When peripheries like Cornwall and Burgundy were folded into the expanding Tudor and Capetian states, no concept of national self-determination was readily available to help their élites mobilize peasant resistance.

The impetus for unification nationalism, however, was largely exogenous. The rulers of the many different states and principalities in Germany and Italy were induced to form a national state in order to defend their interests against the threat posed by the highly effective direct-rule states of France and Great Britain. Nationalist ideals came into their own during this process. Ironically, these ideals came back to haunt both Britain and France: they were adopted in Wales, Brittany, and Corsica to resist further extensions of direct rule in the twentieth century. In this way Herder and Mazzini provided the shoulders for an Irish nationalist like James Connolly to stand on.

Conclusion

The rise of direct rule had major consequences for the development of peripheral nationalism, the most common type of nationalism, as well as for unification nationalism. Since direct rule invariably decreases the power of local authorities, its advent provides them with a strong incentive to resist (Tambiah 1996). The local authorities in culturally distinctive peripheries, therefore, are often tempted to play the peripheral nationalist card in their efforts to keep the centre at bay (Brass 1991).[39] Direct rule can spur peripheral nationalism even in culturally distinct regions (like nineteenth-century Wales and the Spanish Basque Country) whose traditional authorities have assimilated to the culture of the centre. In such regions it can afford political space to new kinds of leaders who attempt to mobilize the culturally distinct peasantry on nationalist grounds.

This logic has a key implication. Variations in peripheral nationalism among the territories of an empire ought to be explained by the timing of direct rule. The development of peripheral nationalism in the various nations of the Ottoman Empire is consistent with this expectation: the sequence of nationalist mobilization is largely accounted for by the onset of direct rule in each territory.

Direct rule plays a somewhat more indirect role in the genesis of unification nationalism. When combined with state-building nationalism, it fosters both economic and military efficiency.[40] Unification nationalism then emerges as a reaction to the increased efficiency of direct-rule states. 'Greatness awaited peoples who could act together as brothers in harmony with one another and with their government, while weakness and ignominy threatened rulers so alienated from their people as to remain incapable of using unstinted popular support' (McNeill 1986: 51). Thus the seeds of German and Italian unification are to be found in the Napoleonic conquests. Likewise, the origins of direct rule in Japan are defensive: its impetus can be traced to the Admiral Perry's sudden appearence in Edo Bay in 1853.[41]

Although the extension of direct rule in a multinational polity is a necessary condition of the two most important types of nationalism, it is far from a sufficient one. The first consequence of direct rule is likely to be state-building nationalism, which aims to destroy the social basis of peripheral nationality. By rendering the boundaries of nation and governance unit congruent, its success erodes any potential for peripheral nationalism. It follows that peripheral nationalism can emerge only when the institutions of direct rule fail to assimilate the distinct nations within a state.

Assimilation is likely to occur only under certain kinds of conditions, however. Also needed, perhaps, is a political opening: the most significant determinants of serious nationalist conflict in the contemporary world are transitional political regimes undergoing democratization, and states that have weathered significant power shifts. Presumably these institutional changes offer new opportunities for political entrepreneurs to build constituencies, and therefore make all kinds of collective action more likely (Gurr 1994: 364).

CHAPTER 6

The Salience of National Identity

AS Chapter 5 shows, nationalism comes in several varieties. Despite their differences, these types of nationalism have at least two elements in common. In the first place, they are enacted in the name of a politically self-conscious nation. In the second, they engender a demand for national sovereignty. Yet culturally distinct groups do not necessarily become politically self-conscious nations. Nor do politically self-conscious nations necessarily demand sovereignty. The present chapter discusses the conditions governing the salience of national identity. The reasons why self-conscious national groups might demand sovereignty are explored in Chapter 7.

That people are more liable to make sacrifices—including the ultimate sacrifice, their own lives—for their nation than for many other kinds of groups is ample testament to the power of national identity:

Group-consciousness is never exclusive. Men find themselves members of different groups at the same time. With the growth of the complexity of civilization, the number of groups of which men find themselves a part generally increases. These groups are not fixed. They have changing limits, and they are of changing importance. Within these pluralistic, and sometimes conflicting, kinds of group-consciousness there is generally one which is recognized by man as the supreme and most important, to which therefore, in the case of conflict of group-loyalties, he owes supreme loyalty. He identifies himself with the group and its existence, frequently not only for the span of his life, but for the continuity of his existence beyond this span. This feeling of solidarity between the individual and the group may go, at certain times, as far as complete submergence of the individual in the group (Kohn 1944: 16).

Why should the nation be able to exercise this kind of grip on the mind? It is commonly held that national identities are intrinsically salient.[1] Nations are thought to have greater durability than many other kinds of groups. Their durability is reflected in the nation's putative historical continuity.[2] Because nations are associated with a homeland, they can persist over time despite changing membership: 'A group's persistence is fostered to the degree that its property remains unalienable . . . As the transitoriness of the individual is reflected in the destructability of his property, so the indestructibility of the association is mirrored in its inalienable and non-assignable tenure of possessions' (Simmel 1898: 676). Such groups resemble the maw of the lion into which everything can enter, from which nothing ever comes out.

Some believe that the multiplex social ties between members of the same nation foster the shared values that are ultimately responsible for national identity. In contrast to other kinds of groups:

a nation forms a social, economic, and political alignment of individuals from different social classes and occupations, around a center and a leading group. Its members are united by more intensive social communication, and are linked to these centers and leading groups by an unbroken chain of connections in communications, and often also in economic life, with no sharp break in the possibilities of communication and substitution at any link (Deutsch 1966: 101).

This leads, among other things, to 'widespread preferences for things or persons of "one's own kind" in such matters as buying and selling, work, food and recreation, courtship and marriage' (Deutsch 1966).

Yet the conclusion that nations are salient because of their durability and shared values begs too many questions. Clearly the salience of nations is variable, not constant. Some nations (like Cornwall) disappear, others (like Euzkadi in Spain or the Kurds in Iraq) are rent with internal conflict. Some nations-in-the-process-of-being-built (like Biafra) never seem to stay the course. For others (like the Italian Northern League's Padania), the verdict is still out. The 'nation' does not provide any essential basis for social identity.[3] Like all other social identities, national identity is imagined, constructed, assembled from characteristics that, in altered circumstances, can become the basis of quite different kinds of social identities. To know why membership in national groups sometimes comes to the fore, one must understand the dynamics of identity formation in general. This chapter contends that the establishment and maintenance of a cultural division of labour is decisive for the salience of national identity.

The Roots of National Identity

Nationalism ultimately rests on cultural distinctions, but the meaning of cultural distinctiveness is ambiguous. How different must a group's language, religion, or social mores be to qualify it as culturally distinct? Is Tuscan Italian different from Genoese Italian? Is Black English (née ebonics) a different language than standard English? What of religious distinctions? Do Dutch Catholics practise a distinct religion from Mexican Catholics? Do Reform Jews and Hasids adhere to different religions? The growing conflict between these last groups in the New York suburbs and in Jerusalem certainly lends some credence to the notion.

Questions of this sort have no definitive answers. The boundary between a language and a dialect is fuzzy. Likewise for that between religious denominations. Instead of searching for iron-clad criteria of cultural distinctiveness, it is more fruitful to ask whether the content of social categories is largely determined by insiders or outsiders. Tourists in Italy take the view that all native speakers speak Italian, but native speakers themselves attend to differences in regional dialects. These very same Italians are likely to regard themselves as homogeneous when comparing themselves to Austrians, however. Much the same can be said for the Jewish groups in New York and Jerusalem: an overarching Jewish identity is likely to emerge only when Jews compare themselves to gentiles.[4]

Evidently, the attribution of cultural distinctiveness is a social construction that is highly sensitive to shifting contexts.[5] Yet this point challenges social research that imputes subjective states merely on the basis of crude measures of linguistic and religious behaviour. This wreaks havoc with quantitative empirical investigation. In such research, cultural distinctions are usually derived from crude counts of linguistic and religious behaviours. I will also adopt that convention here, but merely for the sake of exposition.

However it is measured, linguistic and religious behaviour has no necessary implications for one's social identity. Social identity is that part of the individual's self-concept deriving from membership in groups. Although the term 'identity politics' is bruited about endlessly these days, it is far from clear why people come to primarily identify with one kind of group—say, a nation—rather than another—say, a class. Whereas some culturally distinct groups develop national identities, others do not.[6] Large societies are inherently diverse. They comprise people of varying ages, genders, wealth, education, classes, religions, sexual orientations, and languages. They also include people of different heights, weights, hair and eye colour. In principle, any one of these distinctions—or categorical markers—might serve as a basis for the development of a social identity.

Social identities are parasitic on group formation: one can only identify with a given group when such a group actually exists. Yet group formation is not an indiscriminate process, but a highly selective one. One of Sherlock Holmes's adventures begins with his amazement on reading a newspaper announcement of a meeting of the League of Red-Headed Gentlemen. Holmes was puzzled about the very existence of such a group: whatever could induce redheads to form a voluntary association in Victorian London? After investigating, the famous sleuth is relieved to discover that the announcement had been a hoax; no such group had ever existed. By contrast, the announcement of a meeting of the League of Black-Skinned Gentlemen in contemporary London would occasion no comparable astonishment on anyone's part.

Why are we unsurprised to hear of the latter group, but amazed to hear of the former? Groups form in two disparate but mutually reinforcing ways: on the basis of values and of propinquity (Simmel 1955*b*). Although the end point of each process is often the same, the starting-points are different.

In the first kind of group formation (think of a motorcycle or gliding club), people who already share some common value seek one another out and establish a social network on that account. (After some time, they may come to share a joint location, as well.) Although many such values are idiosyncratic and therefore unpredictable (like the love of motorcycles), one important source of value-based group formation is quite predictable. *Groups crystallize around markers that have systematic implications for individual welfare.*[7] The reason for Holmes's puzzlement now becomes clear. We doubt that having red hair systematically affects peoples' welfare,[8] but we know that having a black skin often does.[9]

What holds for groups holds for social identities, as well. They, too, arise on the basis of age, gender, class, religion, skin colour, and language only to the degree that these markers systematically affect their incumbents' welfare (Eriksen 1993: 138). Consider two industrial regions of a mythical Muslim-controlled state each made up of Hindus and Muslims. In Region α both owners and managers, on the one hand, and workers, on the other hand, are as likely to be Hindu as they are to be Muslim. In Region β, any given owner and manager has a .95 probability of being Muslim, and any given worker has a .95 probability of being Hindu. If, as is likely, both Hindus and Muslims prefer to be owners and managers rather than workers, then the salience of religion in this society will be higher. When Hindus feel that, no matter how diligently they work and how well they behave they have no prospects of being owners or managers, they are likely to feel resentful. In this kind of social structure, Hindus will tend to envy Muslims and covet their positions; Muslims, on the contrary, are likely to fear Hindus.

In the second kind of group formation (think of a neighbourhood association), *people who already share a common location establish a social network on that account.* (After some time, they may come to share common values, as well.) For example, shifts in social networks were crucial in determining changes in social identity in nineteenth-century Paris (Gould 1994). Whereas the participants in the revolution of 1848 adopted a working-class identity, the Paris communards of 1871 identified themselves primarily as residents of neighbourhoods. The explanation of this shift in identity lies in differences in the composition of social networks in the two periods. In 1848, Parisian social networks were composed of people who worked in the same occupations. This kind of network favoured workers' class identification. However, after Hausmann's massive urban renovation projects between 1852 and 1868, workers were dispersed from the centre of Paris to the outlying suburbs. In these areas, the resulting social networks were perforce determined by ties of residence rather than by occupation. This fundamental rearrangement of the patterns of social life favoured social identities formed on the basis of neighbourhood rather than class.[10]

Since they arise on the basis of both values and propinquity, most people have multiple social identities. What determines the relative salience of these identities? This question has inspired considerable research in social psychology. The most extensive treatment is found in research on social identity theory (Tajfel 1982: 172; Turner 1987: 173; Van Knippenberg 1993: 68; Mullen 1992: 166). This theory assumes that individuals seek to maximize their self-esteem and that one important means of doing so is by striving to achieve a positive social identity.[11] The individual's multiple social identities may be ranked on a hierarchical scale of status, or social honour. The higher a group's status, the greater the self-esteem conferred by membership in it.[12]

Social identity theory suggests that individuals will identify with high-status groups because this identification contributes to their self-esteem. Likewise, individuals will avoid identifying with low-status groups for the same reason; hence, they will identify with high-status groups unless there are objective or psychic barriers to so doing. When individuals cannot exit from a low-status group—and hence must depend on it for support and other resources—they will have an interest in changing the attributes of their group in a positive direction.[13] Thus, people are especially likely to identify with a group when membership is determined ascriptively and the prospect of exit is slight (Wright *et al.* 1990).[14] The differential stratification of groups, and their relative permeability, are key determinants of the relative salience of social identities.

When people are treated by others as members of a distinctive group, they identify with others similarly treated (Brewer 1979;

Tajfel 1981). The greater the welfare consequences of a given marker, the more likely that the marked will identify with those who are similarly marked. And the larger the number of people who identify with a given marker, the more advantageous it is for others to identify with it, as well. Therefore, laws and customs that mandate distinctive behaviour toward people with given markers strengthen identification with the affected group (Hughes and Hughes 1952: 101)—but only among those who cannot exit. Nazi anti-Semitism increased Jewish social identity among a people that had begun to assimilate to German culture. Croat hostility to Serbs during the Second World War did the same for Serbian identity.

The bulk of social identities in the modern world probably arise from more mundane and less visible sources, however. The mere use of official categories, such as census classifications, can promote group identities (Alonso and Starr 1987). *Cultural divisions of labour* are among the most important sources of social identity. These consist of distributions of culturally marked individuals in an occupational structure (Hechter 1978).[15] A cultural division of labour has two separate dimensions: hierarchy and segmentation. Hierarchy refers to the variance in average occupational prestige of the culturally distinct groups. It is associated with systematic patterns of cultural disadvantage in various measures of welfare, including income, schooling, and even health outcomes (Williams 1994; Williams and Ecob 1999). Hierarchies tend to persist because groups at the apex of a hierarchy profit from the labour of those beneath them. Segmentation refers to the variance in these groups' corresponding occupational specialization. It fosters—and, in turn, is fostered by—the establishment of culturally distinct social networks.[16]

It is easy to see why an extremely hierarchical cultural division of labour—like the Indian caste system—produces highly salient social identities. By establishing a definite status ranking between groups, this kind of stratification system necessarily assigns a certain quantum of social honour to each. It is this quantum of social honour, rather than the existence of cultural similarity *per se*, that is responsible for the construction of the relevant social identities.[17] Unlike hierarchy, segmentation has no constant impact on social identities. Social identification in a segmented cultural division of labour is strengthened only when the interests of the given segment come into play.

How the Cultural Division of Labour Structures Social Identities

The implications of cultural division of labour for the salience of social identities can be best appreciated by a brief comparison of three societies.[18] The simplest configuration is drawn from Quebec in the 1940s, a largely rural society made up of only two cultural groups, and subject to little immigration. The Caribbean island of Aruba, which has a complex history of conquest and immigration, offers a more elaborate configuration. The cultural division of labour in United States *c.* 1970 is the third and most complex example.

Quebec (1940)

One of the most pristine examples of a cultural division of labour in the sociological literature is found in Everett Hughes's ethnography of a small industrial city typical of most of the settlements in the Canadian province of Quebec (Hughes 1943). In 1937, the small industrial city Hughes refers to as Cantonville was made up of only two cultural groups, English and French speakers. Traditionally, Cantonville had been predominantly Francophone, but a small English population had lived there for a long time. When new factories were set up by outside corporations seeking to take advantage of Quebec's cheap electricity, this spurred a new English immigration. The English held all positions of authority in the new factories; in addition, they monopolized the highly skilled jobs (Hughes 1943: table 17, appendix A).

Why did most of the best paying and highest prestige jobs go to Anglophones rather than Francophones? Despite the stark hierarchy of the Cantonville cultural division of labour, the mechanisms of job allocation were far from overt. Hughes was able to peer inside what is too often a black box by studying the way that personnel decisions were made in firms:

The appointment of a major executive or technician is . . . a vote of confidence. Within it are included several component judgments—to wit, that the man knows his technique, that he can and will work satisfactorily in the interest of the appointing authorities, and that he can and will win the confidence and best efforts of his colleagues and subordinates. For some jobs, the appointers may not trust a candidate who cannot be safely and comfortably entertained at dinner; for others, the degree of required social acceptability may be less. In some cases, a personally unpleasant or undesired expert can be thrown in the faces of colleagues and subordinates; in others, it seems best to cater to the prejudices of subordinates rather than to those of the appointing superiors. In general, there is probably a strong bias in favor of appointing for higher positions a man of the kind liked and trusted by the appointing group. Ethnic background, religion, and even 'the old-school tie' might enter into the case—not in the spirit of looking after one's friends but with the conviction, which might be true, that efficiency is best served so. For almost any position in industry it may be assumed that there is a certain range between the lower limit of necessary skill and knowledge and the upper limit which can be commanded for the money and social rewards offered. The tendency of modern industry is to push toward the ceiling of efficiency. But within the range of indifference there are generally a number of men available. Within this range judgment is likely to be conservative with respect to personal qualities. This is not the point at which industrial organizations take the long chance . . . The road to the higher executive decisions is opened to a man by a series of such votes of confidence, each of which gives him access to a new field of experience and to association with the men whose good will is necessary for the next step. At each step on this road the individual himself gathers power to make judgments about others, and to make gestures which affect the judgments of others with respect to his equals and his subordinates. In this an industrial organization is like any other human society, with its various circles of close associates, its hierarchy of prestige and authority, and its interplay of social gestures and which settle the fate of each individual . . . In [Cantonville] it is evident that French Canadians as a group do not enjoy that full confidence of industrial directors and executives which would admit them easily to the inner and higher circles of the fraternity—and fraternity it is—of men who run industry. This situation prevails throughout the province of Quebec. (Hughes 1943: 52–4)

Thus the Cantonville cultural division of labour divided language groups and was extremely hierarchical. Since language was the principal axis of group stratification, this cultural division of labour gave linguistic identities great salience. No wonder that linguistic identity has proven to be the bedrock of subsequent nationalism in the province of Quebec.[19]

Aruba

A much more complex, if still relatively hierarchical, cultural division of labour developed on the Caribbean island of Aruba (Cole 1993). Aruba's indigenous population was Amerindian. During the pre-Columbian era, the island was populated by various Arawak Indians from what is now the Venezuelan mainland, temporary residents engaged in fishing expeditions or escaping conflicts with stronger groups. These Indians survived Spanish colonization because the island had little to exploit. When the Dutch annexed the island in 1636, the Spanish abducted the Indians from the island and their descendants never returned. (Other Indians, however, did come to Aruba later.)

Dutch merchants arrived in Aruba in the early nineteenth century from Curacao, bringing African slaves who worked as domestic servants, as well as on small aloe and cochineal plantations. The Indian population, which was not permitted to own African slaves, instead captured 'red Indians' from the mainland, thus reinforcing the Indian part of the population. African slaves were emancipated in 1864; many left, and the remaining ones were clustered in the less fertile parts of the island. This mixed population then was joined by 'high-class' Spanish refugees fleeing civil war in Venezuela late in the century. By the end of the colonial era, the lower class Iberian immigrants and Indians, plus the remaining Africans, had merged to become a *mestizo Papiamento*-speaking working-class community, but with distinct regional prejudices between the many *barrios*, and with closely knit networks. The élite of the island were the Dutch and high-born Spanish, mainly merchants (often smugglers) and administrators.

In the 1920s an American-owned oil terminal was set up in the island to tranship and refine oil from the nearby Maracaibo basin. By the Second World War, this had become one of the largest Exxon oil refineries in the world, and a flood of new immigrants followed. Because of their commercial skills, the European 'real Arubans' could take advantage of the opportunities in the refinery sector, opening banks and expanding their trade. In contrast, the Indian-Arubans, who had few relevant skills or experience, either took unskilled jobs in the refinery or remained on their homesteads. Rising consumption expectations also caused many Indian-Arubans to default on loans, and lose their property to European Arubans, leaving a political rift between urban and rural Arubans.

The refinery recruited English-speaking skilled workers from the Dutch Windward Islands and the British West Indies. These immigrants—the pick of the Caribbean labour force—became the core of the African-Aruban population. Often these workers had been employed in Cuba which employed sophisticated technologies similar to those then used in oil refining. There was a complete social separation in the refinery town between the West Indian immigrants and the White American managers of the refinery. Despite their economic skills, these Black immigrants were at the bottom of the social ladder. However, since they identified with disparate islands of origin, they did not form a solidary group. They were largely dependent on wage labour and relied much less on community networks. With the refinery, new immigrants from Asia, Europe, and the Middle East arrived to develop new commercial activities, which often developed into family or homeland corporate communities (See Figure 6.1).

Eventually these communities dominated specific sectors of production: the Chinese as food wholesalers, the Eastern Europeans as retailers of fashion goods, Syrians and Lebanese as commodity traders (Cole 1994). Soon these immigrants became the dominant commercial force on the island. By the late 1970s, the Aruban cultural division of labour looked like this: expatriates and European-Arubans occupied management and professional positions; African-Arubans occupied domestic and service positions, but also many professional and technical jobs; Indian-Arubans predominated in production and rural employment, as well as in commercial and clerical positions and in public works. Since 'race' is the principal axis of stratification in the Aruban cultural division of labour, the Aruban population is arranged into three racially defined groups: Euro-Arubans, Indo-Arubans and Afro-Arubans.

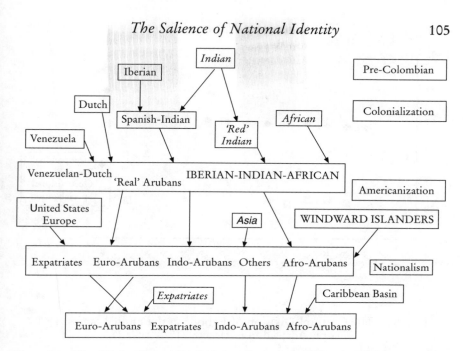

FIG. 6.1. The Four Phases in the Development of Aruban Society. Time measured vertically, socio-economic status horizontally
Source: Cole (1993: fig. 1)

The salience of race in Aruba is underlined by the nature of the island's political cleavages. Each racial group is affiliated with a distinctive political party (Cole 1994).

The United States (1970)

The well-known history of conquest and immigration in the United States resulted in a far more diverse population than Aruba's. The American cultural division of labour—computed from individual-level data on the occupational prestige and specialization of racial and ethnic groups culled from the 1970 census—reflects this complexity (see Figure 6.2). For present purposes, it is important to note that the resulting picture is neither extremely hierarchical nor segmental; indeed, in contrast to Quebec and Aruba the cultural division of labour in the United States is strikingly flat.[20] Whereas Blacks and Hispanics were

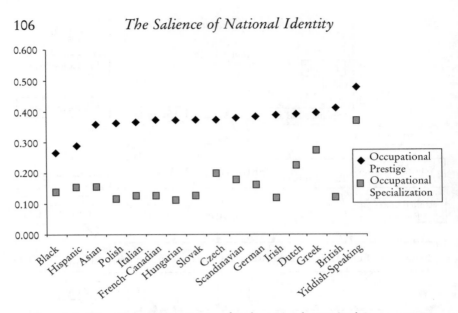

FIG. 6.2. The Cultural Division of Labour in the United States, 1970
Source: Adapted from Hechter (1978: table 1)

clearly concentrated in less prestigious occupations, differences
among the remaining ethnic groups were few. Apart from Yiddish
speakers and Greeks, who were both rather occupationally specialized, there were few dramatic differences in intergroup segmentation. In such a relatively horizontal and non-segmented
cultural division of labour, salient ethnic identities should be rare—
save among African-Americans and Hispanics, whose average
locations are considerably subordinate to those of all other groups.
Evidence about ethnic identity drawn from attitude surveys (Alba
1990) and on intergroup marriage patterns (Hechter 1978) is
largely consistent with this expectation. All told, ethnic divisions
in American politics are much weaker than in Quebec and Aruba.
    This informal survey of the cultural division of labour in three
societies lends support to the notion that strong social identities
are the by-products of hierarchy and segmentation. Quebec's aus-
terely hierarchical cultural division of labour based on language
spurred linguistic identities among both Francophones and Anglophones. When groups subject to a hierarchical cultural division of
labour are territorially concentrated (as in Quebec relative to the

rest of Canada), this provides optimal conditions for the development of peripheral nationalism.[21] Aruba's more complex, but still predominantly hierarchical, cultural division of labour based on race gives racial identity pride of place. The absence of racial territorial concentration inhibits nationalism there, however. The United States cultural division of labour offers infertile ground for the growth of highly salient ethnic identities, save among Blacks and Hispanics. Nor is there any scope for peripheral nationalism, since—unlike the Inuit of the Canadian North (Chartrand and Prattis 1990) or the Russians in Estonia (Mettam and Williams 1998)—none of these ethnic or racial groups is territorially concentrated.[22]

Since both hierarchical and segmental cultural divisions of labour favour the establishment and maintenance of separate social identities, they provide an important social base for the development of nationalism if the relevant groups are territorially concentrated.[23] Recall from Chapter 2 that the territorial concentration of nations distinguishes them from other culturally distinct collectivities, including religious, ethnic, and racial groups. Whereas ethnic or religious identities are often associated with sacred sites or places of origin, 'it is not an essential part of having the identity that you should permanently occupy that place. If you are a good Muslim you should make a pilgrimage to Mecca at least once, but you need not set up house there. A nation, in contrast, must have a homeland' (Miller 1994: 20). Since nations are territorial, they have the potential of attaining political sovereignty.[24]

Sources of the Cultural Division of Labour

Cultural divisions of labour can emerge via three distinct routes.[25] The first route is by conquest. Examples include the English settlement of Ireland in the sixteenth century (Hechter 1999), and the Russian domination of the Soviet Union (Kaiser 1994: 381–2).

A cultural division of labour also can arise as a by-product of institutional arrangements that provide certain kinds of collective rights. The Treaty of Union that tied Scotland to England in 1707 is a prototype. On joining the new British polity, this treaty allowed the Scots to retain several of their traditional institutions (the Kirk, the legal and educational systems). Thus a number of specific and often high prestige occupations in the educational, legal, and clerical professions have been reserved for incumbents who must be trained in specifically Scottish ways. There is little doubt that lawyers in Scotland face considerable professional competition, but they will seldom face competition from *English* lawyers because the two types of law are incommensurable. Recent constitutional devolution in Spain has led to similar results. The Catalan government, for example, employs more than 100,000 people.

The third route is as a consequence of immigration. Cultural differences are often correlated with differences in skills, or human capital (Sowell 1994: ch. 1). German immigrants specialized in building pianos in colonial America, Tsarist Russia, France, Australia, and England; Gujeratis have set up business enterprises from Fiji to virtually the whole coast of East Africa; and Italian fishermen have settled throughout the Mediterranean as well as in San Francisco, Argentina, and Australia. In both Quebec and Aruba, the arrival of new factories stimulated the immigration of a highly skilled managerial class to run the factories and refineries. Of course, not all immigrants are so skilled.

A cultural division of labour can also emerge as a result of employers' attempts to minimize the price of labour. This may occur for two quite different kinds of reasons. On the one hand, labour costs often vary with cultural differences. On average, the members of groups coming from less developed regions of the world economy will be less costly to employ than those coming from more developed regions (Bonacich 1972).[26] If they have comparable skill, then labour from poorer regions may drive out labour from richer ones. To minimize the threat from low-cost immigrants, high-cost labour may seek to either exclude immigration altogether (this is an aim of Le Pen's Front National in France, for example), or, failing that, attempt to set up a caste system in which low-cost labour is either prohibited from certain ranges of the occupational structure or paid less wages than the privileged ethnic sector of the labour force.

On the other hand, there may be higher costs of employing mixed groups of incompatible workers than in employing more homogeneous workers (Sowell 1994: 84–7). Sometimes these costs arise because the groups demand different working conditions. At the turn of the last century, for example, many Jewish immigrants from Eastern Europe did not want to work on Saturdays (their Sabbath). Since at this time factories operated six days a week, factory owners employing both Gentile and Jewish workers would have had higher costs (of scheduling and coordination) than those who employed either all-Jewish or all-gentile workers. Under these conditions, market pressures would favour the survival of religiously homogeneous work forces. When American factories changed to a five-day working week, enabling both Jewish and gentile workers to observe their Sabbaths, both groups could be employed by the same firm without it having to bear these costs.

Once a local cultural occupational specialization occurs, by whatever means, social networks are likely to guarantee its diffusion:

As turnover occurs and the firm expands, established workers pass word of available jobs among friends and relatives, collaborating with and supporting them once they join the work force. Those new workers therefore prove more reliable and effective than others hired off the street, and all concerned come to associate job with the [cultural] category, so much that owner and workers come to believe in the superior fitness of that category's members for the particular line of work. (Tilly 1998: 13, see also ch. 5)

If cultural divisions of labour are a primary foundation of social identity, then under what conditions do these patterns of intergroup stratification persist? After all, national identities are generally not here today and gone tomorrow. If the conditions generating social identities were transitory, then national identities would not endure.[27] Now it is easy to understand why premodern societies might be riddled with cultural divisions of labour: in societies with highly restricted markets for labour and capital, dominant groups can lord it over subordinate ones indefinitely in the absence of exogenous shocks. Nationalism, however, is a creature of the modern world, not the premodern one. Why then are cultural divisions of labour not undermined by the mobility of labour and capital in modern market economies? Why are they not sub-verted by the rise of universal public education and bureaucratic recruitment (on the basis of merit rather than cultural privilege) in private enterprise and government?

The Persistence of Cultural Divisions of Labour

Economist George Akerlof (1984) has attempted to understand how the caste system—the most extreme example of a hierarchical cultural division of labour—can persist in a competitive market economy. Akerlof's model assumes that information in the real world is incomplete and costly. Given the cost of information and the need for it, people typically make predictions about the beha-viour of individuals based on a small number of easily observable indicators. Membership in distinct cultural groups provides a typical source of such indicators. When membership is highly visible, non-members can predict the behaviour of members on the basis of indicators like language, religion, skin colour, sex, and age.

Akerlof's model begins with a stylized caste system drawn from a portrait of marriage customs in India. In such a society people are divided into mutually exclusive castes. The members of these castes must behave according to a particular code of behavior. With respect to marriage, the code specifies rules as to who may marry whom, payment of the dowry, the timing and performance of the marriage rites, and so forth. The code dictates that violators will be outcasted and forced into polluting occupations. Outcastes are not allowed to eat with caste members, including their own parents and siblings, nor touch them or their food. If they fail to comply, their own children will be outcasted and suffer the same fate. Further, people who fail to ostracize the outcastes will themselves be outcasted.

In a caste society any transaction that breaks the caste taboos changes the subsequent behaviour of uninvolved parties toward the caste-breakers. Thus, if a brahmin should knowingly hire an outcaste cook, that brahmin would be outcasted, and the cook would be unable to get another job. Under these circumstances, those who fail to follow, or to enforce, caste customs cannot reap much profit. If the punishment of becoming an outcaste is predicted to be sufficiently severe, the caste system will persist. Akerlof argues that the predictions of the caste code become a self-enforcing system of social relations.

The possible intervention of third parties is crucial for the persistence of the caste system. If people know the relationship between, say, the untouchable and touchable castes, then they are able to predict how the members of each caste will relate to them. Such predictions can lead to an equilibrium—a self-fulfilling prophecy that supports the caste code even among those who are immune to its ideology.

The caste equilibrium is maintained because no one firm can make a profit by offering a higher wage to either untouchable or outcaste workers. For a firm to pay more than the going wage, it must employ outcaste labour in skilled or unskilled jobs. Suppose a new firm does offer untouchables more than the going wage. It must use some of this labour in skilled jobs, or else it cannot compete with firms that continue to pay untouchables the going wage. If it does this, however, then the firm will have no customers: any customer will be outcasted because the firm has violated the caste code by giving untouchables skilled jobs. Further, if word about its hiring practices got out, the owners of the firm would be outcasted, as well. Since outcasting is much more costly than the benefit of buying a good at a lower than market price, the firm would never hire untouchables for skilled jobs. This caste equilibrium will break down only when there are coalitions of individuals who can make themselves better off by engaging in collective action.[28]

For present purposes, this analysis has one critical implication. In urban settings, cultural divisions of labour can only be sustained over the long run by state policies. Although the caste equilibrium may persist in village India, where monitoring costs are low, it is very unlikely to do so in large urban settings. Indeed, the model suggests that it would be difficult to maintain a caste system in modern urban settings, if not impossible. This is because at the heart of the model lies an implicit assumption that violations of the caste code are common knowledge throughout the system.[29]

While it is realistic to assume that the strictures of the caste code are known in modern cities, the idea that third parties have much capacity to outcaste violators of the caste code seems far-fetched. Monitoring costs in cities with labour mobility are likely to be high—save for the members of racial groups, who are phenotypically distinctive. If so, then the probability of sanctioning for violating the caste code will be low: the wages given various categories of workers within the firm can hardly be expected to be public information. Hence, the persistence of caste systems and cultural divisions of labour among culturally distinctive groups in urbanized societies is due not so much to self-enforcing mechanisms like those highlighted by Akerlof, but to political ones.

This provides culturally distinct groups with an interest in controlling state policies, or at least those policies that are most directly relevant to their welfare. The demand for sovereignty arises from just such an abiding interest.[30]

CHAPTER 7

The Demand for Sovereignty and the Emergence of Nationalism

THE French Revolution challenged the legitimacy of existing state regimes, putting into question the previously held view that any government's right to rule was independent of the will of its subjects. As a result, self-determination began to displace more traditional legitimations of rule, such as divine right (Kedourie 1960: chs. 2–3). Little more than a century later, the norm of national self-determination was lent great weight by the Treaty of Versailles. No doubt, this norm was instrumental in the wave of decolonization movements that swept across post-war Asia and Africa. Today, the United Nations Charter includes self-determination as a fundamental human right (Tilly 1993).

Nations that attain sovereignty have the privilege, and the obligation, of determining much of their own fate. The economic success of Bismarck's Germany and that of the four tigers of South-East Asia would have been inconceivable in the absence of sovereignty. This is not to say that sovereignty offers any guarantee of economic success. When the twenty-six counties of southern Ireland seceded from the United Kingdom, Ireland was the least developed of all British territories. Irish nationalists claimed that sovereignty would usher in a new era of prosperity. In fact, however, the Irish economy stagnated under protectionist policies that held sway until the 1990s.[1] At that point the government began to encourage foreign investment; as a result of this new policy, Ireland became the fastest growing economy in the European

Union (Ó Gráda 1997). Similarly, some native American tribes have used their own sovereignty to build gambling casinos that have significantly enriched their coffers.[2]

Moreover substantial amounts of political autonomy, a state of affairs falling short of sovereignty, can affirm national culture, as well. Quebec offers an apt illustration. Although it is part of the Canadian federation, Quebec has attained considerable political autonomy—enough to have enacted the most far-reaching language legislation in the world. Although the province experienced high post-war rates of immigration prior to the 1960s, two out of every three immigrants put their children in English-speaking schools. Thereafter, successive nationalist governments attempted to stem the tide of anglicization by adopting a series of increasingly stringent language laws (O'Donnell 1997). Canada became officially bilingual in 1969, and French became obligatory in English schools. By 1974, French became Quebec's sole official language. In 1977 the famous Bill 101 restricted the number of students who could attend English-language schools and attempted to establish French as the language of the workplace. Bill 178 (1988) banned the use of languages other than French in outdoor commercial signs. The United Nations condemned this law as violating basic human rights in 1993, at which point the ban was lifted.

These language laws have had dramatic effects.[3] On the one hand, they greatly increased the use of French in the workplace. From 1961 to 1991 the number of jobs in Francophone-owned companies increased from 47 per cent to 65 per cent of the total (Québec, Conseil, 1995: 46). On the other, they encouraged an out-migration of many enterprising Anglophones, as well as a number of important corporate headquarters. The recent history of Quebec therefore reveals that support for nationalist policies is widespread and growing, even though these policies have reduced the province's overall economic well-being (Coté and Johnston 1995). While the 1980 referendum on sovereignty was favoured by 40.4 per cent of the province's voters, the corresponding percentage in 1995 was a near majority, 49.4.[4]

Evidently, sovereignty can provide nations with important economic and cultural benefits. By dint of their solidarity and spatial concentration, all nations have the potential of attaining sovereignty, but not all of them demand their own state apparatus. Many Bretons in France regard themselves—and qualify by the present definition—as a nation, yet relatively few of them have ever sought to establish an independent state. By no means does nationhood imply nationalism.[5] Sometimes realism tempers desire: groups perceiving that demands for sovereignty will bring down the full force of repression from central rulers back off rather than publicly advertise their true political preferences (Kuran 1996). Sometimes desire tempers realism: even though secession is an unlikely outcome in the best of circumstances, certain groups pursue it anyway.

The demand for sovereignty is a necessary but insufficient condition for nationalism. Whereas the desire for sovereignty may be pervasive in a given nation, various institutional barriers to collective action can dampen the prospects for nationalism. Accordingly, this chapter begins by exploring the reasons why the demand for sovereignty varies in peripheral nations that are subject to direct rule. It concludes by considering some institutional impediments to collective action that may have the paradoxical effect of inhibiting non-violent nationalist groups at the expense of violent ones.

The Demand for Sovereignty

What accounts for variation in the demand for sovereignty? Not the growing acceptance of an international norm of self-determination. Since the interpretation of this norm is shaped by other norms of legitimacy (Strang 1996), any such explanation ultimately lapses into infinite regress. Instead, the answer is better sought by considering the relationship between the nation and its host state.

Self-determination is a universal good: people always prefer to act on the basis of their own desires rather than those of others.[6] This proposition is as true for groups as it is for individuals. The !Kung of the Kalahari (discussed in Chapter 3) disperse in the rainy season because this allows each family the self-determination to do what it wants, when it wants to. Still, if self-determination is universally valued, why do people ever settle for anything less? Presumably, to gain other goods that self-determination cannot provide. Recall that to procure a regular supply of water in the dry season !Kung families join larger groups around water-holes, even though doing so subjects them to social control that limits their freedom of action. Their seasonal movements appear to follow a simple rule that trades off self-determination against access to water. The rule looks like this: when there is an ample supply of water, opt for self-determination; in dry seasons, when water is scarce, join larger groups.

Although self-determination is a universal good, therefore, it is neither the only such good, nor the most fundamental one. In some circumstances the desire for self-determination wins out, but in others the very same people forego it to attain a more valued good. Access to water always trumps self-determination in the Kalahari desert because it is more fundamental for the family's survival.

This little story has implications for explaining variations in the demand for sovereignty, for nationalism is all about the pursuit of national self-determination.[7] All things equal, the members of any nation would prefer to be sovereign rather than ruled by another nation, for this would provide maximum national self-determination and thereby superior governance. As one Yugoslav political theorist puts it, 'Why should I be a minority in your state when you can be a minority in mine' (Gligorov 1994)?

But sometimes more fundamental goods can trump sovereignty. One such good is economic welfare. Whereas sovereignty would provide the members of national groups with self-determination, concern for their own economic welfare may exert a countervailing appeal. Incorporation in a large, economically dynamic state can convey important economic and political benefits to peripheral nationalities. Large markets are generally more efficient than small ones: Britons pay more for their books than Americans, and (at least in 1990) it often cost more to fly from Sydney to Perth than to London, even though the latter route is several times more distant. Since the collective goods provided by the central government are subject to economies of scale that reduce their cost, large states can also reap governance efficiencies.

Large size can also convey major political advantages to a state. Consider defence, which is high on the list of any government's obligations. When a wooden spear represents the ultimate weapon, even family groups may be capable of mounting their own defence. In a world of Trident submarines, however, an adequate defence lies beyond the capacity of small states. In this way advances in military technology alter the trade-off between sovereignty and security. As the cost of defence rises, smaller, poorer polities are induced to join larger bodies for protection at the expense of some of their sovereignty. In our world, untrammelled sovereignty is beyond the capacity of all but a handful of large states. Therefore, it stands to reason that the members of peripheral nations may be willing to sacrifice some self-determination to profit from inclusion in a larger, albeit multinational, state. This willingness undercuts the demand for sovereignty.

The demand for sovereignty among peripheral nations, therefore, varies with its net benefits. And the net benefits of sovereignty are affected by international as well as domestic considerations. Two international factors of note concern the prevalence of barriers to trade and regional defensive alliances. The economic advantages of large states are principally due to barriers to international trade. When these barriers are high, the size of the domestic market matters a great deal. To the participants in free trade zones, such as the European Union, size alone has little economic consequence for a state, however. Hence the growth of free trade in the world economy should stimulate the demand for sovereignty in peripheral nations. Participation in regional defensive alliances (like the North Atlantic Treaty Organization) removes a large part of the responsibility for defence from the governments of small states. This, too, should stimulate the demand for sovereignty in peripheral nations.

One obvious domestic factor affecting the cost of sovereignty is the weakness of the host state's economy. If the peripheral nation believes that it can prosper by seceding from a weakened host, then the demand for sovereignty should rise. This situation often leads to the fragmentation of multinational states.

Moreover, systematic value differences among national populations, and corresponding inequities in the allocation of government-provided goods, will tend to increase the demand for sovereignty. Inequities in the allocation of *universally valued* government-provided goods—such as defence, public health, economic growth, and social order—have direct implications for the demand for sovereignty. Garbage collection is a case in point. Most people could not care less about who picks up the garbage. Flemings and Walloons in Belgium may agree about few public issues these days, but both groups want the garbage to be collected. Employment issues aside, all that matters is that somebody do the job, and that it be done as efficiently as possible.[8]

While there is no quarrel about the desirability of such collective goods, questions about the fairness of the state's allocation of them can be expected to arise. Does the centre ensure that all communities have equal access to garbage collection, police protection, welfare programmes, transfer payments, government investment schemes, universities, and the like? Much of the political fray in democratic societies pits one region against others in the quest for such state-provided goods and services. To the extent that national groups are systematically disadvantaged by these allocations, this raises the net benefit of sovereignty to them, thereby increasing the demand for it.

In addition to these commonly shared values, nations—by definition—also have *distinctive* ones. The members of a peripheral nation lodged within a multinational state share values with respect to matters of production, as well as matters of consumption. A nation's *production* values are distinct to the degree that its territorial ecology affords it a comparative advantage for producing specialized goods and services. Some territories are blessed with ample mineral resources, others have locational advantages with respect to long-distance trade, others are well-suited for particular kinds of agricultural production. Economic specialization may also result from central state policies, from path-dependent investment decisions, and from cultural factors, such as the skills of the regional labour force as determined by the type of schooling to be found there.[9] Whatever its causes, this productive specialization invariably gives people who are dependent on the territorial economy common values with respect to the pricing and supply of inputs (save those for labour), as well as the distribution and pricing of outputs. These distinct values often lead to demands for tariffs and other protectionist measures, as well as for specific kinds of labour policies. To the degree that a nation's production values are ignored by the centre, the demand for sovereignty may rise.

Consider the Civil War, the prime example of peripheral nationalism in United States history. Many Southerners considered the Confederate South to be culturally distinct from the Yankee North (Genovese 1994).[10] In addition, the South had an economy that was largely driven by exports of primary products (especially cotton, grown in plantations using slave labour), but the North-Eastern economy depended more on commerce and manufactures. These differences in production gave the South and North-East opposing preferences with respect to tariffs (the North-East tended to be in favour, to protect their infant manufacturing industries, the South against, to promote its cotton exports), labour laws (the North-East favored free labour, the South slave labour), and federal promotion for infrastructural improvements (the North-East favoured these subsidies, the South did not). Despite these opposing preferences, political stability was achieved by instituting a balance rule that offered each region protection against domination by the other (Weingast 1998). In the thirty-one years between 1819 and 1850, parity between slave and non-slave states was maintained as the United States incorporated new territories. The breakdown of this rule led Southerners to fear that the federal government would no longer tolerate their production values. This raised the benefit of sovereignty to the South. One reading of the Civil War (not the only reading, of course) is that it was a conflict over the particular production values that would determine subsequent federal legislation (Moore 1966). As this example implies, countries with mixed economies are less likely to manifest distinctive production values than those with highly specialized ones.

That the demand for sovereignty increases when people believe it will promote the nation's economic welfare is well illustrated by the recent history of Italy's Lega Nord (Northern League). This is a growing political party that seeks the secession of the wealthier northern half of Italy, a region it terms Padania.[11] The Lega Nord claims that although Padania is one of the most economically advanced regions in Europe, its economic prospects are hampered by its connection with Rome and the less developed Mezzogiorno. In 1997, for instance, it offered Northern voters the opportunity to renounce their obligation to shoulder a share of Italy's massive debt which, in its view, threatened Italy's inclusion in the European Monetary Union. The size of the debt, not coincidentally, was blamed on profligate central government spending on—here is where the cultural distinctiveness comes in—Mafia-dominated political patronage (Lega Nord 1997).

Whereas a nation's production values are always constrained by the ecological distinctiveness of its territory, its *consumption* values flow directly from the nation's cultural distinctiveness.[12] An individual's birth into a distinctive cultural group tends to determine (at least initially) a whole set of preferences with respect to consumption. Thus, many Hindus are revolted by the prospect of eating meat; Americans are unwilling to eat dogs and cats; many Jews and Muslims are repelled by pork; Quebecois prefer that their children (and those of non-English-speaking immigrants) be schooled in the French language; Abkhazians desire to live under their customary law rather than a standard Russian code (Anchabadze *et al.* 1993).

The problem is that states do more than provide universally valued goods; in addition, some of the goods that they provide are culturally exclusive.[13] Nearly everybody wants free public education, but education can be conducted in any number of languages. People care a great deal about what their children are taught, and with what effectiveness. Few Americans would willingly allow their taxes to fund public schools operating exclusively in Japanese, and vice versa:

State policy on these matters tends to be dictated by the most powerful groups in society: In great centralized nations the legislator is obliged to give a character of uniformity to the laws, which does not always suit the diversity of customs and of districts; as he takes no cognizance of special cases, he can only proceed upon general principles; and the population are obliged to conform to the requirements of the laws, since legislation cannot adapt itself to the exigencies and the customs of the population, which is a great cause of trouble and misery (Tocqueville [1835] 1969).

Further, few political decisions are culturally neutral:

All political decisions differentially affect social groups . . . [because] members will differ with respect to a wide range of other attributes that can be directly affected by political decisions . . . This means that governmental policies and actions cannot be neutral in their impact on groups, although the impact often is trivial and sometimes is not obvious at the time it occurs (Lieberson 1994: 652).

Official languages empower some groups at the expense of others (Tollefson 1991). Official religions benefit some groups at the expense of others. Ethnic discrimination in state employment—or in arranging for transfers—benefits some groups at the expense of others.

On this account, when nations demand different *kinds* of state-provided goods, this poses problems for democratic governance:

Among a people without fellow-feeling, especially if they read and speak different languages, the united public opinion, necessary to the working of representative government, cannot exist. The influences which form opinions and decide political acts, are different in the different sections of the country. An altogether different set of leaders have the confidence of one part of the country and of another. The same books, newspapers, pamphlets, speeches, do not reach them. One section does not know what opinions, or what instigations, are circulating in another. The same incidents, the same acts, the same system of government, affect them in different ways; and each fears more injury to itself from the other nationalities, than from the common arbiter, the state (Mill 1861: 291–2).

People may demand sovereignty as the best means of attaining their consumption values and of protecting, or advancing, their national culture. For this reason, John Stuart Mill argued that the boundaries of governments should coincide in the main with those of nationalities.

This is far too sweeping a claim, however. There is no reason why states must treat peripheral nations in a uniform manner. Central governments may respond to distinctive national values in varying ways. If the bulk of the members of the nation desire the production of distinctive collective goods (say, public education in their own language, rather than the language of the centre), the centre may provide it to them. If the nation largely adheres to a distinctive religion, the centre may give its blessings to those who practise it. If the nation has an overwhelming economic special-ization—say in the production of a given primary product—the centre may facilitate exports by refraining from enacting protec-tionist policies that may be demanded by constituents in other territories.

If the state were merely an impartial arbiter, or referee, for the production and distribution of different collective goods among various national constituencies, then it would matter little which particular group controlled it. So long as all regions were guaran-teed a chance to get their most preferred state policies—say, on some rotating basis—then this arrangement might go a long way to satisfying peripheral interests. As a result, the demand for sov-ereignty would be tempered. If nationals have a very strong desire for a policy that they believe the centre will *never* enact, however, then sovereignty becomes a more attractive option.

Although cultural issues are often considered to be indivisible—and on this account not subject to compromise (Bell 1975)—this view is profoundly mistaken. There is no inherent reason why states cannot split the difference when it comes to cultural issues, as they are wont to do regarding economic ones. Although the French state *could* designate Breton or Arabic as official languages, it has not seen fit to legitimate any language other than French. The German state has a adopted a similar policy regarding the German language. The reluctance of states to countenance multi-cultural language policies is not a feature of language, but of politics. Cultural policies—like those mandating the language of instruction in public education, or those privileging certain reli-gions—need not be zero-sum. The Belgian state has two official languages, Switzerland has four. The United States has no official church. It stands to reason, therefore, that the greater the respon-siveness of the central state to the distinctive values of national groups, the lower their demand for sovereignty (see Chapter 9). 'No taxation without representation' is a peripheral nationalist trope.

If the demand for sovereignty is a function of its net benefits, then it should also vary between individuals in a given nation. This insight should cast light on the social bases of nationalism.

Social Bases of Nationalist Movements

Whereas nationalist movements often justify themselves as the protectors of a threatened culture, to most people national cultures are a collective good. As such, support for a national culture is subject to free riding. However, to a small minority within the nation, the protection of national culture is a *private* good. Since teachers, priests, and entertainers owe their livelihoods to the persistence of specific languages or religions, nationalist ideals may have greater resonance among the incumbents in these occupations.[14] Similarly, Confederate plantation owners probably were more supportive of sovereignty than merchants. In general, people whose welfare largely depends on the maintenance, or growth, of ties between their nation and other parts of a multinational state will be suspicious of nationalism. As the fate of industrial workers is more likely to depend on extra-regional markets than that of free professionals, government employees, and workers in service occupations, this is one reason why support for nationalism is predominantly found among white-collar and tertiary-sector employees (Rogowski 1985*b*: 376).

People who desire to live in a state dominated by co-religionists (a primary element in the nationalism of nineteenth-century Utah, and of the present-day Republic of Ireland, Israel, and Pakistan), or the speakers of their language (Catalonia and Quebec) are likely to support nationalism, at least in part, because they expect their labour-market position to improve as a result of their ability to compete in a smaller pond (Frank 1985). This may help explain why so many of the nineteenth-century European nationalist movements had cultural workers—writers, journalists, lawyers, clerics, teachers, and academics—at their base (Alter 1989: 68).[15]

Fragmentary as it is, this evidence suggests that the social base of nationalism rests, at least in part, on people who expect to profit from sovereignty individually. This conclusion has one important, and controversial, implication. Contrary to some claims (Gurr 1994; McRoberts 1980; Pinard and Hamilton 1986), there is no reason why nationalism must be confined to economically disadvantaged groups. The members of economically advantaged nations are no less likely to favour an outcome that enhances their personal welfare. The nationalism that asserts exclusive rights over revenues from the sale of Scottish and Biafran oil, as well as that propounded by the likes of Italy's Lega Nord, are to be understood in this light.

Some variation in the demand for sovereignty, therefore, is due to structural factors. Thus economic and military globalization tends to increase the demand for sovereignty by reducing the net benefits of attachment to multinational states. The same is true for the economic independence of the periphery from the core. Last, the more the peripheral culture has been institutionalized, the greater the net private benefits of sovereignty to people who owe their jobs and social standing to maintenance of this culture.

Yet these structural factors are not likely to account for rapid shifts in the appeal of sovereignty. Political contingencies and social crises probably explain the greatest fluctuations in the demand for sovereignty (Alter 1989: 76–82). Because these events are seldom foreseeable, shifts in the demand for sovereignty are not wholly predictable. As Chapter 5 reveals, French hegemony after Napoleonic victories first sparked German nationalism; the Rhine Crisis of 1840 and conflict over Schleswig-Holstein provided another impetus. Failure of the 1848 revolution and restoration of Habsburg rule in northern and central Italy stimulated the demand for nationalism there. In Ireland, the Home Rule movement did not take off until the agrarian crisis at the end of the 1870s. Irish tenant farmers, previously unmoved by nationalist appeals that were couched in terms of the pursuit of abstract collective goods, became inspired by speeches promising an end to landlordism and the rights of people to the soil. Today, media coverage of events like state visits are often the occasions for nationalist incidents: President Clinton's visit to Indonesia, for example, led to large demonstrations in East Timor.

The Emergence of Nationalist Organizations

Whereas the demand for sovereignty is a precondition for the emergence of nationalism, it does not foreordain it. Nationalism requires the existence of organizations dedicated to pursuing national sovereignty. However intense the demand for sovereignty may be, nationalist collective action is unlikely to emerge in the absence of pre-existing social groups formed to provide their members with insurance, welfare, and other kinds of private goods.[16]

Such groups are necessary for at least two reasons. First is the free-rider problem, which is exacerbated in the case of nationalist political parties. Since sovereignty is, above all, a collective good, it is vulnerable to free riding. This often prevents a nationalist party from getting off the ground. Second, even if the free-rider problem is somehow overcome, fledgling nationalist parties cannot readily convince prospective members that sovereignty is a realistic prospect. As scepticism abounds about the attainment of sovereignty, nationalist parties are unlikely to arise *de novo* even in circumstances most favourable to it. Pre-existing solidary groups solve these problems by offering a variety of private goods to their members. Once people are already organized in a group, they can be mobilized to seek other types of goods, including some collective ones (Hechter 1987: ch. 4; see ch. 3 above).[17]

For example, the Nonconformist churches provided an organizational base for the development of Welsh nationalism (Hechter 1990*b*). In the early 1700s, Nonconformity spread rapidly in Wales because, unlike their counterparts in the Church of England, its ministers preached to the Welsh in their own language. Services prominently featured singing and emotionality. In addition, the Nonconformist chapels provided for injured, sick, and dying members and their families from church funds. Their Sunday Schools offered the only opportunity for most Welsh people to become literate. The chapels also gave their members opportunities to develop abilities for public speaking, administration, and democratic debate.

That the chapels also acted as insurance groups is underscored by their antagonistic relationship with secular mutual benefit societies that emerged later. Following the extension of legal privileges to friendly societies in 1793, a host of new mutual benefit societies arose in Wales. These new friendly societies typically met at pubs and provided welfare and entertainment—many of the same kinds of private goods that the Nonconformist chapels did—along with drink. Nonconformist ministers stressed temperance as a means of preserving control over their flock. The principal alternative to drinking societies in Wales was the chapel.

The Welsh nationalist agenda began as an elaboration of Nonconformist political concerns. The ministers and members of the chapels sought separate consideration for Wales by Parliament on the issues of education, temperance, and the disestablishment of the Church of England. More than spiritual entities, the chapels were citadels from which attacks were mounted on English landowners and churchmen. Much Nonconformist activism focused on the taxes paid to the English government for support of the Church of England. Since Dissenters had their spiritual and welfare needs met through their chapels, they had little desire to pay money to support a competing institution. Some Nonconformist townspeople simply refused to pay the church rate, although legally the Church of England was the only place to obtain a marriage or funeral.

Nonconformist ministers directly organized protests against tithes to the Church of England. They agitated for disestablishment to break the Anglican monopoly of performing social functions such as weddings and funerals. They demanded government support for their schools. The chapels were also the power behind the first Act to treat Wales as a separate legislative unit, the 1881 Welsh Sunday Closing Act. This Act, which legally closed pubs on Sundays, also attacked the chapel's principal competitors in Wales, the friendly societies.

In similar fashion, German nationalism was kindled in a variety of youth organizations and fraternities (Düding 1987), and the Gaelic Athletic Association was an important base for the development of Irish nationalism (Mandle 1987). Finally, voluntary associations played a key role in the birth of African nationalist movements (Wallerstein 1961).

Institutional Barriers to Collective Action

If collective action emanates from voluntary associations, then the prospects for nationalism are affected by the nation's institutional completeness (Stinchcombe 1975: 605–6). This institutional completeness, in turn, depends on the central state's tolerance of nationally distinctive cultural and political organizations. Multinational states vary in their openness to the establishment of these associations (Hechter and Levi 1979). The point is obvious in comparing democratic and non-democratic polities. Less well appreciated are the significant differences in openness among democracies, however.

For example, the French state historically has been much less tolerant of cultural diversity than the British. Despite Whitehall's control over education and other social services, schools vary widely in terms of curriculum as well as languages of instruction. Although English remains the official language, Welsh has been taught in the elementary schools in Wales since 1888 (Morgan 1963). Moreover, as has been seen, Nonconformity gained a major foothold in Wales, and as a result the Church of England was eventually disestablished there. In contrast, the French state has long made clear its emphasis on religious and cultural standardization (Hayward 1973). Catholicism is by far the dominant religion, and French is the only official language for teaching and governmental business. Until recently, Breton was not taught in schools, which have a highly uniform curriculum. Traditionally, the French state erected numerous legal and administrative barriers to the maintenance of the Breton language and culture (Berger 1972; Reece 1979).

The origin of this distinction between Britain and France is found in the administrative arrangements of the two countries. In brief, France enacted a more thoroughgoing form of direct rule than Britain. Since the sixteenth century, the French administrative system has been extremely hierarchical, and this tendency was strengthened by Napoleon. Various agents—*commissaires, intendants*, and now prefects—mediated the link between centre and periphery. As a result, the local administration is subordinated to and controlled by the centre (Machin 1977; Ridley and Blondel 1969; Tarrow 1977: 48–58).

In principle, Britain has lagged behind France in delegating administrative responsibility to organizations below that of the national ministry (Barker 1944; McKenzie and Grove 1957: 262–75). None the less, for centuries there have been administrative offices within the national bureaucracy that both recognized and ostensibly represented the distinct concerns of particular regions, especially Wales, Scotland, and Northern Ireland (Ashford 1977; Duchacek 1970).

The difference between British and French tolerance of cultural diversity is mirrored in their legislation affecting peripheral regions. At least since the late nineteenth century, the British parliament has passed numerous laws not only directed at Wales specifically, but granting it special privileges in regard to education, housing, and other governmental functions. In 1997, Scotland was granted its own parliament and Wales an assembly. France has never devolved comparable authority to Brittany or any other region; until quite recently its laws have been aimed at promoting similarities—rather than recognizing distinctiveness—among its culturally distinct peripheries.

Electoral laws also have implications for the development of nationalist parties. Some electoral mechanisms, most notably proportional representation, foster multipartism, which lowers the obstacles to the formation of nationalist parties.[18] Others, such as those based on single-member districts, discourage third parties.

The Strategic Use of Nationalist Violence

Institutional barriers to collective action affect the set of strategies available to nationalist groups. Where the institutions allow these groups to have ample voice, the range of strategies available to nationalist groups is at a maximum. For this very reason, nationalist demands will tend to be made by parties and through other legitimate political channels. In institutional settings that restrict voice—due to state repression (the African National Congress under apartheid), or to the tyranny of the majority (the Protestants in Northern Ireland)—relatively few strategies are available to nationalist groups. In conditions that preclude exit and voice (Hirschman 1970), the strategic use of violence comes into its own.

Violent tactics can be adopted strategically for a variety of reasons.[19] The most obvious reason is to raise the centre's costs of controlling a restless periphery. Because they are loath to part with territory, central authorities are always interested in suppressing peripheral nationalism. However, when the relative cost of controlling a nationalist group increases due to militant resistance, states are more disposed to grant sovereignty to them. The two most notable cases of pure secession in the twentieth century—those of Norway and Ireland—both can be interpreted in these terms (Chapter 5).

Part of the strategic appeal of violence also comes from its undeniably attention-getting nature. The restive Kosovar Albanians provide just the most recent case in point. When Serbia imposed direct rule in Kosovo in 1989, Kosovar nationalists initially sent activists to Norway to study non-violent resistance. As a result, the territory was largely peaceful. But then things changed:

As Kosovo's Albanians see it today . . . the lack of drama in their land lulled Washington into a false belief that there was always another day to work things out—and room to naïvely hope that Mr. Milosevic's brutal Serbian regime could be reformed. It is ironic that the Dayton accord of 1995, which produced the uneasy peace in Bosnia, was probably the signal event in the formation of an armed insurgency in Kosovo. The leadership in the capital, Pristina, watched in disbelief as the fate of Kosovo was never raised in Dayton, and as other Yugoslav groups that had mounted armed rebellions achieved recognition and even independence. It was especially galling that the self-styled Bosnian Serb republic, which had overseen the expulsion and murder of tens of thousands of Muslims, obtained quasi-legitimacy in Dayton while Kosovo was ignored. 'It was a terrible, terrible, lesson,' said a minister in the self-styled government who asked to remain unidentified. 'We learned that violence works. It is the only way in this part of the world to achieve what you want and get the attention of the international community.' (Hedges 1998a).

Northern Ireland, which has been a virtual laboratory for the study of nationalist violence, provides further evidence of the strategic basis of nationalist violence. Although thousands of people have died since the beginning of the Troubles in 1969, it is striking how controlled this violence has been. Violence between Catholics and Protestants has never escalated into a genocidal fury. Limits on violence are due to microcontrols such as the avoidance provided by segregation and situational variations in relationships (Darby 1987: 155–6). The Irish Republican Army's use of 'legitimate targeting', which was designed to maximize political support of its Catholic constituency, is further evidence of its strategic use of violence (Darby 1994).

Finally, groups can employ violence strategically to polarize a conflict to their advantage. To illustrate, in late October 1992, some of the Croatians who had fled towns in Krajina that had been taken by Serb forces returned to their former homes in the company of United Nations troops. They soon discovered that Serb gunmen had desecrated the graves of their ancestors. Serbs had pulled the covers off Croatian tombs and machine gunned their remains. Surely this bizarre event must provide evidence of irrationality— it must take some very odd passions to make Serbs waste valuable ammunition on Croats who were already long dead.

An event that on its face seems little short of bizarre—firing machine gun rounds into a cemetary full of people who are already dead—may have a strategic rationale. The Serb gunners' behaviour may have been consciously designed to heighten the salience of the boundary between Serbs and Croats. Under Tito's regime, this boundary had been downplayed, and considerable social integration (represented, for example, by relatively high rates of exogamous marriage) had occurred between these two communities. In such a context, desecrating Croat cemeteries had a predictable effect: it instantaneously heightened the salience of the Serb/Croat boundary:

In both Serbian and Croatian culture ancestral graves are endowed with great significance. For example, ceremonies are held and offerings made regularly at the graves of important family members. Serb gunners knew this, of course, knew that the Croats knew it, and knew that the Croats knew that they knew it. Desecrating cemeteries is part of a calculated plan by Serb extremists to make ethnic cohabitation impossible by spreading and deepening hatred across groups. Likewise for the Serb policy of systematic rape in the Bosnian war. Such measures do more than just make Bosnian Muslims or Croats too angry to live with Serbs in the future. *They are also calculated to make it more difficult for less virulently nationalist Serbs to live with Muslims or Croats, due to fear of reprisal or discrimination* (Fearon 1994).

These policies were extremely successful. According to a Bosnian Serb who is now a refugee in Serbia, 'It's not that I wouldn't want to go back . . . If things could be the same as they were before I would go back in an instant. But on all sides there's been too much hatred, too much bloodshed. I'd be afraid of the first Muslim who lived next door' (Fearon 1994: 5–6 n.).

Whereas in the 1980s many Serbs were loath to identify with nationalist symbols carrying symbols, a decade later the climate had changed so much that the failure to affirm Serbian identity often would be sanctioned (Glenny 1993). The first targets of the Serb paramilitary units that swept into multiethnic Bosnian villages were those Serbs who favoured ethnic integration (Mozjes 1994: 167). Spending time and effort to desecrate Croat cemeteries makes strategic sense given the knowledge that it can produce fear and hatred on the part of Croats. In turn, extremist Serbs could predict that Croats would react militantly.[20]

While it is easy to appreciate that, in certain circumstances, nationalist groups might strategically adopt violent means to attain their goals, is it a mystery to understand why individuals might bear very high risks of injury, punishment and even death to help bring the collective good of sovereignty to their nation? The use of violent means will tend to attract members who are skilled or specialized in violence, and will discourage others who are neither skilled nor interested in it. To the degree that members are dependent on a solidary group that adopts violent means, they may be willing to take great risks. Membership in American inner-city youth gangs is one case in point (Jankowski 1991); membership in the Sicilian Mafia is another (Gambetta 1993). There are, after all, many risky occupations. Although it is dangerous to be a policeman, a fireman, or to build skyscrapers, that people can be found to fill these jobs causes no great consternation. Why should membership in violent nationalist groups be so different? Whenever nationalist violence occurs in the absence of highly solidary—that is, organized—nationalist groups, this theory cannot account for it.[21]

Conclusion

The economy, institutions, and policies of direct-rule states can each affect the net benefit of sovereignty to peripheral nations, and hence the demand for it. Incorporation in an economically stagnant or declining state offers little benefit to the periphery; hence, economic weakness increases its demand for sovereignty. State institutions and policies can be more or less responsive to the distinctive values of peripheral nations. The less responsive they are, the greater the demand for sovereignty will be. The same logic accounts for variations in the demand for sovereignty among different groups within a given nation. Those groups most dependent on the central state for their material or cultural welfare should be least supportive of nationalism.

Yet the demand for sovereignty is far from the whole story. Nationalism cannot emerge without an underlying substrate of voluntary associations—or analogues such as non-voluntary trade diasporas, kin groups, or religious institutions (Landa 1994). Since sovereignty is a collective good, and a highly unlikely one at that, nationalist groups tend to face severe organizational problems. As a result, they often develop as a by-product of other kinds of social groups, such as churches and voluntary associations, that provide their members with private goods. Group formation, however, is also affected by state policies and institutions. It is fostered in societies with maximum freedom of association, and inhibited to the degree that these freedoms are limited. In this fashion, state policies and political institutions exercise a much more subtle effect on the prospects for nationalism.

Multinational states encompass nations whose production and consumption values systematically diverge from the centre. These values are not easily accommodated by unitary governments. The demand for sovereignty is determined in good part by the government's responsiveness to these distinctive national values. States whose policies foreordain the members of a nation to being perpetual losers in the competition for state-provided goods lay themselves open to nationalist violence.

CHAPTER 8

Containing Nationalism

ALTHOUGH nationalism often inspires artistic, intellectual and political ferment, it is sometimes implicated in civil war and the most egregious acts of violence.[1] At its worst, nationalism inspires xenophobia, ethnic cleansing, and genocide. Can this dark side of nationalism ever be contained? If nationalist excess is a natural, if unfortunate, product of human nature—if it represents the recrudescence of 'the old Adam'—then despite our best efforts, it will be with us forever. If, however, nationalist conflict is the result of particular kinds of social structures and events, as the theory in this book claims, then its course ought to be substantially affected by social institutions.

What kinds of institutions might be able to contain nationalism's worst excesses? Expert opinion is sharply divided, but the present analysis suggests that nationalist conflict will decline only under three types of conditions: those that increase the costs of collective action in general, those that lower the salience of national identity, and those that decrease the demand for national sovereignty.

Although conditions that increase the cost of collective action—like the institutional barriers discussed in Chapter 7—are important historically, they are not at all specific to nationalism (Hardin 1981; Lichbach 1995). Clearly, the cost of collective action is at a maximum in repressive regimes. Regimes that limit freedom of assembly and tightly regulate the activities of voluntary associations can keep almost any kind of collective action at bay, given sufficient enforcement capacity. Despite their other shortcomings, repressive governments in the Soviet Union and Yugoslavia did manage to succeed in containing nationalist conflict.

Yet global economic interdependence, and the increasing power of third parties—like the United Nations, the North Atlantic Treaty Organization, and the International Monetary Fund—are raising the costs of repression. Meanwhile, the advent of new communications technology is dramatically lowering the cost of collective action, making nationalism ever more likely.[2] To some degree, these heightened prospects for nationalist collective action come at the expense of central authorities. This is especially clear with respect to the media. In most countries, the broadcast media have been government-controlled, and in authoritarian regimes this control usually extends to newspapers, as well. In spite of some governments' attempts to regulate access to the Internet,[3] the advent of new communications technology may well threaten this centralized control.[4] Patrolling the Internet is likely to prove beyond the capacity of most authoritarian governments.

The upshot is that new communications technology is a spur to democratization throughout the world. Although repression may have been reasonably effective in containing nationalism in the past, its future role in this respect likely will diminish. If so, this conventional means of containing nationalist conflict will be increasingly unavailable.

Is national identity likely to wane? Ultimately, this kind of social identity rests on distinctive national production and/or consumption values. To a large extent, these values are nurtured by the stratification of culturally distinct groups, or by their capture of key institutional sectors. Since neither capitalism, socialism, nor any other post-industrial social formation has managed to eradicate cultural stratification, in spite of policies like affirmative action, and since immigration leads to ever new forms of it, this source of national identity is likely to remain with us in the foreseeable future. While many particular nations—like the Cornish and Frisians in England—have faded into the mists of history, new ones—like the Ossies in Germany, or the residents of Hong Kong in China—can be expected to make their début. Moreover, there is scant reason to suspect that cultural groups will voluntarily cede any control they may have over educational, judicial, and religious institutions. Although its locus is bound to shift over time, there is little reason to expect national identity to wane in the future.

The best hope for containing the destructive elements of nationalism therefore hinges on conditions that decrease the demand for sovereignty among national groups. Such groups demand sovereignty to enact a governance structure that is more accountable to them. Whereas distinctive national values will tend to persist, the responsiveness of central states to these distinctive values can be affected by institutional arrangements that, at least in principle, are modifiable. This chapter suggests that institutions which increase the central state's accountability to national minorities should reduce the demand for sovereignty, and hence the potential for nationalist conflict.[5]

Would-be institutional designers have several prominent ideas to consider on this score: consociationalism, electoral laws, and that variant of indirect rule known as federation. As indirect rule has been a *leitmotiv* of this book, federation receives the lion's share of attention.

Consociationalism

Consociationalism—this now musty term is borrowed from Althusius, who was last encountered in Chapter 3—has been advanced as the most suitable form of governance for multinational, as well as multiethnic, societies (Lijphart 1977, 1984). The idea at its root is that intergroup conflict can be tempered by having the leaders of the various nations participate in decision-making as a cartel. In addition, consociational governance entails two other defining characteristics. The leaders of each nation are armed with veto powers over government decision-making. And the principle of proportionality reigns in elections, as well as in the allocation of collective goods. In consequence of these measures, consociational regimes offer their constituent nations a high degree of self-governance. Governance in Switzerland often has been hailed as a consociational success story (Steiner 1974). Many objections have been levelled against this conception, however. Giving each national group a veto is a recipe for governmental inaction. Beyond this, what is to prevent these autonomous national leaders from attempting to secede? Consociational rule has further draw-backs: it avoids popular participation, and it relies on élite bar-gaining carried out in secrecy.

Although consociational thought bears a superficial resemblance to the present theory, it differs in its inattention to individual-level analysis. As a result of this inattention, consociationalists make two highly questionable assumptions. In the first place, they assume—but do not explain—the existence of a mechanism that welds the interests of national leaders and followers into a cohe-sive group.[6] In the second place, they assume that politicians will form cartels that cut across the boundaries of national groups, but there are reasons to doubt this.[7] By promoting group as against individual rights, consociationalism tends to inhibit intergroup cooperation. It is at least as likely that leaders will use consoci-ational institutions to gain maximum resources for themselves rather than to defuse intergroup conflict (Brass 1991: 245). The breakdown of consociational regimes in countries like Lebanon before 1970 would appear to bear out these concerns. Even Arend Lijphart, the theory's strongest advocate, conceded long ago (1977) that the evidence supporting consociation is at best mixed.

No doubt, intergroup cooperation is better fostered by institu-tions which create interests that *span* group boundaries. The most enduring and effective arrangements to reduce intergroup conflict are likely to be based on internal incentives rather than external constraints.[8] Electoral systems can provide one source of such incentives.

Electoral Systems

Electoral systems affect the nature of political parties, those who are represented in parliament, and the groups that govern. They translate electoral votes into parliamentary seats, provide the means by which representatives are held accountable by con-stituents, and influence political discourse by encouraging parties to couch electoral appeals in specific ways (Reynolds 1999: ch. 3). Electoral systems vary between plurality/majority types, which tend to channel votes into two large parties, and proportional types, which aim to reduce the disparity between a party's share of votes and its parliamentary representation.

It is often claimed that electoral systems affect intergroup conflict in multinational societies, but how they do so is not self-evident. Whereas systems based on a plurality rule can lead to the tyranny of the majority, proportional systems increase minority representation. Since perpetually unrepresented minorities are likely to become restive, electoral systems based on proportionality would seem to reduce intergroup conflict in these circumstances. Although proportionality promotes minority representation, however, this may not necessarily reduce intergroup conflict because it provides no incentives for inter-party coalitions. One source of these incentives is an electoral system that encourages 'vote pooling' across group boundaries (Horowitz 1991). In such a system, political stability is to some degree self-enforcing— a crucial advantage, since multinational polities are often particularly ill-suited to the exercise of third-party enforcement. One such electoral system was designed in Malaysia.[9]

Donald Horowitz (1991) touts the Alternative Vote as an electoral system that provides optimal incentives for vote pooling. Under the Alternative Vote, the winning candidate in a district must gain an absolute majority of the votes. If no candidate wins over 50 per cent of the first preferences, then the lowest polling candidate is eliminated and his or her second preferences are redistributed to candidates remaining in the race. The process continues until someone reaches the winning threshold. These vote pooling incentives only come into play if no single party is likely to win an absolute majority of the district's votes. To the degree that nationality determines party preference, however, constituencies must be culturally heterogeneous (as in the Malaysian example cited above) to promote vote pooling. Lijphart (1991), however, contends just the opposite—that proportional representation provides superior incentives for intergroup accommodation. Unfortunately, this debate cannot be settled empirically because there are hardly any empirical cases of the Alternative Vote. It is possible, however, to simulate the likely consequences of the alternative vote in elections on different constituency structures with a given distribution of national groups. Andrew Reynolds (1999) does so for a number of Southern African countries. Whereas Horowitz emphasizes the independent influence of the electoral system's incentives on political behaviour, Reynolds's study provides little support for the vote-pooling capacity of the Alternative Vote.[10] All told, his evidence suggests that electoral incentives tend to be swamped by other kinds of incentives.

Federation

If neither consociationalism nor electoral systems alone are adequate to resolve nationalist conflict, then what about that form of indirect rule known as federation?[11] Federation is an institutional arrangement, taking the form of a sovereign state, that is distinguished from other such states solely by the fact that its central government incorporates regional units into its decision procedure on some constitutionally entrenched basis (King 1982: 77).[12] Federations all employ indirect rule, but their forms can vary widely. For example, the degree to which federal units are formally equal is always an empirical question (in the United States, for example, the Rhode Island voter for the Senate has twenty times the power that her California counterpart has). Further, federations have different degrees and types of decentralization:

In distinguishing federation from other forms of state organisation most commentators consider it as a decentralised political system possessing a constitutional government in which constituent territorial units are involved in a politics of accommodation. The nature and scale of the divisions of powers between the centre and the region can be distinguished from other forms of political devolution by virtue of the fact that regional autonomy and representation are not only more devolved but are constitutionally guaranteed.[13] The centre does not have the judicial right to abolish, amend or redefine its territorial units. Thus in federations, regional units are in effect truly local states with local state rights. Citizen representation is also uniquely based on a regional principle which . . . is the chief distinguishing feature of federation. (Elazar 1994: p. xv; see also Smith 1995: 7–8)

By granting some powers to a national unit, federation clearly offers one way of resolving at least some of the policy conflicts that are likely to arise in a multinational state.

The notion that federation is well-suited for the governance of large, culturally heterogeneous territories has an ancient pedigree in social thought; it has also been forcefully advocated by the political scientist William Riker (1964). According to Riker, federation is the outcome of a bargain between rulers of the central state and leaders of the territorial subunits. As in all bargains, this one only works because it appeals to both parties. Federation enables the territorial subunits to attain some degree of political self-control while profiting from access to the greater resources and military protection that is afforded by membership in large polities.[14] At the same time, the federal bargain offers central rulers a relatively cost-effective means of maintaining their state's territorial integrity.

However, recent events—including the collapse of federations in the Soviet Union, Yugoslavia, and Czechoslovakia, and the continued thirst for secession among the cultural minorities in federations like Canada and Spain—have led many scholars to question the ameliorative effects of political decentralization. These events suggest the very real possibility that, far from inhibiting nationalist conflict, federation exacerbates it instead. Still other observers argue that federation has no determinate effects on nationalist conflict at all. Evidently, the nature of the relationship between federation and nationalist conflict is highly contentious.

Does federation reinforce nationalism by empowering national leaders, and whetting their appetites for even greater powers or privileges? Does it erode nationalism by enabling nations to satisfy their demands within the existing state? Or does it have no determinate effects at all? Debates about the direction of one particular bivariate relationship usually entail disagreements about the underlying causal mechanisms. This is clearly the case here.

Why Federation may Intensify Nationalist Conflict

The causal mechanism responsible for this effect is due to the very nature of federation. Federation diverts some government functions—and hence resources—from the centre to territorial sub-units. Federation may stimulate nationalist conflict because it provides potential nationalist leaders with patronage and other resources that can be mobilized for nationalist ends. Federation also tends to provide institutional supports for nationalism:

Federalism . . . is an important source of institutional capacity because it pro-vides a set of political levers and access to resources that make group mobil-isation more likely. While often put in place as a means of accommodation and cooptation, federal institutions can be quickly turned to new agendas when a coopted leadership is replaced or changes its preferences (Meadwell 1993: 200; see also Nordlinger 1972: 32; Roeder 1991).

In addition to the material incentives to nationalist mobilization that it may provide, federation also may have cognitive implica-tions. When nations are given many of the accoutrements of real states, this also encourages people to think and act according to national categories (Brubaker 1996).[15] Further, federation may be better suited to resolving material differences between subunits than cultural ones:

We can cope with, and even indeed welcome, different types of material arti-fice, but cannot with equal ease accept conflicting rules about 'correct' social and political behaviour. Conflicts between rules have a way of translating out as conflicts over things, as where a native population reverts and seeks to retain all ancestral land, whether tilled or not, in contrast to the expansion-ist settler who will justify the appropriation of any land by those who will render it productive. Two such rules, and two populations so ruled, will not achieve community in peace (King 1982: 47–8).

Thus, federation may provide both material and cognitive sup-ports for nationalist conflict. This view has at least one clear policy implication: *to contain nationalist conflict, local leaders should be offered meaningful, substantial careers in the central government* (Laitin 1998). By this means, nationalist leaders will be trans-formed into stakeholders committed to the maintenance of the central regime.

The historical record provides ample evidence linking federation with nationalist conflict. The United States Civil War broke out in a federation; Pakistan—another federation—lost Bangladesh. Following the attempted secession of its eastern region (1967–70),

Nigeria has managed to avoid secessionism by creating new territorial subunits tending to cut across national boundaries. The only socialist states to dissolve following the climactic year of 1989—the Soviet Union, Czechoslovakia, and Yugoslavia—also just happened to be federations.

Soviet policies to defuse nationalism by coopting regional élites by devolving authority backfired (Kaiser 1990). Federation, perversely, encouraged congeries of local groups to form nations where none had previously existed. In each union republic, the titular nationality used its position to develop its own version of great power chauvinism, limiting the rights of its own minorities (save, of course, for Russians) when possible. Georgia became a protected area of privilege for Georgians. They received the bulk of the rewards of the society, the leading positions in the state, and the largest subsidies for cultural projects, while the Armenians, Abkhazians, Ossetians, Ajarians, Kurds, Jews, and others were at a considerable disadvantage in the competition for the budgetary pie. Although Soviet leaders apparently enacted this policy to coopt indigenous élites, when these élites began tilting towards nationalism, the Soviets abruptly ended the policy in 1934–8.

If Soviet federation generated nationalism, so did the subsequent attempt to increase central control. Recentralization proved impossible in an increasingly complex economy; even when regional leaders were motivated to act in the centre's interest, they lacked the information necessary to do so. Hence, the only policies they could pursue were nationalist in outcome (Kaiser 1994: 331). Similarly, the recent increase in Quebec's regional authority does not seem to have dampened the fate of the separatist political party. Despite taking over the Quebec government—and the subsequent passage of language legislation protecting French and the Francophones—a near-majority of Quebecois voted for separation in 1995. Nor has Spain's devolution of power to the Basque region put its separatist party (ETA) out of business.

Why Federation may Inhibit Nationalist Conflict

The opposing view is also based on an intuitively appealing causal mechanism. Since federation is a form of indirect rule, the theory in this book suggests that it ought to reduce the demand for sovereignty. On this account, federation should also serve to mute nationalist conflict.[16] Since nations are culturally distinctive by definition, individual members' values reflect (to some degree) these distinctive national values. Although members of national groups share values—minimally, those relating to the attainment of wealth, power, and prestige—in common with all the other inhabitants of a given multinational state, they also share a set of values derived from the national culture that are distinctive. Typically, these values include preferences to speak a distinct language and practise a distinct religion.

As discussed in Chapter 7, governments provide a range of collective goods. Some of these goods—like defence—are universally valued by inhabitants. Others—like education in a particular language, and state support for a particular religion—appeal to only a portion of the state's inhabitants. Whereas some universally valued goods may better be provided centrally,[17] goods that are valued only by a segment of the society are better provided locally (Oates 1972). Local provision of these goods is superior because it increases the likelihood that the right mix of goods will be produced—that mix which is most consistent with the distinctive values of the national group.[18] As federation involves the devolution of (at least some) decision-making to localities, it increases local self-governance. To the degree that at least some of the units in a federal system constitute nations, then federation should have the effect of inhibiting nationalism. Since sovereignty is neither more nor less than self-governance, it follows that to the degree that federation increases a nation's self-governance, its demand for sovereignty must be correspondingly reduced.[19]

This reasoning implies that the less self-governance a nation has in a multinational state, the greater the possibility of nationalist conflict. Assuming that nations make up at least some of the constituent local or state subunits in a multinational polity, then the greater the powers of the central government relative to those of state and local governments, the greater the nationalist conflict. A constitution that minimizes the state's control over disposable, transferable revenue and rights presents a very small target for nationalists. It stands to reason that local politicians are less likely to play the nationalist card when their constituents see less benefit in sovereignty. This view has quite a different policy implication: to contain nationalism, *the central rulers of multinational states ought to grant political devolution to mobilized national minorities.*

In spite of the apparent failures of federation alluded to above, this argument also commands ample supportive case-study evidence. Many central rulers have turned to federation as a means of reducing nationalist discontent, and they continue to do so. Britain's recent offer of devolution to Scotland and Wales was welcomed by voters in both lands, with the more thoroughgoing devolution in Scotland more enthusiastically supported than its relatively anaemic Welsh counterpart. When Labour handily came in first in both Scottish and Welsh legislative elections in May 1999, Tony Blair claimed that the voting results vindicated his party's devolution strategy.[20] Spain and Belgium have recently undergone significant constitutional moves from unity toward federation as a means of resolving national conflicts (Forsythe 1989), and even France—traditionally, the archetypal unitary state—has granted Corsica a certain amount of devolution (Savigear 1989). In the Spanish, Belgian, and British cases, very significant powers have been granted to the relevant subunits.

Central government repression of the Sikh independence movement in the Punjab has led to the greatest violence that India has faced since independence (Tambiah 1996: 263). Thus federation has been viewed an essential palliative in India:

Conflict resolution in multiethnic states must focus on center–regional relations and elite group interactions. Policies of state centralization which at the same time select regional collaborators in their policies from among particular ethnic group elites will ultimately produce counterelites within the regions to challenge their regional rivals and the centralizing state allied with them. Under some circumstances, such countermovements may turn secessionist. Consequently, state leaders who wish to avoid such movements will have to consider decentralization of power and economic decisionmaking and decentering ethnic group relations by playing the role of mediator in regional conflicts rather than intervening directly in them except as protector of those without power (Brass 1991: 244).

Centralization has been the bane of South Asian societies, but in Switzerland federation has been widely celebrated (McGarry and

O'Leary 1993: 31; Smith 1995: 14).[21] Finally, the federal United States has experienced little in the way of nationalist conflict since the Civil War (Glazer 1977). This evidence suggests that federation may indeed mute, if not inhibit, nationalist conflict.

There is yet a third view of these matters. Some scholars claim that nothing general can be said about the effects of decentralization at all because it can occur on a practically infinite number of dimensions (King 1982). Centralization of expenditure may be the key factor, rather than political decentralization. Much depends on the precise nature of the governing institutions (Habermas 1994), especially the party system.[22] These caveats derive from the historical record, but there are also theoretical reasons why decentralization may not have a determinate effect on nationalism. Instead, nationalism may result from path-dependent contingencies that cumulate in 'reputational cascades' (Kuran 1998). On this third view, therefore, *neither systematic cooptation of local leaders nor devolution ought to have determinate effects on the containment of nationalist conflict*.[23]

Evidently, the nature of the relationship between federation and nationalism is contentious. Each view is grounded in a plausible causal mechanism and consistent with at least some of the relevant empirical evidence. Finally, these rival views cannot be distinguished on purely theoretical grounds, for each can be derived from exactly the same instrumental motivational assumptions. Is there any relationship at all between political federation and nationalist conflict? If so, what might its nature be?

Some New Evidence

Until recently, there was no means of assessing the proposition that local decision-making decreases nationalist conflict. Now, however, two different sources of evidence sets can be merged to shed some light on the question. The first, *Minorities at Risk*, consists of a large cross-national data set based on newspaper reports of nationalist conflict since 1970 (Gurr 1993). These data contain variables describing various types of collective action carried out by national groups, as well as measures of the various conditions these groups face in their host states. The second consists of a cross-national data set on *Government Finance Statistics* collected by the

International Monetary Fund that documents the degree to which government revenues and expenditures are centralized in a large number of countries.

Nationalist conflict is measured by two indicators of anti-regime activity: *rebellion* (including political banditry, terrorist campaigns, guerrilla activity, and protracted civil war), and *protest* (including expressions of verbal opposition, symbolic rebellion, and demonstrations). These indicators characterize the mean level of rebellion and protest events for all the ethnically distinct groups in a given state.

Although there are many different types of centralization, fiscal centralization is key, for any decentralization that occurs without granting budgetary power to a subunit is well-nigh hollow. The *Government Finance Statistics* data set contains four variables that indicate the degree of fiscal centralization in each country. These indicate the revenue collected and expenditures made by each level of government in every country by year.

Using these measures, new light is cast on the relationship between decentralization and nationalism (Hechter and Takahashi 1999). First, centralization does indeed have a significant effect on nationalist collective action. Second, protest and rebellion events behave quite differently in these data. Although centralization is positively associated with rebellion events, it is negatively associated with protest. This suggests a possible reconciliation of the two opposing arguments in the literature. Whereas decentralization may provide cultural minorities with greater resources to engage in collective action, leading to a rise in protest events, at the same time it may erode the demand for sovereignty. Since secession is always an uncertain prospect, and groups tend to be more averse to uncertainty than individuals are, this decrease in the demand for sovereignty ought to reduce the incidence of nationalist rebellion.[24]

If nationalist groups engage in violent tactics as a means of pursuing sovereignty, then rebellion should be more likely to occur among groups with the greatest opportunity to attain this end (McAdam *et al.* 1996). Groups concentrated in territories that already have their own governance structures—such as American states, Canadian provinces, or French *départements*—can make a more plausible demand for sovereignty than groups concentrated in regions lacking a governance structure.[25]

To determine if this logic holds, the rebellion indicators from the *Minorities at Risk* data set were reconstructed by excluding all non-spatially concentrated groups, as well as those concentrated groups whose territory does not coincide with some intermediate-level political boundary.[26] The countries in bold italic have at least one minority group that is concentrated in a region with its own governance structure, while countries in regular font lack such a group. Figure 8.1 clearly shows that centralization is strongly associated with nationalist rebellion. These results should not be overinterpreted. Fiscal centralization is an indirect indicator of local decision-making, and both the meaningfulness and comparability of measures of fiscal centralization have been questioned (Bird 1986). Further, due to data limitations, the number of countries in this analysis is relatively small. Despite these caveats, the consistency of the results is impressive across three decades of recent history.

Yet two questions remain. In the first place, since most of the violent nationalism during the 1980s occurred in less developed countries—such as Uganda, the Philippines, and Indonesia—is the relationship depicted in Figure 8.1 merely an artifact of the overall level of economic development? On the one hand, people may be less inclined to take action against central governments in rich states because they have more to lose from the resulting disorder, or because they think they have more to lose on account of the greater communication capacity of central governments in developed societies. On the other, since democracy may be associated with economic development, so, perhaps, is fiscal decentralization.

Decentralization and economic development are so highly correlated that their independent effects cannot be estimated unless separate analyses are carried out for developed and less developed countries. When this is done, the results are consistent with the theory in this book. Among less developed countries—those most prone to nationalist violence—the relationship between centralization and nationalist rebellion holds even when Gross National Product per capita is controlled (Hechter and Takahashi 1999).

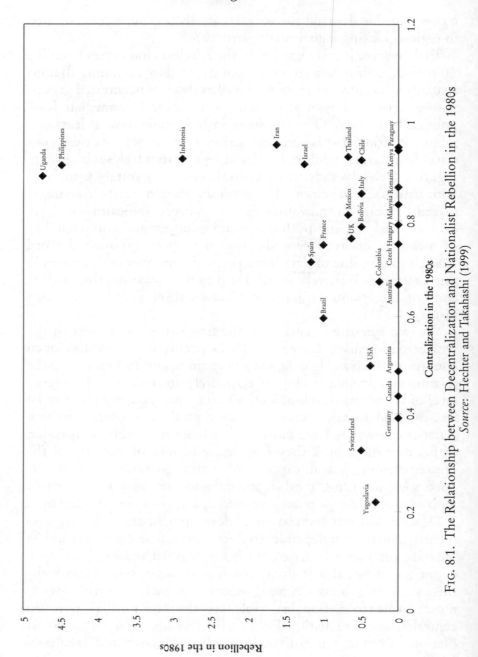

Fig. 8.1. The Relationship between Decentralization and Nationalist Rebellion in the 1980s
Source: Hechter and Takahashi (1999)

In the second place, how robust is the relationship? There is at least one reason to wonder. Yugoslavia's placement in the extreme south-western part of the scatterplot for the decade of the 1980s would seem to imply that this should be the country that is most *immune* to nationalist rebellion. Yet in the very next decade the country was plunged into a severe and prolonged civil war and the term 'ethnic cleansing' entered the English vocabulary. If, as Figure 8.1 suggests, nationalism is contained by political decentralization, then how can Yugoslavia's fate be accounted for?[27]

While decentralization inhibits nationalist rebellion, it also stimulates nationalist protest. Herein lies a quandary. Decentralization is a spur to mobilization among minority nations, for it places greater resources (especially government jobs) in the hands of national leaders. As long as these leaders see a benefit in remaining part of the host state, decentralization ought to contain nationalist rebellion. If the central state implodes, however, then it has little to offer peripheral leaders and fragmentation is the likely consequence.[28]

The discussion of federation and nationalist conflict heretofore has been based on the implicit premise that the key dynamics are endogenous—that is, located within state territory. But that premise is questionable: time and again nationalism has been strongly affected by exogenous forces (Chapter 5). A country that decentralizes as a means of containing nationalist violence is at risk of fragmenting when its centre declines due to exogenous shocks such as military defeat or fiscal crisis. This was Yugoslavia's fate.

Decentralization and Fragmentation in Yugoslavia

From 1948 to 1991 Yugoslavia had managed to contain nationalism, despite the disparate production and consumption values of its various republics.[29] The country was held together by a constitutional order enforced by the resources of the central (federal) state that was explicitly designed to mitigate conflict between its constituent nations. Although the nature of this order varied over time in its degree of centralization (Cohen 1995: 26–38; Ramet 1992: ch. 14), the constitution aimed to provide equality among republics, as well as security for national minorities within each republic. Its goal was to prevent any single national group from gaining political dominance over the state. Federal policy depended on cooperation from republican leaders, who had the capacity to veto any decision.

All federal activities were required to take the proportional representation of individuals by constituent nationality into account. Nationalities were also guaranteed freedom of cultural expression. Individuals retained their national right to self-governance even if they lived outside their home nation's republic, and the choice of a national identity was voluntary. The manifestation of nationalism, however, was regarded as a threat to the social order and outlawed.

As a socialist state, Yugoslavia guaranteed its citizens subsistence, and central and local governments shared responsibility for individual welfare. Public-sector employment was the primary source of living standards. The economy was sustained by substantial amounts of foreign aid, largely from the United States (Rusinow 1977: 44–7), as well as access to foreign credits and capital markets. The basis of this exogenous support was geopolitical, and owed to the regime's neutrality during the cold war.

During the 1980s, however, a deadly combination of exogenous economic and political shocks weakened the central government's ability to maintain this constitutional order. Yugoslavia shared in the worldwide economic recession of the 1980s. To revive economic growth, the government appealed for assistance from the International Monetary Fund and similar bodies. Some assistance was offered, but only on the basis of commitments that the central government would enact policies promoting economic privatization and cut public expenditures for welfare, public employment, and social services.

The government accepted these conditions, but—partly due to them—living standards began to decline. Unemployment and inflation soared. By requiring constitutional revision, the debt-repayment regime turned normal disputes between central and regional governments into constitutional conflicts (Burg 1988: 11–13). The republics best able to adapt to the economic and political reforms of the debt-repayment package—Slovenia and Croatia—sought increasing autonomy from the centre. Those that were disadvantaged by these reforms argued for recentralization. The upshot was a constitutional crisis that was carried out between republican leaders seeking to enhance their control over economic and political resources within their territories (Cohen 1995 offers a detailed narrative).

Many other countries faced austerity measures in the 1980s but did not suffer Yugoslavia's fate. Yugoslavia had the misfortune of being the only multinational state that faced another kind of exogenous shock. The central government's ability to withstand peripheral nationalism was dealt a severe blow by the abrupt and unanticipated end of the cold war. Yugoslavia had profited greatly from its neutrality in the cold war. The demise of the Soviet Union sharply decreased the country's strategic value to the United States, however. It also ended forty years of American-backed guarantees of financial assistance and support for Yugoslav independence and integrity.

This combination of exogenous economic and political shocks so weakened the central government that its ability to contain nationalism was effectively destroyed. Although the centre attempted to prevent the secession of Slovenia and Croatia by force, it no longer had sufficient resources to prevail. Here, too, exogenous forces played a significant role; Germany's recognition of the sovereignty of Slovenia and Croatia spelt Yugoslavia's final chapter. Once the constitutional guarantees for minority rights were null and void, there was little to restrain intergroup violence.

At least two important lessons can be learnt from the Yugoslav case. On the one hand, its complex decentralized constitutional provisions managed to contain nationalism for four decades; this is no mean feat. Although the constitution was designed to keep the country territorially intact, its extreme decentralization made it difficult for the centre to adapt to exogenous economic shifts. On the other hand, the Yugoslav federation relied too heavily on the country's strategic position in the cold war. When—against all expectations—the cold war ended, the centre's resource base was substantially diminished.

Clearly decentralization can proceed so far that it courts fragmentation, which can be another source of intergroup violence. Yugoslavia in the 1980s was described as the most fragmented polity in the world (Stanovčić 1988). The relationship between decentralization and nationalist violence is likely to be U-shaped rather than linear. *If too little decentralization causes rebellion, then too much is likely to engender fragmentation.* To contain nationalist violence, therefore, a balance must be struck between peripheral regions' dependence on the centre for military and economic resources, and the autonomy to pursue their own production and consumption values. Federation is no panacea for nationalist violence in relatively centralized states,[30] but it does offer substantial hope for mitigating nationalism's dark side. This institutional remedy is much less difficult to prescribe than to implement, however.

Implementing Decentralization: The Role of Procedural Justice

Why should the members of peripheral nations trust effective central rulers to permanently cede authority and not regain power whenever it suits them? New federal constitutions are exceedingly difficult to devise and sustain. Suppose that before a federation is institutionalized, the majority group could announce a constitutional plan that would guarantee the minority enough political power to reduce the appeal of secession. Why should the minority believe that the majority would not scrap the plan at its earliest convenience? What can the majority do to make a power-sharing plan credible (Fearon 1994)?

Even if new institutions manage to be erected and sustained despite these obstacles, intergroup cooperation is by no means assured. To endure, intergroup contracts must be flexible; but to become established they must be specific. These conditions are difficult to attain simultaneously, but they may not be impossible. A constitution made in a Rawlsian fashion, as if from behind a veil of ignorance, conceivably might come to be regarded as fair by all parties.[31]

To be convincing, central leaders must find a way to credibly commit themselves to upholding their institutional commitments.

Their credibility will be enhanced when the government provides for maximal procedural justice. The essence of fairness is perceptual (Sheppard *et al.* 1992: 9).[32] Overall fairness evaluations concern outcomes, the procedures that determine outcomes, and the system that generates both outcomes and procedures. However, since both procedures and the overall system of governance are largely unobservable, people try to infer them from outcomes that are more readily observable. When people think that a particular decision is unfair, but that the procedure that generated the decision was fair, they are less likely to act on that perception to change the outcome. Procedures perceived as fair can significantly influence perceptions of the fairness of a specific outcome (Thibaut and Walker 1975; Tyler 1990).[33]

Procedures are regarded as fair if they entail adequate checks and balances to minimize arbitrary bias, ensure that no one entity dominates the process by providing ample opportunity for voice in decision-making,[34] and assure a neutral, accurate, and thorough process. Fair procedures inherently legitimate multiple interests. Whereas these strictures apply to the governance of any kind of organization, procedural justice in particular agencies is key for the reduction of nationalist violence. Here the police take pride of place. A multinational police force that takes a strong stand against intergroup violence is one highly visible indicator of a government's commitment to enacting procedural justice for the members of all its national groups: 'A highly visible display of force at the command of the police under the direction of a government that insists on uniform evenhanded application of protection and control by the police, and that is ready to call quickly on additional strength to back them when necessary, is usually an effective deterrent to the outbreak of civilian riots' (Tambiah 1996: 333).

For procedural justice to be something more than mere rhetoric, all parties—the centre and its subunits—must share a high degree of common knowledge. Francis Bacon once complained that all governments are obscure and invisible. Since most government policy-making occurs in settings with extremely low visibility, and the effects of given policies are often difficult to discern with certainty, this opacity reduces the state's accountability to national minorities. Common knowledge makes it possible to determine the degree to which procedures are just on a day-to-day basis. It also allows subunits to observe the rationale behind resource allocations made to other groups in the state. Procedural justice increases the capacity to maintain corporate integrity in the face of distributional inequality.

The relevant information in multinational states is vast and complicated. Attaining common knowledge, therefore, is exceptionally problematic in this setting.[35] To the extent that it can be attained at all, two institutions appear to play a crucial role. The first is a free press. Newspapers and broadcast media controlled by national minorities presumably have an incentive to monitor the relevant allocation decisions of the central government. The second means of providing the requisite common knowledge is via political representation. Since state allocation decisions are invisible to most constituents, political representation at the center is one means of legitimating budgetary allocation and other policies determined by the central government. Thus, contrary to much received wisdom (such as Elster *et al.* 1998: ch. 7), there are institutional means at hand by which states can contain the dark side of nationalism. Sovereignty need not be—indeed, it seldom is—all-or-nothing (Tully 1995). By enacting just procedures, institutional changes can be wrought that serve to decrease nationalist conflict.[36]

Finding the optimal institutional design to mitigate intergroup conflict is not like purchasing clothes off the rack, however. Institutional designers are most likely to succeed by giving due consideration to each country's particular history and situation. Admittedly, institutions promoting procedural justice are difficult to implement. Thus guarantees of human and minority rights have been included in all constitutions in the former Yugoslavia since 1991 but have never been enforced (Hayden 1998: 48). Resistance to procedural justice occurs even in the most stable of democracies. The view, held by a majority of African-Americans, that O. J. Simpson was framed for murder by a White-dominated police force and jury reveals that the Black community's doubts about American procedural justice have persisted long after the civil rights movement of the 1960s. Even so, the task of promoting procedural justice is far less daunting than that of altering the balance of power between national groups. In principle, all individuals in the society stand to gain by the implementation of procedural justice, whereas a change in the balance of intergroup power is always costly for members of the losing group.

How can central rulers in democratic states find the political will necessary to make the appropriate institutional changes? After all, granting greater autonomy to peripheral nations is bound to be a contentious issue. At a minimum, it increases complexity and rigidity, and detracts from the transparency and efficiency of government. Beyond this, however, it constitutes a commitment to minority cultural protectionism.[37] Just as economic protectionism benefits a small number of producers at the expense of the multitude of consumers, cultural protectionism has similar effects. Why then should the majority agree to subsidize a minority culture at its expense? This question is far from academic: it arises not only in existing multinational states, but also in political units in the making, like the European Union.

Making Minority Cultural Protectionism Politically Feasible

If cultural protectionism only benefits the members of the national group, then why would voters in non-peripheral territories have any reason to support it? In the absence of their support, minority cultural protectionism can only arise on the basis of naked power. Yet the preponderance of power in democratic societies always resides with the cultural majority. As the cases of Norway and Ireland reveal, nationalist movements occasionally can make enough of a nuisance of themselves to win outright secession. But such pure secession is rare (Chapter 5). What is more likely to occur is a situation in which the festering sense of national discontent breaks out from time to time in sporadic episodes of violence.

The best means of instituting minority cultural protectionism is by making the, admittedly counterintuitive, claim that the majority will profit from it. Asserting that political devolution will reduce nationalist violence is one such argument. However, this claim is only likely to be credible too late in the game—once nationalists have already armed themselves and created viable paramilitary organizations. Nationalists therefore would be well advised to contend that minority cultural protectionism provides benefits to the majority other than the reduction of violence.

One such contention is that peripheral autonomy is desirable simply because it preserves cultural diversity. Like biodiversity, cultural diversity may result in future social pay-offs that are impossible to foresee. For example, past laws permitting Asian immigration to the United States have resulted in an unintended benefit to all Americans. Now that the Pacific Rim has become such a dynamic part of the world economy, these laws have provided the United States (unlike the European Union, which was much more restrictive concerning immigration) with considerable cultural capital that can aid in promoting investment in and trade with Asian economies. Likewise, as global markets act to increase the uniformity of urban life, people are increasingly hankering for contrasting cultural experiences (known in the industry as 'adventure travel'). As a result, the demand for ethnic restaurants and tourism is escalating. Quebec's distinctiveness from the rest of Canada probably makes it a more interesting tourist destination for Anglophone Canadians and United States residents alike. Louisiana's cajun country has long been a magnet for domestic tourists for just this reason (Esman 1984; Wood 1984).

Still, cultural diversity is hardly a tangible or non-contentious good. Worse, many people believe that it threatens political unity and social order:

If citizenship is membership in political community, then in creating overlapping political communities, self-government rights necessarily give rise to a sort of dual citizenship, and to potential conflicts about which political community citizens identify with most deeply. Moreover, there seems to be no natural stopping-point to the demands for increasing self-government. If limited autonomy is granted to a national minority, this may simply fuel the ambitions of nationalist leaders, who may be satisfied with nothing short of their own nation-state. Democratic multination states which recognize self-government rights are, it appears, inherently unstable for this reason (Kymlicka 1996: 122).

That social order emanates from, and is supported by, common values is intuitive. The notion also has a distinguished scholarly pedigree: it pervades much social and political theory. None the less, it is quite mistaken: order can be provided more efficiently in a society made up of different national groups, each having distinct values, than in a culturally homogeneous society (Hechter *et al.* 1992).

However counterintuitive this outcome may be, it occurs because a viable central state can profit from the social control activities of its constituent national groups. The solidarity of national groups can contribute to state-wide social order by regulating the behaviour of their members. The members of highly solidary groups must divert a large proportion of their private resources (especially, but not limited to, their *time*), in order to comply with extensive corporate normative obligations. This leaves them with fewer private resources to be invested at their own discretion. Rational people will not hesitate to use force and fraud if these are the most efficient means of satisfying their desires. Acts of force and fraud decrease social order, however. Absent the state, the only constraint on people's use of force and fraud is the amount of resources available to them. Assume for the moment that people with identical amounts of resources have the same probability of engaging in force and fraud. If so, then the members of highly solidary groups contribute more to social order than other individuals because, all things equal, they are subject to greater social control.[38] To the degree that national solidarity is enhanced by institutional autonomy this sets the stage for a more efficient social order—provided that the central government remains a viable source of relevant collective goods.

This principle has already been encountered in Chapter 3. Central rulers were forced to grant their agents total authority over peripheral localities because the technology on offer did not permit direct rule. Political decentralization invariably led to legal heterogeneity because central rulers had no means of enforcing their dictates throughout their realm. Nowadays this restriction does not hold. Modern transportation and communications technology affords central authorities the unprecedented capacity to enforce the law uniformly throughout state territory. Yet even under modern conditions, there is an incentive to decentralize, for cultural minorities will be given short shrift when central authorities reserve decision-making powers for themselves.

Although federation is an organizational form that has medieval roots, modern technology gives it new life by allowing local decision-making to coexist with legal universalism. This permits individual rights and cultural autonomy to be safeguarded at the same time.

A Final Word

That nationalism is complex and historically particular is a truism. Nationalism diffuses across political boundaries; its successes in one country often embolden its advocates elsewhere. Its dynamics are affected by unpredictable global economic and geopolitical forces. For these reasons, nationalism would appear to be a subject that resists generalization. No wonder that the literature is dominated by detailed and subtle case studies.

This book has taken a different tack. Despite the role played by unpredictable demonstration effects and exogenous shocks, nationalist prospects are affected by a small set of fundamental mechanisms. Processes of group formation and solidarity help account for the birth of nations and national identities. Once nations have come into being, institutions of governance influence the costs of collective action and the benefits of sovereignty, determining much about the form and intensity of nationalist movements.

Although it is unlikely that nationalism will subside in the future, there is no reason to believe that it will be the most salient form of political conflict indefinitely. I began this book with a story about the fall of class politics in recent history. Such a shift would be anticipated if there had been a marked increase in direct rule—that is, in political centralization. The development of the welfare state during the post-war era in Western Europe and Canada undoubtedly strengthened direct rule in these societies (Fox *et al.* 1981). By extending a wide range of entitlements, the welfare state increased citizens' dependence on the central state at the expense of local authorities. At the same time, the intrusiveness of the state into citizens' private lives has never been greater. Nowhere is this intrusiveness clearer than with respect to family matters: the treatment of wives and children within the privacy of the home—once every man's castle—is now a matter of public concern. Established to defuse class conflict, the welfare state succeeded beyond its architects' wildest dreams. It did so primarily by extending direct rule. Although this very extension of direct rule muted class conflict, it had the unanticipated effect of sowing the seeds of nationalism.

By the same token, we ought not be too surprised if class supersedes ethnicity as a basis of collective action sometime in the future. Under what conditions might this reversal come to pass? One possibility leaps to mind. To the degree that alternative sources of welfare dry up, then organizations based on social class may be expected to return to the fore. The gradual demise of the welfare state in the United States may revive class politics in its wake. If so, Lenin's resting place in Fremont may be a good deal more short-lived than anyone now anticipates. For the moment, however, the apparent unwillingness of Western European voters to dismantle their own welfare states presages a future with more intense nationalist conflicts on the Continent.

NOTES

CHAPTER 1

1. This trend was already visible more than twenty years ago (Bendix 1974: 151); for a recent comparative analysis of unionization, see Western (1997). This conclusion about the declining political significance of class, however, implies nothing whatever about shifts in social mobility—the influence of class origins for subsequent individual attainments. That is quite an independent issue. It is entirely possible that the strength of class politics may wane when patterns of mobility remain constant, or even increase. For a contrary view about the political salience of class, drawn from an analysis of British electoral behaviour, see Weakliem and Heath (1994).

2. Online communication reduces the costs of producing a public good to near zero. Likewise, coordination costs can also be reduced, for people can interact online without regard to physical location or time. Since many of the public goods on the Internet consist of digital information, they can be distributed to any number of people at the same cost. Whereas most other public goods can only be provided collectively, single individuals are able to create public goods on the Internet—for everything posted there becomes a public good. This sharply reduces the impact of free riding, often a critical obstacle to the production of public goods (Boncheck 1995; Kollock 1998).

3. As this technology is also available to central authorities, however, it is by no means certain that nationalist challengers are ultimately favoured by it. Assessing the social impact of new technologies is risky. For example, prior to 1940 the telephone, a major new communications technology, was predicted to have manifold social consequences—including the disappearance of regional dialects, strengthening of challengers to central authority by lowering the costs of collective action, and the weakening of local ties at the expense of global ones. There is little, if any, evidence to support any of these claims (Fischer 1992).

4. Even the USA has grappled with nationalism, however, both in the past (the Civil War) and the present (in Puerto Rico).

5. Indeed, there is no conflict between these two kinds of inquiries. The

interaction of specific initial conditions with general causal mechanisms can yield principled explanations of particular events (Popper 1994).

6. This includes the modification, ritualization, and institutionalizing of customary traditions that occurred in many European societies in the 19th century. In Switzerland e.g. 'Traditional folksongs were supplemented by new songs in the same idiom, often composed by schoolmasters, transferred to a choral repertoire whose content was patriotic-progressive, though it also embodied ritually powerful elements from religious hymnology . . . The statutes of the Federal Song Festival . . . declare its object to be the "development and improvement of the people's singing, the awakening of more elevated sentiments for God, Freedom and Country, union and fraternization of the friends of Art and Fatherland"' (Hobsbawm 1983*a*: 6).

7. The Mexican muralists—including Orozco, Rivera, and Siquieros—who flourished during the revolutionary years are a particularly apt example, but Delacroix's paintings exalting the Greek nationalist movement preceded them by nearly a century. Frank Lloyd Wright made a self-conscious attempt to create an American style of architecture to rival those of the various European styles. Even something as taken-for-granted as landscape styles have a subtly national basis (Daniels 1993). Studies of nationalism and art are surprisingly scant, however (but see Smith 1979, Agulhon 1981, and Leoussi 1988).

8. Examples are legion. Burns's poetry assailed the Anglo-Scottish Union of 1707 for its deleterious consequences for his native land. Pushkin used Russian history for the basis of many of his works. The Brothers Grimm collected German folk-tales and played a leading role in German lexicography. Byron famously took up the cause of Greek independence against the Ottomans. Daniel Deronda, the hero of George Eliot's eponymous novel, seeks to establish a Jewish state in Palestine. The ferment surrounding Irish nationalism at the turn of the 20th century captivated writers as different as Yeats and O'Casey. Literary canons ostensibly representing the nation's underlying common values have even emerged in multicultural societies like the United States and Canada (for an analysis of this process, see Corse 1997).

9. Beethoven wrote music for Goethe's *Egmont*, a tale about the Netherlands' attempt to free itself from Spain. National themes loom large in the compositions of Chopin, Wagner, Grieg, Dvořák, Liszt, Tchaikovsky, Mussorgsky, Wagner, Brahms, Ives, Bartók, Kodály, Sibelius, Elgar, Gershwin, Copeland, Shostakovich, Vaughn Williams and Villa-Lobos, among many others.

10. A bizarre sign of the cultural salience of nationalism in the modern world is Cambridge University Press's refusal, in 1996, to publish a highly recommended scholarly study of ethnicity in the Greek province of

Macedonia for fear that the subject was too controversial and could put at risk the Press's employees in Greece (Barbash 1996). This decision led to the resignation of a number of the Press's editorial board and created a furore in the newspapers. Subsequently, the book was published by another university press (Karakasidou 1997).

11. See Diaz-Andreu and Champion (1995); Dietler (1994); Kohl and Fawcett (1995); Kohl (1998); Silberman (1990). 'The primary function of nationalistic archaeology, like nationalistic history of which it is normally regarded as an extension, is to bolster the pride and morale of nations or ethnic groups. It is probably strongest among peoples who feel politically threatened, insecure or deprived of their collective rights by more powerful nations or in countries where appeals for national unity are being made to counteract serious divisions along class lines' (Trigger 1984).

12. Although we now are inured to tales about the depth of the animosity between Tamils and Sinhalese in present-day Sri Lanka, it should be borne in mind that the salience of this linguistic boundary and the intractability of the resulting intergroup conflict there are both of very recent vintage. Prior to 1983, Ceylon was commonly described as the most successful democracy in Asia, and prior to the 1930s geography— not language—was the principal basis of group identity (Daniel 1996: 8–17). That violence of such intensity can suddenly erupt between groups whose relations have been pacific—a lesson that has been underlined by recent events in Bosnia—is one of the most puzzling features of nationalism.

13. It is difficult to quarrel with Hobsbawm's (1992: 6) acidic complaint that the criteria often used to describe nations—'language, ethnicity or whatever—are themselves fuzzy, shifting and ambiguous, and as useless for purposes of the traveller's orientation as cloud shapes are compared to landmarks. This, of course, makes them unusually convenient for propagandist and programmatic, as distinct from descriptive purposes.'

14. Whether these cultural phenomena are the cause of nationalist politics or the consequence of it is a question that has received little explicit analysis.

15. This definition may have originated with Kohn (1944); subsequently, it was adopted by Gellner (1983), among others. The normative principle that 'the boundaries of governments should coincide in the main with those of nationalities' was already expressed in the mid-19th century by John Stuart Mill (1861: 291–2).

16. This is because motives are internal states that are inherently difficult to observe. Whereas survey researchers often claim to be able to accurately gauge individual motives, their ability to predict the subsequent behaviour of their respondents from these measures has not been impressive. For an analysis that reveals the complexities involved in measuring individual motives see Hechter *et al.* (1999).

17. For the moment, I ignore the possibility that the policies adopted by groups may have effects on the attainment of national sovereignty that are unintended. Thus, it has been argued that Soviet federation—erected in order to curtail nationalism in the Republics—had the ironic consequence of strengthening nationalism in these territories. This issue is discussed in greater detail in Ch. 8.

18. Although the German National Socialist party certainly promulgated some policies that qualify as nationalist by this definition, Nazism also put forward a host of non-nationalist policies (Brustein 1996). To regard Nazism as a type of nationalism—as Breuilly (1993: 3) does—is therefore misguided (Motyl 1990: 51).

19. This must come as news to at least one authority on nationalism (Snyder 1983: 253), who offers a definition that occupies no less than 208 pp. of text! Definitions of this sort can have little explanatory value.

20. There is nothing distinctive about the kinds of collective action in which nationalists typically engage (Motyl 1990: ch. 3). Motyl therefore prefers to define nationalism as a belief system, for this is where nationalism's distinctiveness is said to rest. The present definition of nationalism, however, links collective action with nationalist beliefs and goals. Therefore, nationalist beliefs can occur in the absence of national*ism*. At any given moment, a plethora of political beliefs usually abounds, but most of these do not inspire much collective action.

21. In this respect, it is interesting to note that the demand for 'sovereignty association' in the 1995 Quebec referendum is highly ambiguous. Critics see it as a move to have one's cake while eating it—gaining the political benefits of sovereignty while remaining part of the Canadian economy (see Ch. 7). Similar questions arise concerning the status of Puerto Rico in the USA.

22. This does not imply that the local group is autarchic, because its members must seek wives from other groups. This requirement induces some interdependence between local groups, but governance units are seldom, if ever, wholly autarchic.

23. 'There is no way of telling the observer how to distinguish a nation from other entities *a priori*, as we can tell him or her how to recognize a bird or to distinguish a mouse from a lizard. Nation-watching would be simple if it could be like bird-watching' (Hobsbawm 1992: 5). It seems as if there is hardly any limit to the kinds of markers that can serve to differentiate communities. Thus, the ancient Romans distinguished themselves from the barbarians by the weapons and means of fighting characteristic of each group: *arma virumque cano* (I sing of arms and men) is the beginning of Virgil's *Aeneid*. Other common ethnic markers used in ancient times included hair-styles and burial customs. Tacitus remarks that the Suebi 'comb the hair sideward and tie it in a knot: thus the Suebi are distinguished from the other Germans, and the free Suebi from the slaves' (Pohl 1998: 51). By contrast, culinary customs divide the

Tamils in Sri Lanka: 'nonlinguistic and even nonreligious cultural values turn out to be more significant than language and religion . . . In terms of the kinds of foods eaten (e.g., *idlis*, tōsas, and other steamed, baked, and fried eatables served at breakfast and as snacks), Estate Tamils and Indian Tamils have much more in common than either has with any other group. But what is selected out as being important is the "spicing" of foods—the ingredients that go into making the curry powder' (Daniel 1996: 165).

24. Thus Armstrong (1982) argues that the characteristic architecture of the Moorish house—which is built around a central fountain—symbolizes the oasis, an idealized homeland in the Arabian peninsula. See also Smith (1986: 163).

25. The contacts occasioned by modernization lead to greater awareness of what makes groups distinct (Connor 1972: 343–4). 'The issues at hand, and even the parties involved in them, are not defined by some "objective" facts of history or obvious and visible markers of identity; rather they are a product and a reflection of certain historical *relationships*' (Szporluk 1993: 369).

26. Suffice it to say that this discussion is exclusively concerned with permanent residents. I make no attempt to classify, say, French nationals who may be tourists, students, professionals, managers, or diplomats stationed temporarily in a foreign land.

27. Whereas the advent of computer-mediated communication makes it possible for local nationalist movements to attract resources from all corners of the globe, this will not reduce the fundamental territoriality of nationalism. Virtual nationalism is an oxymoron; the political force of nationalism is inextricably linked to territory, for only bounded territories are at risk of attaining sovereignty.

28. Some reasons for variations in the inclusiveness of nationalist movements are sketched in Ch. 5.

CHAPTER 2

1. Since even most nationalist regions are themselves multicultural, the creation of new national states often leads to 'matrioshka nationalisms' on the part of newly created minorities (Hall 1993). This was the root of much of the violence in the former Yugoslavia. Likewise, the Baltic states now face the demands of Russian-speaking minorities. Should Quebec gain independence, indigenous groups, led by the Mohawk, have promised to launch their own secessionist movement.

2. For a sceptical view of human sociality, however, see Maryanski and Turner (1992).

3. Biological reductionism has long been—and largely remains—among the social scientists' greatest sins. Sir Ronald Fisher (1930) cautions against the blanket refusal to consider the biological bases of human behaviour: 'Unfortunately for the general adoption of such an objective view of things human, as is necessary for the scientific understanding of human affairs, it is often felt to be derogatory to human nature, and especially to such attributes as man most highly values—as if I had said that the human brain was not more important than the trunk of an elephant, or as if I had said that it ought not to be more important to us, if only we were as rational as we should be. These statements would be unnecessarily provocative: in addition they are scientifically void. And lest there should be any doubt upon a matter, which does not in the least concern science, I may add that, being a man myself, I have never had the least doubt as to the importance of the human race, of their mental and moral characteristics, and in particular of human intellect, honour, love, generosity and saintliness, wherever these precious qualities may be recognized. The supreme value which, I feel, ought to be attached to these several aspects of human excellence, appears to provide no good reason for asserting, as is sometimes done, with a petulant indignation not unmixed with spiritual arrogance, that such a low matter as natural causation cannot be of importance to these sublime things. On the contrary, it introduces the strongest motive for striving to know, as accurately and distinctly as possible, in what ways natural causes have acted in their evolutionary upbuilding, and I do now act in making them more or less abundant.'

4. Inclusive fitness theory (Hamilton 1964) explains the prevalence of the nuclear family in human and other species. In this way, the explanation of cooperative behaviour among closely related kin has genetic roots. An outstanding example is found in the prevalence of in-group behaviour among ants (Hölldobler and Wilson 1994). More controversially, kin selection has also been invoked to explain ethnocentrism (Dawkins 1989; Reynolds *et al.* 1987; Shaw and Wong 1989; van den Berghe 1981), but generally only in primitive societies. In order to account for more interesting forms of cooperation, evolutionary theorists have been forced to supplement kin selection arguments with those concerning institutional arrangements—such as rules of descent, residence, and marriage. Such explanations perforce must enter the realm of conscious human action (Dennett 1995).

5. A multilevel selection theory based on Darwinian principles may offer greater explanatory leverage, however (Sober and Wilson 1998). The adequacy of this new approach to the evolution of cooperation among nonrelated individuals remains to be determined at this writing.

6. As membership in families clearly also entails costs, the universality of the nuclear family (Campbell 1966: 276–81) itself must be explained. One rationale for the family consists in its role in the production and nurture of children, who constitute a vital economic resource and provide insurance against loneliness and physical incapacity in preindustrial societies (Posner 1980). This explanation, however, is not compelling in industrial societies, where the instrumental benefits of children are often negative (Friedman *et al.* 1994; Keyfitz 1987). Biological explanations for the family usually rest on arguments about kin selection (van den Berghe 1979).

7. The logic of this argument can usefully be compared with research on group formation among animals (Lee 1994). One of the leading hypotheses in this literature suggests that mammalian group formation is correlated with the spatial distribution of food resources (Macdonald 1983). Whereas the similarities between biological and economic explanations of group formation are striking, the differences are also notable. As the case of nationalism so well exemplifies, humans, in contrast to other animals, are wont to form groups on the basis of ideal interests in addition to purely material ones.

8. The size of the kinship group (e.g. for insurance against hunger)—which is an obligatory sharing group—is determined by two countervailing forces (Posner 1980: 156). The larger the group, the smaller will be the correlated risks (say, of food production), and hence the more insurance will be provided. The smaller and more geographically concentrated the group, the greater its control capacity—hence, the less the moral hazard.

9. The case of the medieval Icelandic Free State suggests that the spatial concentration of resources can promote institutional innovations (Byock 1988; Miller 1990). As in the Kalahari example, when resources are spatially concentrated individuals cluster together to be near them. But the *permanent* spatial concentration of resources often leads to conflict which social institutions alone can resolve. In medieval Iceland, this combination of circumstances led to the establishment of the *Althing*, the world's first parliamentary body.

10. This view of the causes of solidarity, which emphasizes the role of private benefits as the principal means of overcoming the free-rider problem, is not the only possible one. Normative political theorists distinguish between two different motives for contributing to collective goods, such as voting for state welfare policies (Barry 1995). The *insurance* motive is based on my perception that your misfortune might also befall me. Thus by supporting the welfare state, in effect I am paying a premium for insurance in the event of a possible future personal loss. To the degree that the group is composed of free riders—putative welfare queens too lazy to work—the value of this insurance policy decreases, thereby reducing my willingness to contribute. If I believe that free riders will

be unable to claim welfare benefits, however, my incentive to contribute can remain high. The *empathic* motive is quite different. It is based on my recognition that your misfortune (perhaps some birth defect) might have happened to me, but that due to the luck of the draw it did not. Therefore I support welfare policies purely out of my empathy for you, rather than out of a desire to mitigate a possible future personal loss. People motivated by the empathic principle should contribute more readily to the production of collective goods than those motivated by the insurance motive because their contribution is expressive rather than instrumental. Since there is little or no systematic evidence about the determinants of empathic motivation, the following discussion is based on the insurance motive alone. For works on nationalism that share this commitment to instrumental motivation, see Hardin (1981), Kuran (1998), Weingast (1998), Fearon (1994) and Laitin (1998), among others.

11. 'It is one of the profoundest facts about humanity . . . that individuals as well as groups have derived considerable powers and advantages from structures which they have themselves endowed with the energies and qualities from which these reinforcements come . . . Think, for instance, of the idea of the gods, whom men first endowed with all sorts of qualities, worthinesses, and excellencies reflected from human souls. Then the same men used these gods as a source of moral laws and of power to enforce them . . . If in all such occurrences a deep self-deception is concealed, it is surely not without profound utility' (Simmel 1898: 685).

12. This is sometimes known as the second-order free-rider problem (Heckathorn 1989; Oliver 1980).

13. The collection and disbursement of killed meat among hunter-gatherers, the collection and disbursement of irrigated water among horticulturalists, the formation of partnerships to engage in long-distance trade, the establishment of caravans on the frontier all allow for high visibility (Hechter 1990*a*; Sack 1986: 55–6). Once initial groups are formed, more complex ones can be built on their foundations (see Ch. 3).

14. Groups with permanent settlements institute collective property rights (Ellickson 1993) to restrict consumption of the joint good to members alone. 'Although humankind have made stone tools for at least 2.5 million years, the archeological record of property rights is more obscure. Although aboriginals everywhere have had sophisticated property rights and trading traditions, there is no direct evidence that prehistoric peoples maintained such traditions. Property rights over private goods such as land, fishing sites, livestock, and cemetery lots, as well as over public goods such as crests, names, dances, rituals and trade routes preceded the state' (Smith 1991).

15. If territoriality is one means of precluding free riding, it does not imply that group boundaries are impermeable. Trade aside, the exchange of

wives provides a continuing source of individual entries and exits in all such groups. This membership dynamic is far from indiscriminate, however; all told, most such groups could easily maintain high levels of dependence in spite of this mobility. Academic departments in American research universities provide an analogy. Like tribal societies, they prohibit inbreeding; thus new members flow in from other PhD-granting institutions, and graduate students flow out. Since the department largely controls the fate of its members, their dependence on it tends to be very high.

16. How large must a pan-local group be to qualify as a nation? Large enough to be recognized by non-members as a distinct social category, and to be politically and economically viable in the international system. Beyond these requirements, however, there is no hard and fast answer.

17. Even so, the ancient empires were small by modern standards (Riker 1964: 3–4). At its height Rome probably ruled less land and fewer people than are now ruled from cities like Washington, Ottawa, Brasilia, Moscow, New Delhi, Peking, and Canberra.

18. For example, the Internet has made it possible for people to become long-distance nationalists (Anderson 1992).

19. My use of the term 'indirect rule' is, by design, expansive. It is not, therefore, to be confused with Lord Lugard's famous description of 19th-century British colonial administration. In this book, indirect rule encompasses all governance structures in which authority is divided, in one fashion or another, between a centre and constitutent lower level units, such as provinces, states, regions, and localities.

20. The American research university offers a striking contemporary example of indirect rule. Whereas the central administration holds final authority on budgetary and personnel matters, the academic departments—each defined by its own distinctive disciplinary culture—are effectively self-governing (Stinchcombe 1990: ch. 9). Their autonomy is so ingrained that the prospect of being relegated to 'receivership' is regarded as if it were an impending foreign occupation. For somewhat analogous reasons, indirect rule is also ubiquitous in capitalist firms (Miller 1991). There it often leads to corporate inefficiencies that can be redressed by greater reliance on market mechanisms. The focus of the economic literature on the theory of the firm is on the profitability of the corporate unit, rather than how indirect rule limits conflict between the subunit and the centre. What is considered efficient from the point of view of profitability may not be so efficient from the standpoint of system integrity, however.

21. As is discussed further in Chapter 4, direct rule arises at different times in different places. Its advent dates from the late 18th century in France

(and, to a lesser extent, England), but it is being instituted today in the remote western regions of China. The rise of direct rule following Napoleonic reforms in Belgium stimulated Flemish nationalism there (Senelle 1989). The extension of direct rule in Franco's Spain (1939–75) stimulated peripheral nationalism in the regions (Brassloff 1989). Likewise, the growth of the British welfare state also contributed to the growth of Welsh nationalism (Davies 1989). Even the most technically advanced modern states, however, retain certain features of indirect rule in governance.

22. Of course, to the degree that these populations are not dependent on local authorities, the latters' control capacity suffers. This weakens the local leaders' ability to mobilize support for any political end, including nationalism.

23. Ideals are less stringent than ideologies. Unlike ideologies, which consist of a broad and reasonably coherent set of ideas or shared mental models that specify both the means and ends of political action (Denzau and North 1994), ideals imply ends alone (Motyl 1990: 52–3). Nationalism cannot be an ideology because it includes social movements at opposing ideological poles (Hobsbawm 1992: 175–6). For example, some types of nationalism are pro-feminist, others anti-feminist (Kaplan 1997). Woodward (1995: 224) captures this quality by depicting nationalism as an empty vessel. Despite their plasticity, however, ideals are frequently invoked to mobilize collective action by affecting perceptions of grievances, costs, and benefits among potential participants (Snow and Oliver 1995: 586–7). For a discussion of the structural conditions promoting nationalist ideals, see Snyder and Ballentine (1996).

24. Location in social networks probably plays an important role in predicting just who will resist centralization (Gould 1996).

25. Especially so in the wake of decreasing support for culturally distinctive education, as occurred to teachers of Slovak in the late 19th century in the Habsburg Empire (Eley and Suny 1996*b*: 15).

26. An implication is that nationalist sentiment of this kind would be stronger in countries that are most vulnerable to competition from foreign cultures and economic activities (such as Canada and, increasingly, France).

27. In one noted formulation (Acton 1948), it is held that alien rule invariably produces misgovernment. Likewise, the complaints against absentee owners are legion.

28. Even regions whose self-understanding rests primarily on distinctive economic interests—such as the Italian North—may become nationalist. This is because economically distinct regions tend to develop cultural distinctions as well. Further, as the legitimacy of demands for self-determination flows from cultural rather than economic distinctions, this

encourages regional leaders to cloak their movements in cultural hues. Since claims to cultural distinctiveness ultimately are social constructions, there is no ready-made means of falsifying them.

29. Similarly, it has been argued that the members of nations are likely to act more altruistically toward one another (Chai 1996).

30. The creation of Singapore from the Malay peninsula is a notable exception.

31. This interest has no necessary precedence over other interests that might militate against self-determination, however.

CHAPTER 3

1. 'The idea that political and ethnographic or linguistic boundaries should coincide is recent. Formerly, political units were held together by dynastic ties and multiculturalism was the norm' (Kohn 1944: 17).

2. In a provocative paper on the origin of the state, Crone (1986) suggests that primary state formation only occurred twice in world history— once in Mesopotamia, and once in Meso-America. Moreover, she suggests that religion played a more important role than insurance considerations in the development of primary states. Since she offers no mechanism for the diffusion of a common religion among different tribal groups, however, her explanation of the rise of the primary state is implausible.

3. Much of this section is borrowed from Chai and Hechter (1998).

4. 'Few authorities exist who can coordinate the behavior of many families at once. Common understandings may arise giving individual families priority of access to resources within a home range, but it is courtesy and perhaps some anticipation of aggressive defense of a home range, not political control by suprafamilial leaders, that prevents intrusion by an outgroup . . . When a leader is given temporary control of food production, as in the Shoshone rabbit drive, it is always by mutual agreement of participants who recognize the immediate benefits of cooperation. The family group's control of food processing, consumption, and exchange is not affected, and the arrangement ends when the food supply has been harvested or has moved on' (Johnson and Earle 1987: 316).

5. Likewise, the 'surnames'—large clans of predatory bandits—roamed free on the Anglo-Scottish border four centuries later, in the Tudor period (Ellis 1995: 63–77). The far northern English counties of Northumber-

land, Cumberland, and Westmorland retained a distinctive regional sol-idarity longer than any other territories in the realm (Holt 1992; Stringer 1994).

6. For example, from the 11th cent. on the Chinese rural landscape was per-vaded with multivillage leagues to protect against banditry (Kuhn 1980).

7. No doubt many early states were imposed on vulnerable populations by rulers of already-extant states. This is an example of secondary state formation. But how can the existence of the most powerful state be accounted for? There are two choices: either by imposition (in which case, there is an infinite regress of coercive state formation), or volun-tarily, as a product of primary state formation.

8. 'The oldest political system of the Germans had an associative-federative quality; and if the somewhat bold assumption is correct that we can regard century (*Hundertschaft*), clan (*Geschlecht*), and tribal set-tlement (*Gauansiedlung*) as identical, then we have before our eyes in concrete form an association of clans (*Sippenverband*) that is both a political community and a military body. In any event, there is no doubt that in some form or other the organization of the state as well as the military organization of the time depended on the cohesion of clans, and corresponds to what we otherwise, from historical and ethnographic evidence, know about the organization of primitive life. The Germans went into battle as a clan, and the close solidarity produced by blood-relationship, neighborliness, and a complete community of interest may well have provided their tactical formation, the *cuneus* or boar's head (*Eberkopf*), with a substitute for their lack of true military discipline as the Romans knew it' (Hintze 1975: 188). This same point has been made concerning the emergence of relatively centralized authority in African kingdoms (Mair 1977: 141–65).

9. The nomads of the Eurasian steppe offer a paradigmatic example of coer-cive state formation (McNeill 1964).

10. These states were not all cut from the same cloth; the internal organiza-tion of these groups tended to affect the nature of the resulting state. Where the local groups were organized in a participatory manner—as in England, Scotland, Hungary, Poland, and Scandinavia—the resulting regimes were constitutional. Where the local groups were organized in a top-down, non-participatory manner—as in Latin Europe and Germany—the resulting regimes were absolutist (Ertman 1997: 317–18).

11. All primary states arose in river valleys, practising alluvial agriculture. Most, indeed, irrigated their valley land with flood water. The local inhabitants of such societies were uniquely interdependent. 'A number of such groups were expanding across the flood plain. As trade increased, so did their common dependence on the rivers as a communication system. All had an interest in freedom of trade, in keeping the river channel free of piracy and silt, and therefore in diplomatic regulation. At

the same time conflicts arose over water rights and boundaries . . .'
(Mann 1986: 74–6). This hydraulic agriculture led to small protostates
that controlled a limited length and breadth of a floodplain or river
valley—'city states as in Sumer, or the domains of local lords or *nomarchs*
as in China and Egypt, or self-governing village communities as elsewhere in China, or, indeed, virtually *any* form of local government. In
numbers the Sumerian towns may have been typical of capacities generated by irrigation. They usually varied from about 1,000–20,000 in population, with an unknown number of clients in their hinterlands. At most
in the Early Dynastic I period a town would exercise loose hegemony
over its neighbors, a political control over perhaps 20,000 persons. The
radius of such a zone would vary from about five to fifteen kilometers.
These were tiny societies. In Mesopotamia it is especially striking that
the most important cities, Eridu and Ur, and Uruk and Larsa, were
within sight of one another' (Mann 1986: 97).

12. The geographical distribution of core Western European states provides
some supportive evidence. The cores of Western European states formed
in those regions where the threat of subjugation was greatest. Late
medieval Western Europe may be divided into three geographical zones
(Hechter and Brustein 1980), each having a characteristic mode of
production. The first zone was a predominantly rural area dominated by
relatively autonomous landholders. The second was dominated by urban
burghers, who, like the landholders in the first zone, enjoyed a relatively
secure political monopoly. In neither zone was there much threat of
subjugation—hence little incentive to state formation. The third, feudal,
zone was quite different. Although dominated by aristocratic landholders, it was also home to a growing number of urban burghers. In
this area alone dominant groups had reason to fear subjugation by
rising groups of urban burghers whose interests were often antagonistic
to those of the rural landholders. This gave landholders in this zone
an incentive to form states. This may be why the first states tended to
form in the feudal zone of Western Europe. In contrast, the contemporary attempt to build a European Union exemplifies typical obstacles to
the project of state formation. The German and French core has spear-
headed political and economic reforms designed to bring about a continental superstate. The fitful nature of the development of the European
Union has illustrated the tenacity with which member states have
guarded their cultural and economic sovereignty. The preceding analysis suggests that the rise of the European Union will dither until a rival
alliance (such as one linking the USA with countries in the Pacific Rim
and Latin America) poses a threat to the vital interests of the constituent
states.

13. The two processes are not identical, however, because groups can attain
solidarity without a specialized agent of control, whereas societies

cannot attain social order without such an agent—i.e. a state. What accounts for this difference? Societies and groups are different in two crucial respects. Societies are much more geographically extensive, and contain more actors, than groups do; this means they have much higher monitoring costs. Second, due to assortative association, groups in a society are likely to be more heterogeneous than individuals in a group. This reduces the effect of dependence on the attainment of social order, because the same sanctions may not have the same meaning to all groups in society. For these reasons, a state is necessary to attain order in society even though no specialized agent is required to produce group solidarity (Kanazawa 1997: 109 n. 9).

14. This principle also seems to account for the cell structures of smaller groups in which monitoring is particularly difficult, such as underground political and military organizations (Chai 1993).

15. There is a large literature attempting to explain variations in governance among premodern states and empires (D'Altroy 1992; Hassig 1985, 1988; Luttwak 1976; Skinner 1977). These authors all recognize that empires employed a mix of governance strategies, from indirect to direct rule. Most argue that control in these polities varies as a function of the distance from the imperial core, which is best conceived in terms of transport costs and communications capabilities because these have direct implications for military logistics and the ease of economic and political integration. Direct rule is only likely to occur in territories immediately adjacent to the core or in key productive or security areas; elsewhere indirect rule prevails (D'Altroy 1992: 23).

16. Book v of Machiavelli's *The Prince* advises the rulers of newly acquired territories accustomed to living under their own laws to govern indirectly. Hume also proposed a theory of the state based on federal principles that in many respects is reminiscent of Althusius's (Livingston 1998: ch. 13). Much more recently, Simmel (Wolff 1950: 170–7) also regarded a federation of small groups—and the consequent greater ease of surveillance—as a means of securing large-scale order (see also Homans 1950: ch. 18; MacIver 1937: 247–53). This contention is quite at odds with that of the 17th-cent. theorists of sovereignty Bodin, Hobbes, and Bossuet, who championed direct rule as a superior mode of governance.

17. This view bears a striking resemblance to a conclusion based on comparative ethnographic data written nearly four centuries later: 'At each evolutionary stage existing organizational units are embedded within new, higher-order unifying structures. Hamlets are made up of families, local groups of hamlets, regional chiefdoms of local groups, and states of regional chiefdoms. The earlier levels continue to operate but with modified functions' (Johnson and Earle 1987: 322).

18. This implication is consistent with Weber's ([1922] 1978) noted analysis

of the logic of patrimonial domination. Although this Weberian analysis is widely accepted, the high degree of political centralization attained by the Inca Empire has often been considered to be anomalous. The Incas seem to have instituted direct rule in the absence of modern communications technology (Mann 1986: 122–3). At its apex from 1400 to 1430, their rule extended over a physically vast territory comprising nearly one million square kilometres and a population greater than three million. They employed corvée labour to build cities, more than 15,000 kilometres of roads, and large-scale irrigation projects. Recent research, however, suggests that, like all other early empires, they relied increasingly on indirect rule as territorial distance from Cuzco increased (D'Altroy 1992). Further, the robustness of the Inca Empire must have been highly questionable, for it collapsed in the face of Pizarro's meagre force of 106 foot-soldiers and 62 horsemen.

19. Admittedly, the concept of cultural homogeneity is vague. By it is generally meant homogeneity of language, religion, and other cultural markers. Yet how similar must cultural differences be to be considered homogeneous? Is Tuscan Italian the same as Genoese for this purpose? Further, who determines whether cultural homogeneity obtains, insiders or outsiders? A situation that from an external point of view may appear culturally homogeneous—such as the view that all native speakers in Italy speak Italian—is likely to be perceived by members as culturally heterogeneous. Yet those same Italians might regard themselves as homogeneous when they interact with Austrians, for example. From these considerations, it is evident that cultural homogeneity is a social construction which is highly sensitive to interactional contexts (Ch. 6).

20. Traditional rule is based on personal loyalty 'which results from common upbringing' (Weber [1922] 1978: 227).

21. Extensive preindustrial polities were exclusively *federal* in nature (Mann 1986). For example, the relatively extensive control exerted by Imperial Rome rested on the *civitas*. This was made up of a city and its often large rural hinterland, and was a political, social, and economic community (Ertman 1997: 37).

22. But not in China. There, a unitary central officialdom faced little challenge from autonomous regional aristocracies, clerics, or urban élites. As a result, the centre intervened to a much greater degree in economic and cultural realms than elsewhere. In the economy, the centre attempted to stabilize production and distribution, so as to smooth out revenues. In the cultural realm, it promoted moral instruction as a basic aspect of its rule. 'Though Chinese efforts at education and moral training between the twelfth and nineteenth centuries did not lead to a nineteenth-century European-style "nationalism," they do represent efforts by a state to influence belief and behavior patterns of the general population well before such activities were imagined, let alone pursued, in Europe . . .

There is no early modern European government equivalent to the later imperial Chinese state's efforts at dictating moral and intellectual orthodoxy, nor were such efforts particularly important to Europe's state-making agenda, as they were in China' (Wong 1997: 97). Even so, the situation in China remained a far cry from direct rule (Weber [1922] 1978: 1047–51).

23. The role of the *millets* in the governance of the Ottoman state is discussed at greater length in Ch. 5.

24. Even though it was relatively centralized, the English crown could rule its lowland areas more directly than its northern borderlands (Ellis 1995: 40, 46–7, 257–72).

25. 'Faced with peasant resistance to colonial occupation, a resistance often led by clan leaders or chiefs, indirect rule was meant to hitch compliant sections from the traditional leadership of Africa to the colonial wagon and thereby broaden its social base' (Mamdani 1996: 102).

26. Adam Smith ([1789] 1961) claimed that the interests of joint-stock companies and colonial authorities were quite opposed. Joint-stock companies, in his view, were motivated solely by the drive to obtain the largest and quickest profits, whereas the state was interested in promoting colonial economic development to maximize its tax revenues. For a sceptical view of this antimony, see Emerson (1937).

27. Thus, in areas where European peasant communes enjoyed extensive political rights, as in Scandinavia, violent revolts against central authorities were infrequent in the 16th and early 17th cents. By contrast, violent rebellion was much more frequent in the territories of the Holy Roman Empire that were increasingly subject to central rule and confessional uniformity (Imsen and Vogler 1997).

28. The effects of indirect rule in the colonies were rather different. There, strong central authorities having great technological superiority often attempted purposely to strengthen or prop up local elites, encouraging them to develop tribal identities among their subjects, so as to divide and conquer (Vail 1989). 'While the old foundations of social control withered and old strategies of survival crumbled, colonialism provided the basis for new bonds of dependency. Often, the new social control of a chief far outstripped what he had maintained before. British rulers further strengthened new bonds by regarding the population as members of social organizations led by chiefs rather than as people with individual rights and needs. Any concern with economic development in such a context demanded using chiefs, inefficient as they were, as conduits to the population. In these circumstances, the strategies of survival adopted by most of the population necessarily started with the chief's organizational base, the tribe. The tribe was a key organizational ally of the colonial state, and it is impossible to understand the changing nature of the tribe in the twentieth century without noting its relation to the

state. Using the tribal organization, the chief controlled key resources, including material goods, jobs, violence, and defense; some of those resources, chiefs received from the state. In addition, the symbolic importance of tribe was stressed by chiefs as they sought to build the basis of enduring social control. The tribe catapulted forward as a key structure in the modern world' (Migdal 1988: 115–16).
29. See Ch. 8 pp. 149–52.

CHAPTER 4

1. This development was famously described by Max Weber ([1922] 1978) as the victory of monocratic bureaucracy over patrimonialism.
2. Both Denmark and Sweden instituted direct rule a century before France (Ertman 1997: ch. 6), but due to their relative isolation this had few geopolitical ramifications.
3. None the less, Tocqueville's ([1858] 1955) insistence that many of the characteristic trappings of direct rule antedated the French Revolution (save in the *pays d'état* of Languedoc and Brittany) is a reminder that the measurement of direct rule is never unambiguous (see Beik 1985 for a view of the complexity of the relations between royal and local authorities in 17th-cent. France). In brief, the directness of rule varies positively with the ratio of decision-making power held by central authorities to that held by the authorities in governmental subunits.
4. For one reading of the contrasting views, see Silberman (1993). Spruyt (1994) offers a historically informed argument about the rise of the state as against alternative political forms. Axtmann (1993) and Ertman (1997: ch. 1) provide recent reviews of the historical explanations of state-building. For economists' views of state formation see Friedman (1977), Greif *et al.* (1994), Olson (1993), and Wittman (1991).
5. 'The drive towards predominance in their own societies among the earliest states grew out of their interaction with one another in a new state system. Getting the population to obey the rules of the state rather than the rules of the local manor, clan, or any other organizations arose much less from lofty visions of universal justice and what society should be than from the need for political leaders to ensure their own survival. There was a driving compulsion to establish state social control within society, for that was the key that could unlock the doors to increased capabilities in the international arena' (Migdal 1988: 23). Charles Tilly is a leading proponent of the view that war makes the state (see also Porter 1994; Posen 1993*a*).

6. 'The formation of leagues or confederations in defense of common political interests vis-à-vis aggressive princes was characteristic of large-scale
conflicts in very diverse settings, from the urban Comuneros of Castile
to the peasant leagues of rural Germany and France, from the League of
Schmalkalden in Germany and the Huguenot and Catholic leagues in
France to the Covenanters of Scotland and the Confederates of Ireland.
Such leagues or alliances were typically brokered by the local leaders of
insurrectionary movements within previously constituted political units
with long histories of self-regulation—units that were capable not only
of local self-government but also of mobilizing at the local level the
wherewithal of collective defense. Of course, most these largely defensive unions did not survive in the long run, but when they did, the Dutch
and Swiss cases suggest, the historical experience of often 'heroic' collective efforts became deeply embedded in the political culture of the
resulting confederations' (te Brake 1998: 173–4).
7. Thus Weber emphasized both demand and supply factors in his own
account of the rise of direct rule.
8. This is especially so in island territories, like Britain. The state's costs of
revenue extraction are minimized when only a few ports are permitted
to engage in overseas trade (North 1981).
9. De Swaan (1988) offers a comparative survey of the various menus of
collective goods provided by 19th-cent. Western European states.
10. The battle over the Speenhamland Laws in England provides a graphic
illustration of the conflict over the source of welfare for the poor in 18th-
cent. England (Polanyi 1943).
11. In the literature on Western European history, early attempts to increase
the prerogatives of central authorities are often referred to as the struggle between the court and the country. There is consensus that local resistance to direct rule often took the form of anti-state rebellions (Bercé
1987; Brustein 1985; Brustein and Levi 1987; Mousnier 1958, 1970*a*,
1970*b*; Zagorin 1982). These rebellions did not assume a nationalist
guise, however. Instead, appeals to maintain local autonomy were often
couched in terms of loyalty to some pretender to the throne (see e.g.
Worcester's account of the reasons for his participation in the regional
rebellion against King Henry in Shakespeare's *Henry IV, Part I*, Act V,
scene 1). Why did these early efforts at centralization not produce
nationalism? Largely because the available communications technology
did not permit extensive direct rule. In part, the rise of a nationalist
discourse awaited the development of printed media (Anderson 1982;
Calhoun 1997). More fundamentally, however, these limits on technology often kept the centre from assuming enough power to make the
struggle for secession worth the candle (Ch. 5).
12. Since direct rule increased both administrative and economic efficiency,
the resulting gains also enabled the centre to purchase some political

support from citizens by providing them with a greater bundle of collective goods.

13. Linguistic uniformity facilitates direct rule in part by increasing administrative efficiency (Laitin 1992: 8–17). Moreover, cultural identification with the state was a means of increasing the legitimacy of transformed regimes, as well as entirely new ones. 'What else could legitimize the monarchies of states which had never previously existed as such, like Greece, Italy, or Belgium, or whose existence broke with all historical precedents, like the German empire of 1871? The need to adapt arose in even long-established regimes, for three reasons. Between 1789 and 1815 few of them had not been transformed—even post-Napoleonic Switzerland was in important respects a new political entity. Such traditional guarantors of loyalty as dynastic legitimacy, divine ordination, historic right and continuity of rule, or religious cohesion, were severely weakened. Last, but not least, these traditional legitimations of state authority were, since 1789, under permanent challenge' (Hobsbawm 1992: 84). The model of the culturally unified nation state may have been inspired by the democratic *polis*, which was largely ethnically homogeneous (McNeill 1986).

14. For example, when it embarked upon state-building nationalism, interwar Poland used both strategies simultaneously in its dealings with different national minorities. The new state tended to employ exclusive strategies with respect to the ethnic Germans in its western borderlands and to its geographically dispersed Jewish populations. At the very same time it pursued inclusive strategies with respect to the Belorussians and Ukrainians residing in its eastern borderlands (Brubaker 1996: ch. 4).

15. The nature of these inclusive policies has changed substantially in the last two centuries, however. 'It is said that in Spain, during the Inquisition, gypsies who were found guilty of speaking their own language had their tongues cut out. With policies of this sort, it is not difficult to understand why it was possible, a few centuries later, to legislate Castilian as the sole official language of the monarchy. But when Emperor Haile Selassie of Ethiopia pressed for policies promoting Amharic, infinitely more benign than those of the Inquisition, speakers of Tigrey, Oromo, and Somali claimed that their groups were being oppressed, and the international community was outraged' (Laitin 1992: p. xi).

16. Distinctive sports—American baseball, Gaelic and Australian Rules football—also came to embody national symbols but these were popular activities that tended to arise spontaneously, in the absence of state sponsorship.

17. In East Central Europe and the Balkans, the impetus behind direct rule often was exogenous—a result of the new state boundaries mandated by the treaties of Bucharest, Neuilly, and Versailles. Romania, for example, found its territory nearly doubled after 1918. As was common in this

part of Europe, the new Romanian territories were ethnically heterogeneous. In these new territories, ethnic Romanians tended to be of the lowest social status. Not surprisingly, they eagerly supported attempts by the central government to promote Romanian culture in schools and other institutions at the expense of Russian, Hungarian, German, and Jewish subjects of the new state (Livezeanu 1995). These policies did not succeed in muting national diversity in the new state, however. Similarly, attempts by the Greek state to Hellenize the culturally diverse population of Greek Macedonia met with imperfect success (Karakasidou 1997).

18. 'Whereas virtually the entire population supported the Danish armies during the first of the Swedish–Danish wars in 1685 to 1689, they demonstrated a completely different attitude in the Great Nordic War of 1700–21' (Østergård 1992: 4).

19. See e.g. Hobsbawm and Ranger (1983); Hobsbawm (1992); Kennedy (1973); Snyder and Ballentine (1996).

20. Eric Hobsbawm (1993: 92) scathingly recalls 'being submitted to . . . a piece of (unsuccessful) political invention in an Austrian primary school of the middle 1920s, in the form of a new national anthem desperately attempting to convince children that a few provinces left over when the rest of a large Habsburg empire seceded or was torn from them, formed a coherent whole, deserving love and patriotic devotion; a task not made any easier by the fact that the only thing they had in common was what made the overwhelming majority of their inhabitants want to join Germany. "German Austria", this curious and short-lived anthem began, "thou magnificent (*herrliches*) land, we love thee", continuing, as one might expect, with a travelogue or geography lesson following the alpine streams down from glaciers to the Danube valley and Vienna, and concluding with the assertion that this new rump-Austria was "my homeland" (*mein Heimatland*).'

21. The creation of state-wide military forces brought with it a concern for political loyalty. The Prussian commitment to the development of a professionally trained mass army depended on widespread literacy among the recruits. This favoured educational investment. Following the Franco-Prussian War, Prussian educators increasingly saw state-building nationalist ideology as a firmer foundation of social cohesion than religion (Posen 1993*a*: 104–15).

22. Japanese firms in the era of permanent employment are an exception to this rule. Employees faced extremely high exit costs; as a result, they exhibited high of levels of loyalty to their firm and to its symbols (Hechter and Kanazawa 1993).

23. Whereas France was exceptional in its capacity to legislate universal military conscription, a strong indicator of state-building (Levi 1997), even at the end of the 19th century some French people did not know

who Napoleon was. 'J. E. M. Bodley, putting up at an inn by the Durance, close to the spot where Napoleon crossed the river on his way from Elba, asked an old woman if she had known elders who might have seen him there. "*Napoléon*," she replied in her broad Provençal accent, "*connais pas ce nom-là. Peut-être bien c'est un voyageur de commerce.*" ... In 1864, a school inspector in Lozère was incensed to find that at one school he visited not a single child could answer questions like "Are you English or Russian?" or "What country is the department of Lozère in?" Among most of these children, the inspector added bitterly, "thought doesn't go beyond the radius of the poor parish in which they live"' (Weber 1976: 109–10).

24. Thus central rulers in the Prussian royal court and the revolutionary French *parlements* were largely unable to institute national educational systems. Although both regimes were capable of a centralized military administration by 1800, 'universal elementary education would have posed new problems of governance: it required the development of techniques for raising and allotting funds, building schools throughout the realm according to population densities, developing and imposing a standard curriculum, overhauling entrenched local and religious opposition, training and examining teachers for certification, inspecting the condition and performance of each school, disciplining the new and expansive teaching body (which might pose for a government many of the problems that armies are prone to create, including intellectual armies), prodding the local school authorities and getting the children to attend the school, not just on paper, but in person. As a matter of fact, military mobilization might have been a good training ground for an educational *levée en masse*, which was more or less how the Convention went about it, sending its *instituteurs* into the villages in the same way as its recruiters and quartermasters. But it was only a half-hearted attempt: the Convention had other, more pressing business to attend to, and although it passed a series of decrees, they were drafted carelessly and debated only perfunctorily. And the *instituteurs* met staunch opposition in the villages where they had to face the priest on his own ground' (de Swaan 1988: 94). See Posen (1993*a*: 102) for another view of Prussian education.

25. One suspects that similar conclusions might be drawn about contemporary resistance to assimilation on the part of recent immigrants to Western Europe from less developed countries.

26. 'Traditionally, in one small Bourbonnais village near Lavoine, in Allier, "almost all boys at birth were declared as girls," and this subtle avoidance of conscription was still practiced in the 1870's' (Weber: 1976: 296).

27. To appreciate the sweep of the Empire at its apex, consider the official title of its master: Emperor of Austria; King of Hungary, of Bohemia, of

Dalmatia, Croatia, Slavonia, Galicia, Lodomeria, and Illyria; King of Jerusalem, etc.; Archduke of Austria; Grand Duke of Tuscany and Cracow; Duke of Lothringia, of Salzburg, Styria, Carinthia, Carniola, and Bukovina; Grand Duke of Transylvania, Margrave of Moravia; Duke of Upper and Lower Silesia, of Modena, Parma, Piacenza, and Guastella, of Ausschwitz and Sator, of Teschen, Friaul, Ragusa, and Zara; Princely Count of Habsburg and Tyrol, of Kyburg, Görz and Gradiska; Duke of Trient and Brizen; Margrave of Upper and Lower Lausitz and in Istria; Count of Hohenembs, Feldkirch, Bregenz, Sonnenberg, etc.; Lord of Trieste, of Cattaro and above the Windisch Mark; Great Voyvod of the Voyvodina, Serbia, etc. (Jászi 1929: 34).

28. Thus multiple languages persist in these societies despite decolonization and the subsequent attempts of central rulers to impose linguistic uniformity on their populations (Laitin 1992).

CHAPTER 5

1. It has long been customary to refer to 'tribalism' in Africa, and to talk of linguistic and religious conflict in the Middle East and the Indian subcontinent, but the outbreak of peripheral nationalism in western China came as a surprise to many commentators on contemporary politics. Terrorist bombs set in Urumuqi, the capital of Xinjiang, and rioting in the frontier city of Yining in early 1997 signalled the rise of peripheral nationalism among the Muslim Uighurs. Uighur nationalism was stimulated by the immigration of Han Chinese and the subsequent establishment of a hierarchical cultural division of labour there (Tyler 1997).

2. The precise nature of the *millets*, their age, and degree of institutionalization are all highly contested subjects (Grillo 1998: 86–96). For a discussion of analogous institutions designed to provide autonomy to non-territorial cultural minorities, see Coakley (1994).

3. Actually, Crimea was the first province of the Empire to develop nationalism, successfully acquiring its independence in 1774. It was a very special case: Crimea had traditionally been an autonomous vassal state of the Empire and was valued for its strategic geographic position near Russia. Of all the Ottoman provinces, the Khanate (Crimea) maintained more of its independence and sovereignty than any other. 'It was in fact the first self-contained province to break away from the Empire at a time when "nationalism" and "national consciousness" had scarcely emerged

anywhere else' (Fisher 1977: 59). In the century leading up to Crimea's separation from the Empire, the Ottomans increasingly interfered directly in Crimean politics, particularly influencing the deposition and installation of Khans. In their secessionist struggle, Crimean local authorities stressed their glorious past and their link to the Golden Horde.

4. The centre's interference in Serbia's cultural life began in 1766, when the Sultan abolished the Pec patriarchate and subordinated the Serbian church to the Greek patriarch of Constantinople. This intensified the Serbs' sense of national identity. 'The Serbian church became even more of a people's church, spreading the national mythology that idealized memories of medieval Serbia through art, literature, and numerous saints' (MacKenzie 1996: 207). The subjection of the Serbian church ensured that the local clergy would support an eventual Serbian nationalist movement (Ramet 1984).

5. Likewise, Armenian nationalism began during the latter decades of the *Tanzimat* era (Suny 1993). It was fuelled from 1894 to 1915 by a series of brutal campaigns that the Turkish government carried out against Armenians. Following Armenian support of Russia during the war, the Turkish authorities ordered a mass deportation of Armenians to Syria and Mesopotamia which led to more than a half-million deaths. Turkish policies towards Armenians can only be understood if it is appreciated that Ottoman Muslims had themselves been subject to the same kind of brutal ethnic cleansing by Christians in the Balkans, Anatolia, and the Caucausus. For a reading of Armenian–Turkish conflict from the Muslim point of view, see McCarthy (1995).

6. One exception was the province of Iraq. In 1830 Sultan Mahmud II sent an envoy to Baghdad with the aim of replacing the local Mamluk notables with a Turkish governor responsible directly to the central government. The city of Karbala, in particular, attracted the attention of Mahmud, as its commercial development permitted it to become a virtually autonomous city-state in the 1820s and 1830s. In reaction to Mahmud's incursions in Iraq, local notables rallied the population in revolt against the centre (Cole and Momen 1986).

7. It is instructive to compare the fate of Kosovo to that of the separatist province of Aceh in Indonesia (Robinson 1998). Like Kosovo, Aceh had attained a special, relatively autonomous, status from the central authorities in Jakarta. The discovery of substantial reserves of liquid natural gas focused Jakarta's attention on Aceh, however. Moves toward direct rule occurred in order to protect what had become one of Indonesia's greatest sources of foreign exchange. A small separatist movement (Aceh Merdaka) was founded to protest increasing direct rule, but until Jakarta launched a massive military effort to repress it the movement fared badly. At the time of writing, Aceh is the site of some of the greatest national-

ist violence in Indonesia. Christie (1996) provides an analysis of peripheral nationalism in a number of South-East Asian states.

8. For example, the Tamil Tigers of Sri Lanka have obtained surface-to-air missiles from Cambodia, assault rifles from Afghanistan, mortar shells from the former Yugoslavia, and explosives from the Ukraine (Bonner 1998).

9. Like the previous definitions in this book, this one is analytical rather than normative. To some writers, however, the term secession has definite normative connotations. It is used to describe the severance of a presumptively permanent link between a peripheral territory and a central state, whereas 'decolonization' is often used if the link was presumed to have been temporary (Lustick 1993: 22–4). My use of secession conveys nothing whatever about the alleged permanence of the relationship between the territories in question.

10. That the sources of fragmentation are often exogenous to a given polity deserves to be emphasized. For a discussion of the fragmentation that beset Yugoslavia after the end of the cold war, see Ch. 8. Laitin (1998: 327–31) describes the fragmentation of the Soviet Union in light of current theories of international relations, and Bunce (1999) contends that institutional differences among fragmenting states help determine how violent the outcome will be. Finally, the government of Indonesia only began to countenance independence for East Timor (January 1999) after an economic crisis that previously caused the fall of the Suharto regime.

11. Thus the proliferation of secessionist movements in the Soviet Union followed *glasnost'* in time and clearly was precipitated by it throughout Soviet territory (Beissinger 1996).

12. Not all peaceful secessions qualify as pure, however (Young 1995: chs. 10, 11). A handful of other 20th-century political divorces fail to meet this standard. Iceland terminated its union from Denmark in 1944 when the metropole was under German occupation. Likewise, Bangladesh's separation from Pakistan in 1971 does not qualify, because the Pakistani state cannot be considered to have been highly effective at that time. Namibia's independence from South Africa in 1990 was won due to external pressure exerted by the United Nations and by Cuban military forces on the Angolan border. Shortly thereafter the South African regime collapsed. Slovakia's separation from the Czech Republic in 1993 is in key respects different from these other contemporary examples of secession. After the fall of the Soviet Union, the economies of the Czech and Slovak republics were largely incompatible: the latter's economy was highly dependent on non-competitive heavy industrial production. Here too fragmentation was at work, for Slovakia's independence would have been inconceivable at the height of Soviet power. At the end of the day, the new Czech government willingly

accuded to Slovak independence rather than compromising its turn toward a market economy.

13. For more formal analyses of the bargaining situation between centre and periphery see Putnam (1988) and Tsebelis (1990).

14. As the Ottoman case reveals, these third-party reactions can affect the prospective benefits for secessionists, as well. Thus when the USA made it known that an independent Quebec would neither receive special trade benefits nor be welcomed into North American Free Trade Agreement, this weakened popular support for secession.

15. This is one sense in which the analogy between secession and divorce holds (Buchanan 1991). When a third person unilaterally supports one of the parties to a divorce, this is tantamount to rejecting the other party.

16. Of course, the leaders of X are likely to support a secessionist movement in Y when they are at war with Y or otherwise committed to Y's destabilization. Thus, Iraq's invasion of Kuwait in 1991 probably increased the likelihood of American support for Iraq's Kurdish insurgents.

17. In June 1921, the British chief of the Imperial General Staff wrote, 'Unless England was on our side we would fail, and if we failed we would break the army . . . Unless England was on our side . . . it would be madness to try and flatten out the rebels' (Curtis 1936: 451).

18. Thus the variable institutional completeness of Soviet-era nations helps explain variations in their responses to the fragmentation of the USSR (Treisman 1997).

19. Ossie/Wessie conflict in Germany is a poignant example of the problem. At the very time that western Germany is making highly visible moves to come to terms with its Nazi past, eastern Germany—facing high unemployment and poor economic prospects in the wake of unification—has become the breeding-ground for violent neo-Nazi youth groups. The targets of the neo-Nazis are 'leftists, foreigners and others who view themselves as apart from German norms' (Cowell 1998).

20. I borrow the term 'unification nationalism' from Breuilly (1993: ch. 4). As discussed previously, the concept of cultural homogeneity is itself vague. It is clear, however, that the adjective 'cultural' entails more than language.

21. See Ch. 3 n. 12 below.

22. The emergence of the central state in a culturally homogeneous Japan may also constitute an instance of unification nationalism.

23. Neither had become fully national states, however. Britain contained not only England but an Ireland that would secede in 1921, as well as Scotland and Wales, both of which developed significant peripheral nationalist movements in the 20th century. In addition to its struggles with Germany over Alsace-Lorraine, France encompassed Brittany, Occitania, and Corsica, all of which later developed peripheral nationalism.

24. 'Napoleon considered Germany chiefly as a base for Imperial recruitment to his *Grand Armée* and as the object of financial and economic exploitation. The burdensome billetings and devastating marches through the country by foreign armies, the financial burdens, which Prussia in particular had to bear after the Peace of Tilsit, and which [caused] the impoverishment of various sections of the population, were followed by a tariff system which protected the French economy at the expense of the remaining European states, entailing price rises and economic collapse. Thus, the population's original indifference was transformed within a few years into hatred of the occupying power' (Schulze 1991: 50–1). Conspiratorial anti-French associations arose around the so-called Club movement and among student fraternal groups. Beethoven originally named his Third ('Eroica') Symphony *Sinfonia grande Napoleon Bonaparte*. On learning that Napoleon had proclaimed himself emperor of Germany, Beethoven tore up its title-page in wrath and changed the name of the symphony to *Sinfonia eroica composta per festeggiare il souvenire d'un gran uomo* (Heroic symphony, composed to celebrate the memory of a great man) (Taylor and Kerr 1954: 52).

25. The effects of Napoleon's continental blockade against Britain fostered economic prosperity in some German territories (protection against British imports stimulated textile production in Saxony), whereas it led to economic collapse in regions depending on exports to British markets (Kiesewetter 1987). That East Prussia, a monocultural grain export economy, suffered particularly badly as a result of the blockade no doubt contributed to its resistance to Napoleon.

26. Despite the patent insubstantiality of some of the claims in these nationalist treatises, their popular appeal cannot be denied. Thus in his 'Speeches to the German Nation' delivered in 1807–8 to large audiences in French-occupied Berlin, Fichte argued that the German language was superior to its French counterpart. German was a natural language (*Ursprache*) which had grown from living roots, while French was a neo-Latinate language that was superficially living but dead at its roots (Düding 1987: 23). Since language was the only possible basis of nationality in the German territories, Fichte's argument about the natural superiority of German legitimated the pursuit of German nationhood.

27. There were also significant differences. On the one hand, Italy's Restoration states were more vulnerable to international pressure than were Germany's—to a considerable extent, their destiny was decided by statesmen in Vienna, Paris, and London. On the other, the physical presence of the Pope in Italy and the Church's strong hostility to national unification had no German parallel (Riall 1994: 78–9).

28. 'Napoleon reorganised the Italian and German lands along the lines of a reduced number of more rationally administered and territorially bounded states. The modern-minded men who oversaw this

transformation sought to defend these new creations as best they could, sometimes collaborating with Napoleon and sometimes opposing him. Generally speaking these men and their political creations survived Napoleon's defeat. Within this new political framework ideas of German and Italian nationalism were formed . . . in ways which would have been inconceivable under the patchwork *ancien regime* order' (Breuilly 1993: 99).

29. This difference in institutional arrangements in the two territories may have resulted from different combinations of geographic and political conditions. The German territories lay between two great powers, France and Russia, and were dominated by two strong states, Prussia and Austria. To minimize external attempts to stimulate political fragmentation within the territory, Prussia and Austria developed a formal institutional structure. Italy likewise faced a powerful France, but there the Habsburgs were virtually unchallenged and had no need to develop a formal institutional arrangement to exercise their control (Breuilly 1993: 100).

30. The customs union (*Zollervein*) was only one of three important pan-German economic reforms enacted in the early 19th cent. The first reform (*Gewerbefreiheit*) extended the freedom to engage in trade and industry. The last development—and perhaps the one with the greatest effect on German nation-building—was the construction of the German railway network. Although each of these factors contributed to the growth of a pan-German economy, they had no necessary implications for German *political* unification. Further, as might be expected, political fragmentation severely inhibited the establishment of a single German customs union (Kiesewetter 1987). The union was acceded to in much of the territory 'only when economic depression and empty exchequers made further resistance to Prussia impossible' (Henderson 1984: 95).

31. Only about 2.5% of the inhabitants of unified Italy were fluent in Italian in 1870; Cavour declared his loyalty to Italy by saying 'Je suis Italien avant tout'. When Garibaldi spoke to southern Italian peasants about 'Italia', they thought he was talking about his mistress (Gibson 1994: 179).

32. The Northern League has significant political support at the time of writing (spring 1999), and recently a small secessionist movement in Veneto was put down militarily.

33. Likewise, it is instructive to compare the modern German and Italian experiences with that of ancient Greece. Although the members of each *polis* recognized the members of other polities as Greek, nothing like unification nationalism ever developed there (Yack 1996: 203–4). The present analysis suggests that the absence of a Persian state based on direct rule was ultimately responsible for the failure of a Greek polity to

emerge in the ancient world. France, in particular, played such a role for Germany and Italy.

34. 'It was undoubtedly the example of the west, of Great Britain and France, successful and flourishing because they were unified nations, that stimulated the ambitions of other peoples to become unified nations too. The period after 1815 was in Germany a time of rising agitation over the national question, in Italy of the Risorgimento, in eastern Europe of the Slavic Revival. The movement was led by intellectuals, who often found it necessary to instil in their compatriots the very idea of nationality itself . . . Since such ideas could not be fully realized without the overthrow of every government in Europe east of France, thoroughgoing nationalism was inherently revolutionary' (Palmer and Colton 1965: 438).

35. The attempt to build a European Union is a contemporary example of unification nationalism; its fitful development reveals just how torturous a process this is. As was argued in Ch. 3, for further unification to proceed, the threat posed by commercial and political alliances between American states, and between American and Pacific Rim countries, must become more tangible to the member states of the European Union. In the absence of such external threats, there is an insufficient incentive for member states' leaders to forsake their sovereignty; cf. Streeck and Schmitter (1991: 148).

36. A telling example comes from a Bavarian teacher's manual at the turn of the century concerning the teaching of a poem celebrating a costly military victory in the war of 1870–1: 'If during the treatment of such a piece the eyes of our boys do not flash, the cheeks do not glow, the heart does not pound, if the fist is not clenched with the thought: If only I could have ridden there!—then either the discussion or the delivery lacked the proper inspiring fires, or the boy is no good' (Kennedy 1982: 262).

37. Friedrich Meinecke distinguished between state nations (*Staatsnation*) and cultural nations (*Kulturnation*). In state nations of the West, state- and nation-building coincided, so the nation became defined through the political principles of constitution and citizenship. In Germany, where state-building occurred belatedly, the nation became defined as a prepolitical community of culture, language, and ethnicity. This ethno-cultural notion of nationhood became perpetuated over time and planted the seeds for the exclusivist conception of Germanness ever since (Forsythe 1989).

38. This difference has been characterized in terms of various distinctions: e.g. between ethnic and civic, Eastern and Western, *ethnos* and *demos*, and German versus French understandings of nationhood. Like many generalizations, this one is overdrawn. On the one hand, French history reveals the importance of both kinds of self-understandings (Grillo 1998: 121–40). On the other, these baseline tendencies are conditioned by historical particulars that can change as circumstances do. Thus the present

Social Democratic regime in Germany has proposed legislation toward immigrants that is far more culturally inclusive than that entailed in current French policy.

39. Opposition to direct rule was not always based on nationality; often it was based on religion. Breuilly (1993: 76–81) contains a useful discussion of the similarities and differences between *religious* and *nationalist* opposition to the imposition of direct rule. Breuilly concludes that Namier is to a large degree justified saying that religion is a 16th-cent. word for nationalism. There is a fundamental difference between these two bases of opposition, however: unlike the national variety, religious opposition is guided by an explicit ideology (Hobsbawm 1992: 175–7).

40. Although England adopted direct rule early, the origins of *British* nationalism largely arose as a defensive response to direct rule in France: 'Time and time again, war with France brought Britons, whether they hailed from Wales or Scotland or England, into confrontation with an obviously hostile Other and encouraged them to define themselves collectively against it. They defined themselves as Protestants struggling for survival against the world's foremost Catholic power. They defined themselves against the French as they imagined them to be, superstitious, militarist, decadent and unfree' (Colley 1992: 5). See also Newman (1987).

41. Interestingly, the Japanese employed direct rule in their Asian colonies (especially Korea) to a far greater extent than other colonial powers. By concentrating political power in central agencies, rather than relying on local notables (as in indirect rule), this may have inadvertently set the stage for strong states in Korea and Taiwan in the era following the Second World War (Migdal 1988: 272).

CHAPTER 6

1. 'The nation is something to which we are naturally tied. In everything natural there is always something unchosen ... precisely because national ties are not chosen, they have a halo of disinterestedness. All sorts of people are at ease with the idea of national interest. For most people the whole point of the nation is that it is interestless. Just for that reason, it can ask for sacrifices. Dying for one's country, which usually one does not choose, assumes a moral grandeur which dying for the Labour Party, the AMA, or perhaps even Amnesty International cannot rival, for these are all bodies one can join or leave at easy will'

(Anderson 1983: 132). This seems misguided. Nations are not any more or less natural than other kinds of groups—the point is that they are often hard to exit. Nor are nations interestless. People may be willing to sacrifice for nations because they encompass collective rather than individual interests, but this does not distinguish them from other kinds of groups.

2. 'Nations stretch backwards into the past, and indeed in most cases their origins are conveniently lost in the mists of time. In the course of this history various significant events have occurred, and we can identify with the actual people who acted at those moments, reappropriating their deeds as our own. Often these events involve military victories and defeats: we imagine ourselves filling the breach at Harfleur or reading the signal hoisted at Trafalgar. . . . Renan thinks that historical tragedies matter more than historical glories—"sorrows have greater value than victories; for they impose duties and demand common effort." The historic national community is a community of obligation. Because our forebears have toiled and spilt their blood to build and defend the nation, we who are born into it inherit an obligation to continue their work, which we discharge partly towards our contemporaries and partly towards our descendants. The historical community stretches forward into the future too. This then means that when we speak of the nation as an ethical community, we have in mind not merely the kind of community that exists between a group of contemporaries who practice mutual aid among themselves and which would dissolve at the point at which that practice ceased; but a community which, because it stretches back and forward across the generations, is not one that the present generation can renounce. Here we begin to see something of the depth of national communities which may not be shared by other more immediate forms of association' (Miller 1994: 19).

3. 'Nationalism is not engendered by nations . . . To see [nationalisms] as the struggles of nations, of real solidary groups who somehow survived despite Soviet attempts to crush them . . . is to get things exactly backwards . . .' We do not live in a world of nations, but in a world 'in which nationhood is pervasively institutionalized in the practice of states and the workings of the state system. It is a world in which nation is widely, if unevenly, available and resonant as a category of social vision and division. It is a world in which nationness may suddenly, and powerfully, "happen." But none of this implies a world of nations—of substantial, enduring collectivities' (Brubaker 1996: 17, 21).

4. The following example illustrates the effect of social context on the salience of a cultural marker. Although classical Jewish law prohibited shaving with a razor, it did not require the Jew to wear his beard conspicuously long or untrimmed. Where Jews cultivated such an appearance, such as in the Mahgreb and the Muslim or Byzantine East, it was

due no less to the cultural values of the surrounding environment, in which the beard functioned as a badge of masculine honour, than to the demands of Jewish tradition. In those same areas the kabbalists were able to endow the beard with an additional dimension of mystical meaning, regarding it as a symbol of divine splendour which was not to be tampered with in any way. Not surprisingly, where the beard was most venerated, it was also most subject to violent attack or punitive removal. In medieval Christian Europe, by contrast, most Jews opted not to grow their beards in a pronounced manner. This did not prevent Christians from making use of the beard as a symbol of the Jew and his otherness. Jews (and Christians) travelling to the East or the Holy Land would sometimes grow their beards there but remove them upon returning to Europe, apparently so as not to be perceived as an alien Other (Horowitz 1994).

5. The point is an old one. Simmel's [1922] 1955a) essay on *Conflict* is its *fons et origo* in sociology. Freud ([1930] 1961: 68) has a view of one mechanism that might be responsible for these effects: 'It is always possible to bind together a considerable number of people in love, so long as there are other people left over to receive the manifestations of their aggressiveness.' In contrast, most social psychologists, following (Festinger 1954), regard cognitive consistency as the basis of social comparison processes.

6. Thus Father Paisii, an Eastern Orthodox monk who was the father of Bulgarian nationalism, wrote in his manifesto *Slavic-Bulgarian History of the Bulgarian People, Kings, and Saints and of All Bulgarian Deeds and Events . . . for the Benefit of the Bulgarian Nation* (written 1762, unpublished until 1844), 'There are those who do not care to know about their own Bulgarian nation and turn to foreign ways and foreign tongue; they do not care for their own Bulgarian language but try to read and speak Greek and are ashamed to call themselves Bulgarians. O, you senseless and stupid people! Why are you ashamed to call yourselves Bulgarians and do not read and speak your own language? Or had the Bulgarians no kingdom and state? They have ruled for many years and their glory and renown have been known in the whole world and many times they have exacted tribute from powerful Romans and Greeks . . . In the entire Slavic race the Bulgarians have had the greatest glory; they first called their rulers tsars, they first had a patriarch, they first were converted, and they conquered the largest territory' (Pundeff 1969: 101–2).

7. To some degree, of course, people's social identities can be affected by the cultural framings of political entrepreneurs (Snow *et al.* 1986). Nationalist ideologues face daunting challenges, for they seek to assert the feasibility of entirely new political possibilities (Chatterjee 1993). While cultural analyses of social movements place a premium on the

plasticity of social identities, not all frames are equally likely to have popular appeal (Babb 1996). The frames that are most likely to catch on, however, are those that reflect the concrete social experiences of their targets (Sperber 1996). For a compelling depth-psychological analysis of the development of social identity, see Kakar (1996).

8. The key term in this sentence is 'systematic'. It is hard to deny that having red hair has no implications for individual welfare: it may make one more attractive to Jules, and less attractive to Jim. But in England the advantages and disadvantages of having red hair tend to cancel out when considering the totality of one's social interactions. It is in this sense that the trait of redheadedness has no systematic effect on one's welfare.

9. The example leads to a subsequent question: why does red hair have no implications for group formation when black skin does? There never was a slave trade in redheads in the modern world. Further, skin colour is more salient than hair colour because it can be traced back to some putative community or origin (where everyone shared this skin colour), whereas hair colour usually cannot.

10. Further evidence that is supportive of the general thrust of this argument shows how network position leads to differential power (Cook and Yamagishi 1992), and how 'brokers' who serve as the bridges between otherwise disconnected groups are higher paid and advance more rapidly in their firms than others (Burt 1992). In the absence of systematic network data, we must turn to more indirect measures of structural location.

11. The other principal means of doing so is by striving to attain a positive *individual* identity. The critical issue here concerns the trade-off between these two means of increasing self-esteem (Brown 1986).

12. This is as true for the groups that form in American high schools as it is for those that attract these same students later in life (Coleman 1961). American college students are more likely to wear clothes bearing the insignia of their university in weeks following victories of the school's football team than in weeks following losses (Cialdini *et al.* 1989). This kind of identification can also occur over long distances: the successful début of Hideo Nomo, the first Japanese-born baseball player to pitch in the US major leagues, with the Los Angeles Dodgers was greeted with euphoria in Japan (Nightengale 1995).

13. One of the most interesting new forms of low-exit (or no-exit) groups is based on health states, such as the deaf and disabled. The American group Disabled in Action has fought for elevators in subways and against telethons to aid the disabled, which it views as demeaning. 'For the disabled . . . the new advocacy associations allow mutual affirmation to replace individual denial. "When I was growing up, I was terrified of walking into a room of people with disabilities and admit I was one of

them. . . . Now I just love being in a community of people with disabilities.". . . "Even if we have a minor disability, we're still different—because society won't let us forget that we're different." For some disabled people, these differences are the opposite of off-putting. 'I came to see disabled people as beautiful, said Danny Robert, who has multiple sclerosis. "Particularly people on respirators, people in wheelchairs, people who spasm a lot, people who drool"' (Martin 1997).

14. When people are categorized as members of a group on account of visible traits they are powerless to alter (such as age, gender, and skin colour) exit is precluded and their dependence on fellow members is enhanced. This accounts for the greater salience of ascriptive memberships and identities over attained ones. This logic also helps explain the relatively high solidarity of communities of the deaf, the physically handicapped, and communities of lepers, among others (Goffman 1963 provides a general phenomenological analysis; Sacks 1989; Schein 1989).

15. Following Barth (1969), Olzak (1992) views ethnic boundaries as ultimately based on different productive niches. From this perspective, Group α and Group β maintain an ethnic boundary because their 'modes of production' are complements rather than substitutes. On this account, they do not threaten one another—they are non-competitive.

16. Tilly (1998: 91) refers to the mechanism responsible for the persistence of segmentation as opportunity hoarding: 'When members of a categorically bounded network acquire access to a resource that is valuable, renewable, subject to monopoly, supportive of network activities, and enhanced by the network's modus operandi, network members regularly hoard their access to the resource, creating beliefs and practices that sustain their control.'

17. This point helps explain why populations such as Zionist Jews, Kurds, and North American Indians can develop social identities despite being culturally and spatially dispersed.

18. Many writers besides those discussed here have recognized the importance of the cultural division of labour on nationalism (Breuilly 1993: 34; Horowitz 1985: 108–35) without, however, providing much in the way of analysis. In contrast, the hypotheses advanced by Rogowski (1985a) linking the cultural division of labour directly to nationalist outcomes are more sophisticated. As the present analysis makes clear, however, cultural divisions of labour have no direct effects on nationalist outcomes. Instead, they are important determinants of national social identities which are necessary, but insufficient, causes of nationalism.

19. What would happen if all Anglophones were Protestant, and all Francophones Catholic? Then stratification patterns alone could not predict the salience of language or religion; other factors—such as social networks—would come more strongly into play (Gould 1994).

20. Measures of the cultural division of labour taken from official statistics

are bound to understate the true amount of occupational specialization, for some of it derives from criminal activities. Thus the leading role played by Dominican immigrants in the illicit drug trade in the northeast region of the USA is invisible in portraits like this one.

21. The development of peripheral nationalism in the southern counties of Ireland is a paradigmatic case (Hechter 1999). Likewise, the ethnic Romanians, who occupied the most disadvantaged position in the cultural division of labour in Greater Romania, formed the social base of a virulent nationalism aimed at the subjugation of non-Romanian ethnic groups in the interwar period (Livezeanu 1995).

22. There is some debate about the role of the cultural division of labour in generating intergroup conflict. Breakdown in a cultural division of labour may promote interethnic conflict, because then—and only then—members of different cultural groups are likely to be competing against one another for the same kinds of jobs. Competition exists between two populations when the presence of one reduces the opportunities for the other. Ethnic groups can be considered to occupy niches that constitute their means for exploiting the environment. If so, the likelihood of racial and ethnic conflict may be minimized when groups occupy non-overlapping habitats (Olzak 1992). However, Olzak's analysis has been criticized on the basis of sampling bias (Forbes 1997: 104), and its empirical adequacy has also been challenged (Diez-Medrano 1994). Whereas the breakdown of a cultural division of labour may be a necessary condition for ethnic conflict, it is far from a sufficient one (Hechter 1994*a*). At a minimum, variables promoting group solidarity—including dependence and control mechanisms—must also be added to the brew to account for collective action. Even so, it is notable that one of the most egregious examples of intergroup conflict—that between Hutus and Tutsis in Rwanda–Burundi—has been ascribed to a cultural division of labour. Thus, Burundi has been 'described as "the one state in Africa that displays the most systematic and blatant violations of human rights," a state in which the Tutsi minority of 14 per cent (about the same percentage as Whites in South Africa) controls well over 90 per cent of all high governmental, political party, foreign service, private sector, educational, judicial, and health care positions, not to mention its 99.7 per cent of all military positions, top to bottom' (Horowitz 1991: 37).

23. 'For many . . . [cultural groups] in the state, the transition to . . . nationalization of elites was a reaction to the subordinate position in which indigenous intellectuals found themselves (i.e. the ethnic stratification system that was a reflection of the colonial relations between groups at the time). Socially mobilized Latvians and Estonians found Germans in a dominant position. Lithuanians found themselves subordinated to Poles, Georgians and Azerbaydzhanis to Armenians and Russians, Ukrainians and Belorussians to Russians, Poles and Jews. Later Central

Asians and dozens of [nations] in the Russian east found themselves sub-ordinate to the dominant Russians' (Kaiser 1994: 382).

24. 'There are many other competing loyalties in ... any state—ties to class, party, business, union, profession, or whatever. But groups formed of such ties are virtually never considered as possible self-standing, maximal social units, as candidates for nationhood. Conflicts among them occur only within a more or less fully accepted terminal community whose political integrity they do not, as a rule, put into question. No matter how severe they become they do not threaten, at least not intentionally, its existence as such. They threaten governments, or even forms of gov-ernment, but they rarely at best ... threaten to undermine the [state] itself, because they do not involve alternative definitions of what the nation is, of what its scope of reference is. Economic or class or intel-lectual disaffection threatens revolution, but disaffection based on race, language, or culture threatens partition, irredentism, or merger, a redrawing of the very limits of the state, a new definition of its domain. Civil discontent finds its natural outlet in the seizing, legally or illegally, of the state apparatus' (Geertz 1963: 111).

25. See also Horowitz (1985: 109–10). For a detailed analysis of how differences in employment patterns can harden over time by reshaping educational incentives and accentuating differences among ethnic sub-cultures, see Sowell (1994).

26. This may explain why Chinese restaurants have long provided the best value for money in Western societies. If this view is correct, rapid eco-nomic development in China will lead to higher priced Chinese restaur-ants in the rest of the world. This process has already occurred in Hong Kong. It has recently spread to sites—like Monterrey Park, California and Richmond, British Columbia—which have witnessed massive middle-class migration from Hong Kong.

27. This is not to deny that the melting pot sometimes does its work: many culturally distinct groups (especially ethnic groups) have assimilated in the course of history. As this chapter argues, prospects for assimilation rise when cultural markers cease to have implications for individual life chances. For example, declining occupational segregation among Jews in the USA has led to high rates of exogamy and low rates of religious participation—trends that have called into question the very nature and survival of a separate Jewish identity there (Lipset and Raab 1995). Like-wise, many Jews assimilated following the Napoleonic reforms in the German states, and the Jewish community in Kaifeng, China, also grad-ually disappeared into thin air. For a fine-grained analysis of differential linguistic assimilation of Russian speakers in a number of former Soviet Republics, see Laitin (1998).

28. Under certain conditions, these non-caste-compliant firms will be able to attract customers. Since workers will receive higher wages from these

firms, and will be able to purchase a range of goods from them, these firms will also be able to attract workers. Yet the threat to the caste equilibrium is small when the cost of forming a coalition is high. This is the case when the coalition of non-caste firms is large, and exchange with the caste economy is necessary. It is instructive to compare Akerlof's discussion with a more recent attempt to model two other self-enforcing suboptimal equilibria—footbinding in China and female infibulation in Africa (Mackie 1996). The caste labour model differs in at least two respects. First, it is meant to apply to urban as well as rural settings. Second, the caste equilibrium is not Pareto inferior, because—in contrast to footbinding and female infibulation—dominant workers would stand to lose if the system were abandoned.

29. This assumption seemingly is at variance with the emphasis on imperfect information that motivates other parts of Akerlof's model.

30. Caste divisions may persist in the urban setting for *racial* groups, however, for the visibility of the relevant phenotypical marker makes self-enforced outcasting child's play. In this case, the central government can play a vital role in dismantling a race-based caste system by promoting affirmative action policies. This provides disadvantaged racial groups, as well, with a strong interest in state policy.

CHAPTER 7

1. Just as sovereignty had no necessary implications for Irish economic growth, so the recent trend towards decentralized government in Italy has benefited northern regions more than southern ones (Putnam 1994).

2. Thus the directors of the Harvard Project on American Indian Economic Development conclude that 'Among the most powerful arguments for tribal sovereignty is the simple fact that it works. Nothing else has provided as promising a set of political conditions for reservation economic development. Nothing else has produced the success stories and broken the cycles of dependence on the federal system in the way that sovereignty backed by capable tribal institutions has ... In our work, we cannot find a single case of successful economic development and declining dependence where federal decision makers have exercised de facto control over the key development decisions' (Cornell and Kalt 1998: 209).

3. If sovereignty can protect a threatened but extant culture, can it also

foster the creation of new national cultures? Israel offers the most impressive example of sovereignty's power to nurture a new national culture. Since it attained statehood in 1948, Hebrew, once a dead language, has become a vital modern one. As is the case in the economic realm, however, sovereignty alone provides no guaranteed outcomes. Although the Irish government has endeavoured to strengthen the largely disused Irish language—most recently, by establishing an Irish-language television channel—to date its success pales in comparison with Israel's (Ó Gliasain 1988; Ó Laoire 1995).

4. There are two puzzling features about Quebec nationalism. In the first place, why is Quebec still pressing for secession if it already has sufficient autonomy to institute such stringent language legislation? Its proponents respond that English Canada has refused to make constitutional changes on behalf of cultural dualism, as indicated by the failures of the Meech Lake Accord in 1990 and the Charlottetown Agreement in 1992 (Leslie 1996: 136–51). In the second place, if support for secession is in fact growing, then why do the nationalists insist on remaining part and parcel of the Canadian economy? The 1995 referendum bill stipulates that, if it passes, the proclamation of sovereignty 'must be preceded by a formal offer of economic and political partnership with Canada' (Quebec 1995). It can only be that the nationalist government seeks to mitigate the negative economic effects of separation to voters who are otherwise interested in cultural autonomy. This suggests that much of the support for nationalism in Quebec is soft. For 1998 survey data indicating the existence of a large number of ambivalent voters among Francophones, see Pinard (1998).

5. The Zionist group ahad Ha'aman, for example, objected to the pursuit of Israeli sovereignty and instead stressed the goal of achieving an authentic national identity (Breuilly 1993: 71).

6. By no means does this axiom imply that their desires are selfish, however.

7. The term sovereignty refers to the idea that there is a final and absolute authority in the polity. Such an idea is irrelevant in stateless societies, where no such authority exists. The rise of the state was not sufficient to bring this conception to the fore, for states that employed indirect rule do not have a singular locus of absolute authority. In effect, the idea of sovereignty only comes about with the rise of direct rule (Hinsley 1966).

8. In the real world, however, employment issues can never be left aside. Recall that Martin Luther King, Jun., was assassinated during a trip to Memphis, where he had gone to support the unionization efforts of African-American garbage collectors. To underscore the point, Pierre van den Berghe (personal communication) doubts that garbage collection in Belgium 'escapes the politics of ethnic proportionality and territorialism'.

9. This is not to deny that substantial consumption differences can arise within the same nation. This is evidently the case with different social classes. For a detailed analysis of the varying consumption values of various élite sectors of French society, see Bourdieu (1984).

10. Some American historians attribute the South's cultural distinctiveness to the predominantly Celtic heritage of its settlers (Fischer 1989; McWhiney 1988).

11. The Lega Nord makes an effort to cloak itself in nationalist rather than mere regionalist raiment, presumably because this affords it greater legitimacy and political support. To bolster its claims, it cites the well-known research of political scientist Robert Putnam (1994), who argues that differences in political culture between the North and South date from the early medieval period.

12. To some degree, regional production values may determine consumption interests, as well. Thus, the distinct consumption interests of the Nuer (which revolved almost exclusively around cattle) emanated from their pastoral production system, which was shaped, in turn, by the ecological character of the Nuer's territory (Evans-Pritchard 1944).

13. The desire to restrict government-provided goods to people in a given culture leads most states to impose strict entry requirements on immigrants. Without such entry requirements, Israel would soon cease to be a Jewish state; indeed, it would soon become a Muslim one. Most Israelis do not want that to occur. Similar concerns arise in formally multicultural polities like the USA, as well, where the educational status of the Spanish language is a perennial political issue. The possibility that the Chinese government tried to influence the 1996 American presidential election brought forth a storm of protest in Congress. How else can the existence of laws preventing foreign countries from interfering in domestic elections be accounted for?

14. Istvan Szabo's film *Mephisto* tells the tragic tale of a liberal Weimar-era stage actor whose career ambitions (he could only work in the German-language theatre) overcame his antipathy to Nazism. Szabo portrays, in exquisite detail, just how this particular deal with the devil cost the actor dearly. The state itself directly controls many jobs. In some societies, the fraction is well over half. In many societies, the best jobs that most people could get are state jobs of the officialdom or the military. Most jobs in health, education and public services are controlled by the state. Indeed, in such impoverished, subsistence societies as Somalia, Burundi, and Rwanda, the most valuable resource may be government itself. Land runs a poor second, especially if the government can tax the product of land. If my group is in control of government in such a society, I am likely to be much better off than I would otherwise be. Even in Yugoslavia, Serbs benefited from Serbian dominance of the military and the government. With the fragmentation of Yugoslavia, they will lose.

The harsh turn to war came after Croatia, upon declaring independence, replaced Serbs with Croats in the police force in Krajina' (Hardin 1995: 217).

15. However, it is difficult to draw generalizations about the relationship between social class and nationalist activity (Hroch 1985: 179). Some nationalist movements clearly did *not* have teachers at their social base: in 19th-cent. France e.g. teachers had extremely high prestige; therefore, they were not inclined to rock any political boats (Weber 1976: 317–18). Intense nationalist activity tended to distributed unevenly over the territory of the small European nations: e.g. linguistic homogeneity and the closeness of the language boundary are not correlated with the incidence of nationalist collective action (Hroch 1985: 166). Schooling, however, is: in Bohemia, growth in the nationalist movement corresponded to the expansion of primary schooling; in Slovakia, with secondary schooling. Further, nationalist activity tended to occur in part, or entirely, in the most productive and market-oriented parts of the territory occupied by a peripheral nation (Hroch 1985: 172). Such relatively fine-grained conclusions must be treated with due caution, however, for data on the social bases of 19th-cent. nationalism are notoriously poor. There are even large pitfalls in determining the relative numbers of Czechs, Germans, and Jews in early 20th-cent. Prague (Sayer 1996).

16. This conclusion is supported by extensive empirical research on the development of social movements (McAdam 1982; Morris 1984), as well as trade unions (Van Leeuwen 1997).

17. The initial members of any group seeking collective action are likely to be those most committed to its goals. Once a critical mass of adherents has been organized, the group is then likely to attract less ardent recruits. Bandwagon effects of this kind can greatly extend the group's efficacy (Granovetter 1978; Marwell and Oliver 1993). A good example of this process is seen in the struggle for Kosovo in 1998. After the Serbian government attempted to clear ethnic Albanians from those parts of Kosovo bordering on Albania, Albanian Kosovars from all over Western Europe returned to their homeland to join the Kosovo Liberation Army.

18. That states with proportional representation are more likely to have nationalist political parties can be no surprise: the introduction of proportional representation is usually the result of a strategy of institutionalizing potential nationalist conflict (Rokkan 1970: 168).

19. The strategic nature of political violence is well illustrated in a study of the former Soviet Union (Beissinger 1998). Once *glasnost'* revealed the weakness of central authorities, the rate of political contention rose rapidly throughout Soviet territory. The use of violence, however, was more likely in inter-republic border disputes than in secessionist movements. Whereas central authorities were traditionally responsive to nonviolent protests (because their existence called the state's legitimacy into

question), the only means of pressing territorial claims in inter-republican border disputes was by force. The use of violent means is conditioned on a large number of factors, including the loss of central control, the targets of political demands, and the availability of appropriate weaponry.

20. Recent game-theoretic analyses have modelled some conditions that might lead to violent nationalist conflict. The ethnification of Yugoslavian politics has been explained as a rational outcome of a signalling game (Bates *et al.* 1998). In this game, the true political preferences of moderate Serbs (who constitute the majority, and therefore represent the decisive political actors) are unknown. The seriousness of the stakes (such as those due to the proponents of ethnic cleansing) rapidly increase the political salience of ethnic divisions, thus splitting the previously dominant pro-reform (ethnically heterogeneous) coalitions. Further, intergroup violence has been modelled as a breakdown in one of two equilibria responsible for intergroup peace (Fearon and Laitin 1996). The first of these equilibria is sustained by the belief that if the members of one group attack the other, then the victimized group will retaliate indiscriminately against the attackers. Then if violence occurs, it tends to spiral. The second equilibrium relies on quite a different mechanism. In this mechanism, the victims forsake retaliation, assuming that the authorities of the first group will punish the attackers in its midst. In the second equilibrium, the victims' only role is to notify these authorities when there is a breach of peace. Both analyses assume high levels of group solidarity, which is exogenous in each model.

21. This is not to claim that all nationalist violence is the outcome of such mechanisms, nor that this perspective has anything else to say about the phenomenology of collective violence. Riots directed against Jews in Russia during the early years of this century, Chinese in Indonesia during the fall of the Sukarno regime, or gypsies in today's Czech Republic may have occurred spontaneously, without much prior organization. Yet too often violent events described as spontaneous have not been subjected to empirical scrutiny. In this respect, it is significant that a detailed analysis of two such events—the 1983 Sinhalese–Tamil riots in Sri Lanka, and the 1984 Hindu pogroms against the Sikhs in India in retaliation for the assassination of Indira Gandhi—reveals that much of the mob violence in both events was indeed organized and quite purposive (Tambiah 1996: 96, 137). Likewise, when Czechs in the northern Bohemian city of Usti nad Labem demanded that the authorities erect a 15-foot-high wall to separate them from their gypsy neighbours (Perlez 1998), this too smacks of prior organization. Of course, whether collective violence is organized or spontaneous is often a highly politically charged question. For example, there was a fierce debate about the nature of the Hindu violence directed against Sikhs (Tambiah 1996: 110–11). That the issue

usually entails serious political implications makes the need for empirical scrutiny all the more vital.

CHAPTER 8

1. For comprehensive surveys of the literature on nationalist violence, see Beissinger (forthcoming) and Brubaker and Laitin (1998). Brubaker and Laitin argue that the subject should command our attention not so much because this kind of violence is ubiquitous, but because it is so appalling.
2. See Ch. 1 n. 2.
3. In Jan. 1996, the French Minister of Information Technology announced the intention of his government to propose to the European Union a series of measures to ban free access to the Internet (Castells 1997: 268). China sentenced the dissident Lin Hai to two years in prison in Jan. 1999 for sending thousands of Chinese electronic mail addresses to an electronic publication based in the USA that the regime considers hostile to Beijing. Currently, in Chinese Internet cafés access is limited to adults who provide their identification cards.
4. 'The diversification of communication modes, the link-up of all media in a digital hypertext, opening the way for interactive multimedia, and the inability to control satellites beaming across borders or computer-mediated communication over the 'phone line, blew up the traditional lines of regulatory defense. The explosion of telecommunications, and the development of cable, provided the vehicles for unprecedented broadcasting power ... Authoritarian states are losing the battle over media in the Information Age' (Castells 1997: 254–7).
5. This is quite different from the view that nationalism is merely the cynical policy of peripheral leaders to retain or increase their power at the expense of central rulers (Brass 1991). This cynical view takes the loyalty and support of the peripheral masses for granted; it treats them as the dupes of false consciousness. Explanations based on false consciousness cannot be disconfirmed, however: they can always be squared with the facts in some *post-hoc* account. By contrast, I contend that nationalism results from a coincidence of interests between peripheral leaders and masses. But what does this coincidence of interests consist of? In rural settings, it often derives from the dependence of peasant producers on local authorities (Brustein 1988). This dependence often leads peasants to forswear goods offered by the central state. Thus the French peasantry resisted the appeals of state centralizers on behalf of universal

national education in the 19th cent. (de Swaan 1988: ch. 3). In settings where the dependence of masses on leaders has eroded, this coincidence of interests derives from their common demand for the collective goods (including transfer payments) that the central government provides to the region as a whole.

6. The cohesiveness of this relationship is threatened from both sides. On the one hand, leaders may not be able to bind the members of their respective nations to their bargains; on the other, leaders may not be responsive to members' demands. Thus, 'moderately-minded autonomous leaders may be faced with opposition from more secessionist-minded constituents which undermines elite authority to speak or negotiate on behalf of the ethno-regional group' (Smith 1995: 16).

7. There is some evidence e.g. that ethnocentrism increases with education. If so, educated leaders may not be inclined to accommodative politics. 'Even if leaders committed themselves to such a plan at the outset, under democratic, competitive conditions, centrifugal forces from among their own followers and from among their more extreme electoral competitors would easily undermine the durability to the agreement' (Horowitz 1991: 142).

8. A constraint is a constitutional rule that binds only because it was agreed to at the outset. Its binding force is based not on immediate interest, but in the longer range interest in keeping one's word or in abiding by the law. Group rights and consociational solutions are based on constraints. An incentive, in contrast, binds because it is in the continuing interest of the participants. Consociationalists do not pay attention to incentives; therefore, they do not provide any mechanisms that lead to intergroup accommodation. The most important incentives are those operating on politicians and their followers, that 'harness their self-interest to the cause of intergroup conflict reduction, regardless of their personal feelings, that, in a word, make moderation pay' (Horowitz 1991: 154).

9. 'The genius of the Malaysian coalition arrangements . . . was that they forced Malay and Chinese politicians, in heterogeneous constituencies, to rely in part on votes delivered by politicians belonging to the other ethnic group. Those votes would not be forthcoming unless leaders could portray the candidates as moderate on issues of concern to the group that was delivering its votes across ethnic lines. Consequently, compromises at the top of the coalition were supported by electoral incentives at the bottom . . . [this is what is meant by] internal incentives built by constitutional engineers into the structure of the selfish calculations of politicians . . . To frame the utility of incentives in terms of their ability to affect the selfish calculations of politicians, harnessing self-interest to the cause of peace, is, of course, to reject the perhaps-loftier aspiration of dealing with the so-called root causes of conflict. It

is to resort to an approach that does not seek or need to change hearts
and minds in order to succeed' (Horowitz 1991: 155).

10. Reynolds's analysis depends on the assumption that voter preferences
would have remained constant regardless of the electoral system used.
Thus, his simulations do not permit electoral system incentives to affect
the votes cast. As Reynolds acknowledges, this assumption vitiates, to
some extent, Horowitz's claims about the influence of electoral incentives. Reynolds justifies his assumption on the basis of evidence showing
that electoral systems have few implications for multipartism in his
sample of Southern African countries. This finding, he argues, shows that
'electoral system incentives only have an impact at the margins of voter
behavior' because party identification and voting preferences in Southern Africa are 'strongly held, reflecting polities highly polarized along
linguistic, cultural, ideological and regional lines' (ch. 7).

11. The subject at hand is more properly designated as 'federation' rather
than 'federalism'. As King (1982) emphasizes, the former term designates
a social institution, whereas the latter one is a form of political ideology.

12. Lijphart (1977: 42) regards federation as a special case of consociationalism, but this view is clearly mistaken: federation is considerably more
open-ended.

13. Constitutional guarantees, in turn, affect the cost of altering governance
arrangements (Breton and Scott 1980; Seabright 1996).

14. One way of construing federation is as an insurance group for the
various territories of a given state. As in smaller level insurance groups,
such as mutual benefit societies, members (here, the administrative subunits of a given state) are provided with insurance against losses (such as
those due to invasion, or to localized economic or natural catastrophes),
as well as access to credit (loans or transfer payments from the centre).
Moreover, federations, like insurance groups, tend to thrive only when
the risk of loss is relatively low and randomized among members.
Members who routinely suffer losses greater than their contributions to
the central fund threaten to bankrupt the institution. Insurance groups
strive to avoid this threat by enlisting large numbers of members
(thereby reducing the correlated risk), and by enacting various restrictions on membership. For example, groups that insure against sickness
may require a physical examination for admission. Unlike insurance
groups, however, federations have a very small number of members (the
USA has only fifty members, Canada a mere ten), and losses among
members tend not to be randomized. Eastern Germany offers a glaring
example. On entering the German federation in 1989 it was by far the
poorest region; ten years later, it remains quite the poorest. Many
Western Germans therefore face the prospect of subsidizing Easterners
for the duration of their lifetimes. Their willingness to continue this
arrangement is likely to be a function of the amount of the subsidy they

have to bear, as well as the prosperity of the West German economy. In this way, persisting regional inequalities highlight the fragility of federations, raising the prospect of fragmentation should the centre's ability to provide collective goods falter.

15. Analogously, much of the tribalism that divides contemporary African societies is a by-product of the culturally arbitrary political boundaries that were imposed by colonial powers (Mamdani 1996).

16. This advantage is far from costless, however. 'The more decentralized a state is, the more the coordination or negotiation that will have to be carried on between the different jurisdictions. Therefore, the total cost of coordination increases as the degree of decentralization increases' (Breton and Scott 1980: pp. xvi–xvii).

17. There is even some doubt about this. Whether collective goods are optimally produced by central rather than local authorities probably depends on the production functions of these goods—in particular, on scale economies. Defence e.g. probably gains from central provision because it entails large economies of scale. Many other state-provided goods, however, may be optimally provided on a more decentralized basis. The decentralized provision of collective goods, which is a characteristic of federation, is likely to be superior because it sets up a market for governmental rules and regulations, giving incentives for citizens to 'vote with their feet' (Ostrom *et al.* 1961; Weingast 1995).

18. This is one reason why political theorists have traditionally insisted that all true democracies must be small societies (Sale 1980). Plato, for instance, argued that the ideal number of citizens was 5,040.

19. In this respect, it should be noted that surveys indicate that federation is even popular among the inhabitants of regions which are culturally similar to state cores. Thus, popular support for subnational governments (*Länder*) in Germany has risen steeply since their introduction in 1949, and is on the rise in Italy (Putnam 1994: 59). Despite a sharp decline in survey measures of Americans' trust in their central government in the past thirty years, trust in state and local governments has remained at high levels (Jennings 1998).

20. Thus Blair's victory statement: 'In relation to Scotland and Wales, I think the most important elements are that we have made devolution work, and in Scotland it's absolutely clear that the vast majority of people voted for parties that are opposed to the nationalist agenda of independence. . . . People have rejected the notion of separatism' (Hoge 1999). The case for British devolution has been articulated by Bogdanor (1999).

21. Of course, Swiss cantonalism also entails some difficulties of its own. Drawing up of appropriate levels of government and winning consent for them is problematic. Securing such consent has much to do with the way in which local identities overlap in complex ways, so as to reduce the prospects of ethnic tension. The success of cantonalism for the Swiss

federation is largely due to the fact that 'the overlapping boundaries of language and religion . . . have weakened language and religion as divisive forces, for each linguistic group contains representatives of both faiths and . . . vice versa' (Dikshit 1975: 234).

22. Suppose the parties are highly centralized. Then, it would seem that all the constitutional and institutional prohibitions guaranteeing constituent governments against revision of the federal bargain would be ineffectual. If, on the other hand, the officials of the central government do not have partisan supporters operating the constituent governments, they may expect some opposition to their breaking of the guarantees (Riker 1964). Where there is a political party symmetry between the central government and the subunits, this should help integrate the federation. Where there is a notable asymmetry between regional (provincial) parties and central parties, where the latter often lack viable affiliates in the subunits, then this is likely to promote intergroup conflict (Smith 1995: 9).

23. 'In establishing that small differences between two populations may produce large variations in their observed behaviors, this essay suggests that statistical relationships between aggregate ethnic activity and its determinants are bound to exhibit high standard variation' (Kuran 1998: 651).

24. Secession is a fundamentally uncertain prospect for at least two reasons. In the first place, it is impossible to predict how third parties in the international system will react to the new entity. For example, separatists argue that a sovereign Quebec would maintain current economic relations with Canada and would also be included in the North Atlantic Free Trade Association, but they have no means of providing these assurances. In the second place, it is impossible to gauge the stability and effectiveness of any prospective new sovereign government.

25. This contention is supported by empirical analyses of the determinants of secessionism in Russia and Eastern Europe (Beissinger 1996; Treisman 1997).

26. The groups included in the analysis are Amazonian Indians in Brazil, Quebecois in Canada, Indigenous Peoples in Colombia, Slovaks in Czechoslovakia, Basques in France, Papuans, Chinese, and East Timorese in Indonesia, Palestinians in Israel, South Tyrolians and Sardinians in Italy, Igorots in the Philippines, Basques and Catalans in Spain, Jurassians in Switzerland, Malay-Muslims in Thailand, Acholi and Baganda in Uganda, Scots in the United Kingdom, Native Americans in the USA, and Hungarians in Yugoslavia.

27. I owe this question to Adrian Raftery.

28. See Ch. 8 n. 14.

29. Much of the thrust of this section is drawn from Woodward (1995), who provides a compelling analysis of the disintegration of Yugoslavia.

30. Some nationalist violence continues to occur in spite of decentralization.

A virtual natural experiment has been going on the Spanish Basque and Catalan regions, both of which developed strong nationalism since the death of Franco. Despite the high levels of fiscal and political self-governance granted to these regions by recent Spanish constitutional reforms, Catalan nationalism has been notably peaceful, while ETA in the Basque country is among the most violent nationalist organizations in the world. Differences in social structure between the two regions may help account for the difference in nationalist violence (Diez-Medrano 1995). While both Basque and Catalan capitalists opposed secession because of their economic dependence on the Spanish state, initial economic development in the two regions differed markedly. The Basque region specialized in the production of capital goods (steel, shipbuilding, and financial services), whereas Catalonia specialized in the production of consumer goods (textiles). As a result, the Basque bourgeoisie was smaller, more concentrated, and more dependent on the Spanish state and markets than its Catalan counterpart. Because they were less dependent than their Basque counterparts, the Catalan élite was more nationalist. This meant that Catalan nationalism had a much broader base of support than its Basque counterpart. Because the Basque bourgeoisie was anti-nationalist, Basque nationalists were fiercely anti-bourgeois. Not so for Catalan nationalists. As a result, Basque nationalism was far more politically extreme than Catalan.

31. Some contend that this indeed happened in Nigeria. 'The Nigerians had been through severe conflict and civil war, and they did not want a repetition. Since no one could be sure which group might be on the receiving end in any future round of ethnic conflict and civil strife, the Nigerians made, not a bargain but a real constitution, not a contract among groups that knew what their interests would be but a social contract among groups that were not sure what their interests might be next time around. They made a blind, Rawlsian contract' (Horowitz 1991: 150). However, it is not enough to whip up principles that are in some sense fair. These principles have to be *perceived* as fair by, and to, the actual parties involved. What any nation can perceive as fair depends, however, on its historical self-understanding. This requirement makes Rawlsian contracts extremely problematic in the real world. To underline the point, at the time of writing the Nigerian regime bears an unmistakable resemblance to a dictatorship.

32. Perceptions of justice are sensitive both to situational norms and to individual interests. These perceptions are partially determined by situational norms (Zajac 1995: 129). Thus, it is legitimate for an airline to compensate passengers for overbooking, but (at least in the USA) it is not legitimate for a customer to buy a better place in a supermarket checkout line. Likewise, the importance of individual interests motivates Rawls's decision to start off from behind a veil of ignorance.

33. To resolve the dissonance, people often construct rationalizations as to why the decision must be a right one—the decision-maker may have had information I did not have, the decision may have fulfilled a greater purpose I did not know about, and so forth. Such rationalization permits us to live with an 'acceptable' level of injustice in our organizations. However, this conservatism is a double-edged sword. Should a person decide that a given procedure is unfair, it is difficult to change that view as applied to any particular outcome (Sheppard *et al.* 1992: 30).

34. Political inclusion traditionally has been regarded as a means of increasing procedural justice (Dryzek 1996). The basis of the idea is simple. If governance is necessarily secret, then the best way of assuring that a group's interests are consistently taken into account in policy-making is by assuring that representatives of the group are party to the relevant decision-making.

35. The advent of the Internet is likely to substantially increase the scope of common knowledge, however.

36. e.g. Francophone Quebecois were less likely to resist conscription in the Second World War than the First World War due to changes of this kind (Levi 1997).

37. Pierre Eliot Trudeau argued that cultural protection does not even benefit the peripheral nation: 'Precisely because they are such a tiny minority in North America, French Canadians must refuse to be enclosed within Quebec. I am opposed to what is called "special status" ... [because, among other reasons] in the long run this status can only tend to weaken values protected in this way against competition. Even more than technology, a culture makes progress through the exchange of ideas and through challenge' (Trudeau 1968: 139).

38. Evidence supporting this contention comes from a cross-national analysis of crime rates in Japan and other advanced industrial societies. Throughout their lives, Japanese are more dependent on a variety of solidary groups—ranging from families, to schools, to firms, to neighbourhoods—than westerners. Further, because these groups impose high levels of visibility on their members, behaviour is more easily monitored in Japan than other large post-industrial societies. This difference in visibility is associated with corresponding variations in crime rates: Japanese crime rates are much lower than those in the West (Hechter and Kanazawa 1993). Experimental research reveals that when they are beyond the reach of such solidary groups, Japanese are less willing to cooperate with strangers than Americans (Yamagishi *et al.* 1998). There is strong evidence that community solidarity reduces violent crime in the USA, as well (Sampson *et al.* 1997).

BIBLIOGRAPHY

Acton, J. E. E. D. (1948). *Essays on Freedom and Power* (Boston, Mass.: Beacon Press).

Agulhon, Maurice (1981). *Marianne into Battle: Republican Imagery and Symbolism in France, 1789–1880* (Cambridge: Cambridge University Press).

Ahrne, Göran (1994). *Social Organizations* (London: Sage).

Akerlof, George (1984). *An Economic Theorist's Book of Tales* (Cambridge: Cambridge University Press).

Akzin, Benjamin (1966). *States and Nations* (New York: Anchor Books).

Alba, Richard D. (1990). *Ethnic Identity* (New Haven, Conn.: Yale University Press).

Alonso, William, and Paul Starr, eds. (1987). *The Politics of Numbers* (New York: Russell Sage Foundation).

Alter, Peter (1989). *Nationalism* (London: Edward Arnold).

Althusius, Johannes (1964). *Politics*, trans. Frederick S. Carney (Boston, Mass.: Beacon Press; originally published 1614).

Anchabadze, I. D., S. A. Arutiunov, and N. G. Volkova (1993). 'The North Caucasus: The National Situation and Ethnic Problems', *Anthropology and Archeaology of Eurasia*, 31: 12–62.

Anderson, Benedict (1983). *Imagined Communities: Reflections on the Origin and Spread of Nationalism* (London: Verso).

——(1992). *Long-Distance Nationalism* (Amsterdam: Centre for Asian Studies).

Armstrong, John A. (1982). *Nations Before Nationalism* (Chapel Hill, NC: University of North Carolina Press).

Ashford, Douglas (1977). 'Are Britain and France "Unitary"?', *Comparative Politics*, 9: 483–99.

Axelrod, Robert (1984). *The Evolution of Cooperation* (New York: Basic Books).

Axtmann, Roland (1993). 'The Formation of the Modern State: The Debate in the Social Sciences', in Mary Fulbrook (ed.), *National Histories and European History* (Boulder, Colo.: Westview), 21–45.

Babb, Sarah (1996). ' "A True American System of Finance": Frame

Resonance in the U. S. Labor Movement, 1866 to 1886', *American Sociological Review*, 61: 1033–52.

Barbash, Fred (1996). 'Publisher Shelves a Book and Uproar Ensues at Cambridge University Press', *International Herald Tribune* (2 May): 9.

Barker, Ernest (1944). *The Development of Public Services in Western Europe, 1660–1930* (New York: Oxford University Press).

Barkey, Karen (1994). *Bandits and Bureaucrats: The Ottoman Route to State Centralization* (Ithaca, NY: Cornell University Press).

——and Sunita Parikh (1991). 'Comparative Perspectives on the State', *Annual Review of Sociology*, 17: 523–49.

——and Mark von Hagen, eds. (1997). *After Empire: Multiethnic Societies and Nation-Building* (Boulder, Colo.: Westview).

Barry, Brian (1995). *Justice as Impartiality* (Oxford: Clarendon Press).

Barth, Fredrik, ed. (1969). *Ethnic Groups and Boundaries* (London: Allen & Unwin).

Bartlett, Robert (1994). *The Making of Europe: Conquest, Colonization, and Cultural Change, 950–1350* (London: Penguin).

Barzel, Yoram (1999). 'Property Rights and the Evolution of the State', *Economics of Governance*, 1 (in press).

Bates, Robert H., Rui J. P. De Figueiredo, jun., and Barry R. Weingast (1998). 'The Politics of Interpretation: Rationality, Culture, and Transition', *Politics and Society*, 26: 221–57.

Bayley, David H. (1975). 'The Police and Political Development in Europe', in Charles Tilly (ed.), *The Formation of the Modern State* (Princeton: Princeton University Press), 328–79.

Beckett, J. C. (1966). *The Making of Modern Ireland: 1603–1923* (London: Faber & Faber).

Beik, William (1985). *Absolutism and Society in Seventeenth Century France: State Power and Provincial Aristocracy in Languedoc* (Cambridge: Cambridge University Press).

Beissinger, Mark R. (1996). 'How Nationalisms Spread: Eastern Europe Adrift in the Tides and Cycles of Nationalism Contention', *Social Research*, 63: 97–146.

——(1998). 'Nationalist Violence and the State: Political Authority and Contentious Repertoires in the Former USSR', *Comparative Politics*, 30: 401–22.

——(forthcoming). 'Nationalism and Violence', in *Encyclopedia of Nationalism*, ed. Alexander J. Motyl.

Bell, Daniel (1975). 'Ethnicity and Social Change', in Nathan Glazer and Daniel P. Moynihan (eds.), *Ethnicity: Theory and Experience* (Cambridge: Harvard University Press).

Bellah, Robert (1988). 'Civil Religion in America', *Daedalus*, 117: 97–118.

Bendix, Reinhard (1974). 'Inequality and Social Structure: A Comparison of Marx and Weber', *American Sociological Review*, 39: 149–61.

Bendor, Jonathan, and Piotr Swistak (1997). 'The Evolutionary Stability of Cooperation', *American Political Science Review*, 91: 290–307.

Bercé, Yves Marie (1987). *Revolt and Revolution in Early Modern Europe* (New York: St Martin's Press).

Berger, Suzanne (1972). *Peasants Against Politics* (Cambridge, Mass.: Harvard University Press).

Berlin, Isaiah (1992). *The Crooked Timber of Humanity* (New York: Pantheon).

Billig, Michael (1995). *Banal Nationalism* (London: Sage).

Bird, R. M. (1986). 'On Measuring Fiscal Centralization and Fiscal Balance in Federal States', *Environment and Planning, C: Government and Policy*, 4: 389–404.

Blau, Peter (1977). *Inequality and Heterogeneity* (New York: Free Press).

Bogatyrev, Petr Grigorevic (1971). *The Function of Folk Costume in Moravian Slovakia* (Paris: Mouton).

Bogdanor, Vernon (1999). *Devolution in the United Kingdom* (Oxford: Oxford University Press).

Bonacich, Edna (1972). 'A Theory of Ethnic Antagonism: The Split-Labor Market', *American Sociological Review*, 37: 533–47.

Boncheck, Mark S. (1995). 'Grassroots in Cyberspace: Using Computer Networks to Facilitate Political Participation', paper presented at the 53rd Annual Meeting of the Midwest Political Science Association. Chicago, Ill.

Bonner, Raymond (1998). 'Tamil Guerillas in Sri Lanka: Deadly and Armed to the Teeth', *The New York Times* (7 Mar.): A1, A5.

Bourdieu, Pierre (1984). *Distinction: A Social Critique of the Judgment of Taste* (Cambridge: Harvard University Press).

Brass, Paul R. (1991). *Ethnicity and Nationalism* (New Delhi: Sage).

Brassloff, Audrey (1989). 'Spain: The State of Autonomies', in Murray G. Forsyth (ed.), *Federalism and Nationalism* (Leicester: Leicester University Press), 24–50.

Braude, Benjamin, and Bernard Lewis, eds. (1982). *Christians and Jews in the Ottoman Empire: The Functioning of a Plural Society* (New York: Holmes & Meier).

Brayshay, Mark, Phillip Harrison, and Brian Chalkley (1998). 'Knowledge, Nationhood and Governance: The Speed of the Royal Post in Early-Modern England', *Journal of Historical Geography*, 24: 265–88.

Breton, Albert (1964). 'Economics of Nationalism', *Journal of Political Economy*, 72: 376–86.

Breton, Albert and Anthony Scott (1980). *The Design of Federations* (Montreal: The Institute for Research on Public Policy).

Breuilly, John (1993). *Nationalism and the State* (Chicago: University of Chicago Press).

Brewer, Marilyn B. (1979). 'Ingroup Bias in the Minimal Intergroup Situation: A Cognitive-Motivational Analysis', *Psychological Bulletin*, 86: 307–34.

Brown, Roger (1986). *Social Psychology: The Second Edition* (New York: Free Press).

Brubaker, Rogers (1992). *Citizenship and Nationhood in France and Germany* (Cambridge, Mass.: Harvard University Press).

——(1996). *Nationalism Reframed: Nationhood and the National Question in the New Europe* (Cambridge: Cambridge University Press).

——and David D. Laitin (1998). 'Ethnic and Nationalist Violence', *Annual Review of Sociology*, 24: 423–52.

Brustein, William (1985). 'Class Conflict and Class Collaboration in Regional Rebellions, 1500–1700', *Theory and Society*, 14: 445–68.

——(1988). *The Social Origins of Political Regionalism: France, 1849–1981* (Berkeley, Calif.: University of California Press).

——(1996). *The Logic of Evil* (New Haven, Conn.: Yale University Press).

——and Margaret Levi (1987). 'The Geography of Rebellion: Rulers, Rebels and Regions, 1500 to 1700', *Theory and Society*, 16: 467–96.

Buchanan, Alan (1991). *Secession: The Morality of Political Divorce from Fort Sumter to Lithuania and Quebec* (Boulder, Colo.: Westview).

Bunce, Valerie (1999). 'Peaceful versus Violent State Dismemberment: A Comparison of the Soviet Union, Yugoslavia and Czechoslovakia', *Politics and Society*, 27: 217–37.

Burg, Steven L. (1988). 'Political Structures', in Dennison Rusinow (ed.), *Yugoslavia: A Fractured Federalism* (Washington, DC: The Wilson Center Press), 9–22.

Burckhardt, Jacob (1958). *The Civilization of the Renaissance in Italy*, trans. S. G. C. Middlemore (New York: Harper; originally published 1860).

Burt, Ronald S. (1992). *Structural Holes: The Social Structure of Competition* (Cambridge, Mass.: Harvard University Press).

Byock, Jesse (1988). *Medieval Iceland: Society, Sagas and Power* (Berkeley, Calif.: University of California Press).

Calhoun, Craig (1991). 'The Problem of Identity in Collective Action', in Joan Huber (ed.), *Macro–Micro Linkages in Sociology* (Newbury Park, Calif.: Sage), 51–75.

——(1997). *Nationalism* (Minneapolis: University of Minnesota Press).

Campbell, Bernard G. (1966). *Human Evolution* (Chicago: Aldine).

Canny, Nicholas (1998). 'The Origins of Empire: An Introduction', in N. Canny (ed.), *The Oxford History of the British Empire*, i. *The Origins of Empire* (Oxford: Oxford University Press), 1–34.

Castells, Manuel (1997). *The Power of Identity* (Oxford: Blackwell).

Chai, Sun-Ki (1993). 'An Organizational Economics Theory of Anti-Government Violence', *Comparative Politics*, 26: 99–110.

——(1996). 'A Theory of Ethnic Group Boundaries', *Nations and Nationalism*, 2: 281–307.

—— and Michael Hechter (1998). 'A Theory of the State and of Social Order', in Patrick Doreian and Thomas Fararo (eds.), *The Problem of Solidarity* (New York: Gordon & Breach), 33–60.

Chartrand, Jean-Philippe, and J. Iain Prattis (1990). 'The Cultural Division of Labour in the Canadian North: The Implications for Multiculturalism Policy and the Inuit', *Canadian Review of Sociology and Anthropology*, 27: 49–73.

Chatterjee, Partha (1993). *Nationalist Thought and the Colonial World* (Minneapolis: University of Minnesota Press).

Chazan, Naomi (1991*a*). 'Approaches to the Study of Irredentism', in Naomi Chazan (ed.), *Irredentism and International Politics* (Boulder, Colo.: Lynne Rienner), 1–22.

—— ed. (1991*b*). *Irredentism and International Politics* (Boulder, Colo.: Lynne Rienner).

Christie, Clive J. (1996). *A Modern History of Southeast Asia: Decolonization, Nationalism and Separatism* (London: I. B. Tauris).

Cialdini, R. B., J. F. Finch, and M. E. DeNicholas (1989). 'Strategic Self-Presentation: The Indirect Route', in M. J. Cody and M. L. McLaughlin (eds.), *The Psychology of Tactical Communication* (London: Multilingual Matters), 194–206.

Clausewitz, Carl Von (1984). *On War* Trans. M. Howard and P. Paret (Princeton: Princeton University Press; originally published 1827).

Coakley, John (1994). 'Approaches to the Resolution of Ethnic Conflict: The Strategy of Non-Territorial Autonomy', *International Political Science Review*, 15: 297–314.

Cohen, Lenard J. (1995). *Broken Bonds: Yugoslavia's Disintegration and Balkan Politics in Transition* (Boulder, Colo.: Westview).

Cohen, Ronald, and Elman R. Service, eds. (1978). *Origins of the State* (Philadelphia: Institute for the Study of Human Issues).

Cole, Fuan R. I., and Moojan Momen (1986). 'Mafia, Mob and Shiism in Iraq: The Rebellion of Ottoman Karbala, 1824–1843', *Past and Present*, 112: 112–43.

Cole, Sam (1993). 'Cultural Accounting in Small Economies', *Regional Studies*, 27: 121–36.

——(1994). 'Cultural Accounting in a Small Caribbean Island', *Contemporary Economic Policy*, 12: 1–12.

Coleman, James S. (1961). *The Adolescent Society* (Glencoe, Ill.: Free Press).

——(1993). 'The Rational Reconstruction of Society', *American Sociological Review*, 58: 1–15.

Colley, Linda (1992). *Britons: Forging the Nation, 1707–1837* (New Haven, Conn.: Yale University Press).

Connor, Walker (1972). 'Nation-Building or Nation-Destroying?', *World Politics*, 24: 319–55.

Cook, Karen S., and Toshio Yamagishi (1992). 'Power in Exchange Networks: A Power-Dependence Formulation', *Social Networks*, 14: 245–66.

Cornell, Stephen, and Joseph P. Kalt (1998). 'Sovereignty and Nation-Building: The Development Challenge in Indian Country Today', *American Indian Culture and Research Journal*, 22: 187–214.

Corse, Sarah M. (1997). *Nationalism and Literature: The Politics of Culture in Canada and the United States* (Cambridge: Cambridge University Press).

Coté, Marcel, and David Johnston (1995). *If Quebec Goes . . . : The Real Cost of Separation* (Toronto: Stoddard).

Cowell, Alan (1998). 'Neo-Nazis Carving Out Fiefs in Eastern Germany', *The New York Times* (8 Feb.): 1/3.

Crone, Patricia (1986). 'The Tribe and the State', in John A. Hall (ed.), *States in History* (Oxford: Basil Blackwell), 48–77.

Curtis, Edmund (1936). *A History of Ireland* (London: Methuen).

D'Altroy, Terence N. (1992). *Provincial Power in the Inka Empire* (Washington, DC: Smithsonian Institution Press).

Dandeker, Chris (1990). *Surveillance, Power and Modernity: Bureaucracy and Discipline from 1700 to the Present Day* (Cambridge: Polity Press).

Daniel, E. Valentine (1996). *Charred Lullabies: Chapters in an Anthropography of Violence* (Princeton: Princeton University Press).

Daniels, Stephen (1993). *Fields of Vision: Landscape Imagery and National Identity in England and the United States* (Cambridge: Polity Press).

Darby, John (1987). 'Northern Ireland: The Persistence and Limitations of Violence', in Joseph V. Montville (ed.), *Conflict and Peacemaking in Multiethnic Societies* (Lexington, Mass.: Lexington Books), 151–60.

——(1994). 'Legitimate Targets: A Control on Violence?', in Adrian Guelke (ed.), *New Perspectives on the Northern Ireland Conflict* (Aldershot: Avebury).

Davies, Charlotte Aull (1989). *Welsh Nationalism in the Twentieth Century* (New York: Praeger).

Davison, Roderic (1963). *Reform in the Ottoman Empire, 1856–1876* (Princeton: Princeton University Press).

Dawkins, Richard (1989). *The Selfish Gene* (Oxford: Oxford University Press).

De Palma, Anthony (1997). 'To Some Canadians, the Maple Leaf is a Red Flag', *The New York Times* (26 Nov.): A4.

De Swaan, Abram (1988). *In Care of the State: Health Care, Education, and Welfare in Europe and the USA in the Modern Era* (Cambridge: Polity Press).

Dennett, Daniel C. (1995). *Darwin's Dangerous Idea* (New York: Simon & Schuster).

Denzau, Arthur T., and Douglass C. North (1994). 'Shared Mental Models: Ideologies and Institutions', *Kyklos*, 47: 3–31.

Derry, T. K. (1979). *A History of Scandinavia* (Minneapolis: University of Minnesota Press).

Deutsch, Karl (1966). *Nationalism and Social Communication* 2nd ed. (Cambridge, Mass.: MIT Press).

Diaz-Andreu, Margarita, and T. C. Champion (1995). *Nationalism and Archaeology in Europe* (London: University College London Press).

Dietler, Michael (1994). ' "Our Ancestors the Gauls": Archaeology, Ethnic Nationalism and the Manipulation of Celtic Identity in Modern Europe', *American Anthropologist*, 96: 584–605.

Diez-Medrano, Juan (1994). 'The Effects of Ethnic Segregation and Ethnic Competition on Political Mobilization in the Basque Country, 1988', *American Sociological Review*, 59: 873–90.

——(1995). *Divided Nations: Class, Politics and Nationalism in the Basque Country and Catalonia* (Ithaca, NY: Cornell University Press).

Dikshit, R. (1975). *The Political Geography of Federalism: An Inquiry into its Origins and Stability* (Delhi: Macmillan).

Dryzek, John S. (1996). 'Political Inclusion and the Dynamics of Democratization', *American Political Science Review*, 90: 475–87.

Duchacek, Ivo (1970). *Comparative Federalism: The Territorial Dimension of Politics* (New York: Holt, Rinehardt & Winston).

Düding, Dieter (1987). 'The Nineteenth-Century German Nationalist Movement as a Movement of Societies', in Hagen Schulze (ed.), *Nation-Building in Central Europe* (Leamington Spa: Berg), 19–50.

Durkheim, Emile (1965). *The Elementary Forms of Religious Life*, trans. Joseph Ward Swain (New York: Free Press; originally published 1912).

Earle, Timothy (1997). *How Chiefs Come to Power: The Political Economy in Prehistory* (Stanford, Calif.: Stanford University Press).

Elazar, Daniel (1994). *Federal Systems of the World: A Handbook of Federal, Confederal, and Autonomy Arrangements* (New York: Stockton).

Eley, Geoff, and Ronald Grigor Suny, eds. (1996*a*). *Becoming National* (New York: Oxford University Press).

——and——(1996*b*). 'Introduction', in Eley and Suny (eds.), *Becoming National* (New York: Oxford University Press), 3–37.

Ellickson, Robert C. (1993). 'Property in Land', *Yale Law Journal*, 102: 1315–400.

Ellis, Steven G. (1995). *Tudor Frontiers and Noble Power: The Making of the British State* (Oxford: Clarendon Press).

Elster, Jon, Claus Offe, and Ulrich K. Preuss (1998). *Institutional Design in Post-Communist Societies: Rebuilding the Ship at Sea* (Cambridge: Cambridge University Press).

Elton, G. R. (1982). *The Tudor Constitution: Documents and Commentary* (Cambridge: Cambridge University Press).

Emerson, Rupert (1937). *Malaysia: A Study in Direct and Indirect Rule* (New York: Macmillan).

Emsley, Clive (1993). 'Peasants, Gendarmes and State Formation', in Mary Fulbrook (ed.), *National Histories and European History* (Boulder, Colo.: Westview), 69–93.

Eriksen, Thomas Hylland (1993). *Ethnicity and Nationalism: Anthropological Perspectives* (London: Pluto Press).

Ertman, Thomas (1997). *Birth of the Leviathan: Building States and Regimes in Medieval and Early Modern Europe* (Cambridge: Cambridge University Press).

Esman, Marjorie (1984). 'Tourism as Ethnic Preservation: The Cajuns of Louisiana', *Annals of Tourism Research*, 11: 451–67.

Evans, Geoffrey, and Mary Duffy (1997). 'Beyond the Sectarian Divide: The Social Bases and Political Consequences of Nationalist and Unionist Party Competition in Northern Ireland', *British Journal of Political Science*, 27: 47–81.

Evans-Pritchard, E. E. (1944). *The Nuer* (Oxford: Oxford University Press).

Fearon, James D. (1994). 'Ethnic War as a Commitment Problem', paper presented at Annual Meeting of the American Political Science Association, New York.

——and David D. Laitin (1996). 'Explaining Interethnic Cooperation', *American Political Science Review*, 90: 715–35.

Festinger, Leon (1954). 'A Theory of Social Comparison Processes', *Human Relations*, 7: 117–40.

Finer, Samuel E. (1975). 'State- and Nation-Building in Europe: The Role of the Military', in Charles Tilly (ed.), *The Formation of National States in Western Europe* (Princeton: Princeton University Press), 84–163.

Fischer, Claude S. (1992). *America Calling: A Social History of the Telephone to 1940* (Berkeley, Calif.: University of California Press).

Fischer, David Hackett (1989). *Albion's Seed: Four British Folkways in America* (New York: Oxford University Press).

Fisher, Alan (1977). 'Crimean Separatism in the Ottoman Empire', in William W. Haddad and William Oschenwald (eds.), *Nationalism in a Non-National State: The Dissolution of the Ottoman Empire* (Columbus, Ohio: Ohio State University Press), 57–76.

Fisher, Michael H. (1991). *Indirect Rule in India: Residents and the Residency System, 1764–1858* (Delhi: Oxford University Press).

Fisher, Ronald A. (1930). *The Genetical Theory of Natural Selection* (Oxford: Clarendon Press).

Forbes, H. D. (1997). *Ethnic Conflict: Commerce, Culture and the Contact Hypothesis* (New Haven, Conn.: Yale University Press).

Ford, Caroline (1993). *Creating the Nation in Provincial France* (Princeton: Princeton University Press).

Forsythe, Diana (1989). 'German Identity and the Problem of History', in Elizabeth Tonkin, Malcolm Chapman, and Maryon McDonald (eds.), *History and Ethnicity* (London: Routledge).

Fox, Richard G., Charlotte H. Aull, and Louis F. Cimino (1981). 'Ethnic Nationalism and the Welfare State', in Charles F. Keyes (ed.), *Ethnic Change* (Seattle: University of Washington Press), 198–245.

Frank, Robert (1985). *Choosing the Right Pond* (New York: Oxford University Press).

Freud, Sigmund (1961). *Civilization and its Discontents*, trans. James Strachey (New York: Norton & Company; originally published 1930).

Fried, Morton H. (1967). *The Evolution of Political Society* (New York: Random House).

Friedman, David (1977). 'A Theory of the Size and Shape of Nations', *Journal of Political Economy*, 85: 59–77.

Friedman, Debra (1990). 'Toward a Theory of Union Emergence and Demise', in Michael Hechter, Karl-Dieter Opp, and Reinhard Wippler (eds.), *Social Institutions: Their Emergence, Maintenance and Effects* (New York: Aldine de Gruyter), 291–306.

——Michael Hechter, and Satoshi Kanazawa (1994). 'A Theory of the Value of Children', *Demography*, 31: 375–401.

Gambetta, Diego (1993). *The Sicilian Mafia: The Business of Private Protection* (Cambridge, Mass.: Harvard University Press).

Gamble, Clive (1986). 'Hunter-Gatherers and the Origin of States', in John A. Hall (ed.), *States in History* (Oxford: Basil Blachwell), 22–47.

Geertz, Clifford (1963). 'The Integrative Revolution: Primordial Sentiments and Civil Politics in the New States', in Clifford Geertz (ed.), *Old Societies and New States* (Glencoe, Ill.: Free Press), 105–58.

Gellner, Ernest (1983). *Nations and Nationalism* (Ithaca, NY, and London: Cornell University Press).

Genovese, Eugene D. (1994). *The Southern Tradition: The Achievement and Limitations of an American Conservatism* (Cambridge, Mass.: Harvard University Press).

Gewehr, Wesley M. (1967). *The Rise of Nationalism in the Balkans, 1800–1930* (New York: Archon Books).

Gibson, Ralph (1994). 'The Intensification of Nationalist Consciousness in Modern Europe', in Claus Bjørn, Alexander Grant, and Keith J. Stringer (eds.), *Nations, Nationalism and Patriotism in the European Past* (Copenhagen: Academic Press Copenhagen).

Glazer, Nathan (1977). 'Federalism and Ethnicity: The Experience of the United States', *Publius*, 7: 71–87.

Glenny, Misha (1993). *The Fall of Yugoslavia* (New York: Penguin).

Glick, Thomas F. (1970). *Irrigation and Society in Medieval Valencia* (Cambridge, Mass.: Belknap Press of Harvard University Press).

Gligorov, Vladimir (1994). 'Is What's Left Right?', in Janós Matyás Kovacs (ed.), *Transition to Capitalism? The Communist Legacy in Eastern Europe* (New Brunswick, NJ: Transaction), 147–72.

Goffman, Erving (1963). *Stigma: Notes on the Management of Spoiled Identity* (Englewood Cliffs, NJ: Prentice-Hall).

Goldstone, Jack A. (1991). *Revolution and Rebellion in the Early Modern World* (Berkeley, Calif.: University of California Press).

Gould, Roger V. (1994). *Insurgent Identities: Class, Community and Protest in Paris from 1848 to the Commune* (Chicago: University of Chicago Press).

——(1996). 'Patron–Client Ties, State Centralization, and the Whiskey Rebellion', *American Journal of Sociology*, 102: 400–29.

Granovetter, Mark (1978). 'Threshold Models of Collective Behavior', *American Journal of Sociology*, 83: 1420–43.

Greenfeld, Liah (1992). *Nationalism* (Cambridge, Mass.: Harvard University Press).

Greif, Avner, Paul Milgrom, and Barry R. Weingast (1994). 'Coordination, Commitment, and Enforcement: The Case of the Merchant Guild', *Journal of Political Economy*, 102: 745–76.

Griffiths, P., A. Fox, and S. Hindle, eds. (1996). *The Experience of Authority in Early-Modern England* (London: Macmillan).

Grillo, R. D. (1998). *Pluralism and the Politics of Difference: State, Culture, and Ethnicity in Comparative Perspective* (Oxford: Clarendon Press).

Gurr, Ted Robert (1993). *Minorities at Risk: A Global View of Ethnopolitical Conflicts* (Washington, DC: United States Institute of Peace Press).

——(1994). 'Peoples Against States: Ethnopolitical Conflict and the Changing World System', *International Studies Quarterly*, 38: 347–77.

Haas, Ernst B. (1997). *Nationalism, Liberalism, and Progress*, i. *The Rise and Decline of Nationalism* (Ithaca, NY: Cornell University Press).

Habermas, Jurgen (1994). 'Citizenship and National Identity', in Bart van Steenbergen (ed.), *The Condition of Citizenship* (London: Sage), 20–35.

Hachey, T. E. (1973). *The Problem of Partition* (Chicago: Rand-McNally).

Hale, William (1994). *Turkish Politics and the Military* (London: Routledge).

Hall, John A. (1993). 'Nationalisms: Classified and Explained', *Daedalus*, 122/3: 1–28.

Hamilton, William D. (1964). 'The Genetical Evolution of Social Behaviour', *Journal of Theoretical Biology*, 7: 1–52.

Hancock, M. D. (1972). *Sweden: The Politics of Post-Industrial Change* (Hinsdale, Ill.: Dryden).

Hardin, Russell (1981). *Collective Action* (Baltimore, Md.: Johns Hopkins University Press for Resources for the Future).

——(1995). *One for All: The Logic of Group Conflict* (Princeton: Princeton University Press).

Hassig, Ross (1985). *Trade, Tribute and Transportation: The Sixteenth Century Political Economy of the Valley of Mexico* (Norman, Okla.: University of Oklahoma Press).

——(1988). *Aztec Warfare: Imperial Expansion and Political Control* (Norman, Okla.: University of Oklahoma Press).

Hayden, Robert M. (1998). 'The State as Legal Fiction', *East European Constitutional Review*, 7: 45–50.

Hayward, Jack (1973). *The One Indivisible French Republic* (New York: W. W. Norton).

Hechter, Michael (1978). 'Group Formation and the Cultural Division of Labor', *American Journal of Sociology*, 84: 293–318.

——(1987). *Principles of Group Solidarity* (Berkeley, Calif.: University of California Press).

——(1990a). 'The Emergence of Cooperative Social Institutions', in Michael Hechter, Karl-Dieter Opp, and Reinhard Wippler (eds.), *Social Institutions: Their Emergence, Maintenance, and Effects* (New York: Aldine de Gruyter), 13–34.

218 *Bibliography*

Hechter, Michael (1990*b*). 'Nonconformity and the Emergence of Nationalism in Nineteenth Century Wales', in Hans Heinrich Nolte (ed.), *Internal Peripheries in Europe* (Gottingen and Zurich: Muster-Schmidt Verlag),
45–66.

——(1994*a*). 'Review of Olzak, *Dynamics of Ethnic Competition and Conflict*', *European Sociological Review*, 10: 96–8.

——(1994*b*). 'The Role of Values in Rational Choice Theory', *Rationality
and Society*, 6: 318–33.

——(1995). 'Explaining Nationalist Violence', *Nations and Nationalism*, 1:
53–68.

——(1999). *Internal Colonialism: The Celtic Fringe in British National Development* (New Brunswick, NJ: Transaction; originally published 1975).

——and William Brustein (1980). 'Regional Modes of Production and Patterns of State Formation in Western Europe', *American Journal of Sociology*, 85: 1067–94.

——and Satoshi Kanazawa (1993). 'Group Solidarity and Social Order in
Japan', *Journal of Theoretical Politics*, 3: 455–93.

——and Margaret Levi (1979). 'The Comparative Analysis of Ethnoregional
Movements', *Ethnic and Racial Studies*, 2: 262–74.

——and Nobuyuki Takahashi (1999). 'Political Decentralization and
Nationalist Conflict', paper presented at Annual Meeting of the American
Sociological Association, Chicago, Ill.

——Debra Friedman, and Satoshi Kanazawa (1992). 'The Attainment of
Global Order in Heterogeneous Societies', in James S. Coleman and
Thomas J. Fararo (eds.), *Rational Choice Theory: Advocacy and Critique*
(Newbury Park, Calif.: Sage), 79–97.

——James Ranger-Moore, Guillermina Jasso, and Christine Horne (1999).
'Do Values Matter? An Analysis of Advance Directives for Medical Treatment', *European Sociological Review*, 15: 405–30.

Heckathorn, Douglas D. (1989). 'Collective Action and the Second-Order
Free Rider Problem', *Rationality and Society*, 1: 78–100.

Heckscher, Eli F. (1955). *Mercantilism* (London: Allen & Unwin).

Hedges, Chris (1998*a*). 'Another Victory for Death in Serbia', *The New York
Times* (8 Mar.): V5.

——(1998*b*). 'Gun Battles in Serbia Raise Fear of "Another Bosnia"', *The
New York Times* (6 Mar.): A3.

Henderson, William O. (1984). *The Zollervein* (London: Frank Cass).

Heper, Metin (1985). *The State Tradition in Turkey* (Hull: The Eothen Press
at the University of Hull).

Heraclides, Alexis (1990). *The Self-Determination of Minorities in International Politics* (London: Frank Cass).

Hinsley, F. H. (1966). *Sovereignty* (London: C. A. Watts).

Hintze, Otto (1975). 'Military Organization and State Organization', in *The Historical Essays of Otto Hintze*, ed. Felix Gilbert (Oxford: Oxford University Press), 180–215.

Hirschman, Albert O. (1970). *Exit, Voice and Loyalty* (Cambridge, Mass.: Harvard University Press).

Hobsbawm, Eric (1983*a*). 'Introduction: Inventing Traditions', in Eric Hobsbawm and Terence Ranger (eds.), *The Invention of Tradition* (Cambridge: Cambridge University Press), 1–14.

——(1983*b*). 'Mass Producing Traditions', in Eric Hobsbawm and Terence Ranger (eds.), *The Invention of Tradition* (Cambridge: Cambridge University Press), 263–307.

——(1992). *Nations and Nationalism since 1780: Programme, Myth, Reality* (Cambridge: Cambridge University Press).

——and Terence Ranger, eds. (1983). *The Invention of Tradition* (Cambridge: Cambridge University Press).

Hoge, Warren (1999). 'Blair's Party Finishes First in Scottish and Welsh Voting', *The New York Times* (8 May): A3.

Hölldobler, Bert, and Edward O. Wilson (1994). *Journey to the Ants: The Story of a Scientific Exploration* (Cambridge, Mass.: The Belknap Press of Harvard University Press).

Holt, J. C. (1992). *The Northerners: A Study in the Reign of King John* (Oxford: Oxford University Press).

Homans, George C. (1950). *The Human Group* (New York: Harcourt, Brace).

Horowitz, Donald L. (1985). *Ethnic Groups in Conflict* (Berkeley, Calif.: University of California Press).

——(1991). *A Democratic South Africa? Constitutional Engineering in a Divided Society* (Berkeley, Calif.: University of California Press).

——(1992). 'Irredentas and Secessions: Adjacent Phenomena, Neglected Connections', *International Journal of Comparative Sociology*, 32: 118–30.

Horowitz, Eliott (1994). 'Visages du judaïsme: De la barbe en monde juif et de l'élaboration de ses significations', *Annales: Histoire, Sciences Sociales*, 49: 1065–90.

Hroch, Miroslav (1985). *Social Preconditions of National Revival in Europe: A Comparative Analysis of the Social Composition of Patriotic Groups Among the Smaller European Nations* (Cambridge: Cambridge University Press).

Hughes, Everett (1943). *French Canada in Transition* (Chicago: University of Chicago Press).

Hughes, Everett and Helen M. Hughes (1952). *Where Peoples Meet: Ethnic and Racial Frontiers* (Glencoe, Ill.: Free Press).

Hutchinson, John, and Anthony D. Smith, eds. (1994). *Nationalism: An Oxford Reader* (Oxford: Oxford University Press).

Imsen, Steinmar, and Gunter Vogler (1997). 'Commmunal Autonomy and Peasant Resistance in Northern and Central Europe', in Peter Blickle (ed.), *Resistance, Representation, and Community* (Oxford: Clarendon Press for the European Science Foundation), 5–43.

Inalcik, Halil (1970). 'The Heyday and Decline of the Ottoman Empire', in *The Cambridge History of Islam*, ed. P. M. Holt, K. S. Lambton, and Bernard Lewis (Cambridge: Cambridge University Press), 324–53.

——(1976). *Application of the Tanzimat and its Social Effects* (Lisse, Belgium: Peter de Ridder Press).

——(1995). *From Empire to Republic* (Istanbul: Isis Press).

Jankowski, Martín Sánchez (1991). *Islands in the Street: Gangs and American Urban Society* (Berkeley, Calif.: University of California Press).

Jászi, Oscar (1929). *The Dissolution of the Habsburg Monarchy* (Chicago: University of Chicago Press).

Jennings, M. Kent (1998). 'Political Trust and the Roots of Devolution', in Valerie Braithwaite and Margaret Levi (eds.), *Trust and Governance* (New York: Russell Sage Foundation), 218–44.

Johnson, Allen W., and Timothy Earle (1987). *The Evolution of Human Societies* (Stanford, Calif.: Stanford University Press).

Johnson, Gregory (1982). 'Organizational Structure and Scalar Stress', in Colin Renfrew, Michael J. Rowlands, and Barbara A. Seagrave (eds.), *Theory and Explanation in Archaeology* (New York: Academic Press), 389–421.

Johnson, Harry G. (1965). 'A Theoretical Model of Economic Nationalism in New and Developing States', *Political Science Quarterly*, 80: 169–85.

Kaiser, Robert (1994). *The Geography of Nationalism in Russia and the USSR* (Princeton: Princeton University Press).

——(1990). 'The Equalization Dilemma in Yugoslavia', *Geoforum*, 21: 261–76.

Kakar, Sudhir (1996). *The Colors of Violence: Cultural Identities, Religion, and Conflict* (Chicago: University of Chicago Press).

Kanazawa, Satoshi (1997). 'A Solidaristic Theory of Social Order', *Advances in Group Processes*, 14: 81–111.

Kaplan, Gisela (1997). 'Feminism and Nationalism: The European Case', in Lois A. West (ed.), *Feminist Nationalism* (New York: Routledge), 3–40.

Karakasidou, Anastasia N. (1997). *Fields of Wheat, Hills of Blood: Passages to Nationhood in Greek Macedonia, 1870–1990* (Chicago: University of Chicago Press).

Karpat, Kemal (1968). 'The Land Regime, Social Structure, and Modernization in the Ottoman Empire', in William R. Polk and Richard L. Chambers (eds.), *Beginnings of Modernization in the Middle East: The Nineteenth Century* (Chicago. University of Chicago Press).

——(1972). 'The Transformation of the Ottoman State, 1789–1908', *International Journal of Middle East Studies*, 3: 243–81.

——(1973). *An Inquiry into the Social Foundations of Nationalism in the Ottoman State: From Social Estates to Classes, From Millets to Nations* (Princeton: Princeton University Press).

Kayali, Hasan (1997). *Arabs and Young Turks: Ottomanism, Arabism, and Islamism in the Ottoman Empire, 1908–1918* (Berkeley, Calif.: University of California Press).

Kedourie, Elie (1960). *Nationalism* (London: Praeger).

Kennedy, K. D. (1982). 'Lessons and Learners: Elementary Education in Southern Germany, 1871–1914', in *Education* (Stanford, Calif.: Stanford University).

Kennedy, Paul (1973). 'The Decline of Nationalistic History in the West, 1900–1970', *Journal of Contemporary History*, 8: 77–100.

Keyder, Caglar (1997). 'The Ottoman Empire', in Karen Barkey and Mark Von Hagen (eds.), *After Empire: Multiethnic Societies and Nation-Building* (Boulder, Colo.: Westview), 30–44.

Keyfitz, Nathan (1987). 'The Family that Does Not Reproduce Itself', in Kingsley Davis, Michael S. Bernstam, and Rita Ricardo-Campbell (eds.), *Below-Replacement Fertility in Industrial Societies: Causes, Consequences, Policies* (Cambridge: Cambridge University Press).

Kiesewetter, Hubert (1987). 'Economic Preconditions for Germany's Nation-Building in the Nineteenth Century', in Hagen Schulze (ed.), *Nation-Building in Central Europe* (Leamington Spa: Berg), 81–106.

King, Preston (1982). *Federalism and Federation* (London: Croom Helm).

Kiser, Edgar, and Joachim Schneider (1994). 'Bureaucracy and Efficiency: An Analysis of Taxation in Early Modern Prussia', *American Sociological Review*, 59: 187–204.

Kohl, Philip L. (1998). 'Nationalism and Archaeology: On the Constructions of Nations and the Reconstrions of the Remote Past', *Annual Review of Anthropology*, 27: 223–46.

——and Clare Fawcett, eds. (1995). *Nationalism, Politics and the Practice of Archaeology* (Cambridge: Cambridge University Press).

Kohn, Hans (1944). *The Idea of Nationalism* (New York: Macmillan).

Kollock, Peter (1998). 'The Economies of Online Cooperation: Gifts and Public Goods in Cyberspace', in Marc Smith and Peter Kollock (eds.), *Communities in Cyberspace* (London: Routledge).

Kuhn, Philip A. (1980). *Rebellion and its Enemies in Late Imperial China* (Cambridge, Mass.: Harvard University Press).

Kuran, Timur (1996). *Private Truths and Public Lies* (Cambridge: Harvard University Press).

——(1998). 'Ethnic Norms and their Transformation through Reputational Cascades', *Journal of Legal Studies*, 27: 623–60.

Kymlicka, Will (1996). 'Social Unity in a Liberal State', *Social Philosophy and Policy*, 13: 105–36.

Laitin, David D. (1992). *Language Repertoires and State Construction in Africa* (New York: Cambridge University Press).

——(1998). *Identity in Formation: The Russian-Speaking Populations in the Near Abroad* (Ithaca, NY: Cornell University Press).

Landa, Janet T. (1994). *Trust, Ethnicity, and Identity: Beyond the New Institutional Economics of Ethnic Trading Networks, Contract Law, and Gift-Exchange* (Ann Arbor, Mich.: University of Michigan Press).

Lapidus, Gail W., and Victor Zaslavsky, eds. (1992). *From Union to Commonwealth: Nationalism and Separatism in the Soviet Republics* (Cambridge: Cambridge University Press).

Laponce, Jean A. (1960). *The Protection of Minorities* (Berkeley, Calif.: University of California Press).

Larsen, Karen (1948). *A History of Norway* (Princeton: Princeton University Press).

Lee, P. C. (1994). 'Social Structure and Evolution', in P. J. B. Slater and Tim R. Halliday (eds.), *Behavior and Evolution* (Cambridge: Cambridge University Press), 266–303.

Lega Nord (1997). 'Welcome to Padania: Official World Wide Web Site (10/29/97)': http://www.leganordsen.it/eng/index.htm.

Leoussi, Athena S. (1998). *Nationalism and Classicism: The Classical Body as National Symbol in Nineteenth-Century England and France* (London: Macmillan).

Leslie, Peter M. (1996). 'The Cultural Dimension', in Joachim Jens Hesse and Vincent Wright (eds.), *Federalizing Europe? The Costs, Benefits, and Preconditions of Federal Political Systems* (Oxford: Oxford University Press), 121–65.

Levi, Margaret (1988). *Of Rule and Revenue* (Berkeley, Calif.: University of California Press).

——(1997). *Consent, Dissent, and Patriotism* (Cambridge: Cambridge University Press).

Lewis, Bernard (1977). *History: Remembered, Recovered, Invented* (Princeton: Princeton University Press).

Lichbach, Mark (1995). *The Rebel's Dilemma* (Ann Arbor, Mich.: University of Michigan Press).

Lieberson, Stanley (1994). 'Understanding Ascriptive Stratification: Some Issues and Principles', in David Grusky (ed.), *Social Stratification* (Boulder, Colo.: Westview), 649–56.

Lijphart, Arend (1977). *Democracy in Plural Societies: A Comparative Exploration* (New Haven, Conn.: Yale University Press).

——(1984). *Democracies: Patterns of Majoritarian and Consensus Government in Twenty-One Countries* (New Haven, Conn.: Yale University Press).

——(1991). 'The Alternative Vote: A Realistic Alternative for South Africa?', *Politikon*, 18: 91–101.

Linz, Juan J., and Alfred Stepan (1996). *Problems of Democratic Transition and Consolidation* (Baltimore, Md.: Johns Hopkins University Press).

Lipset, Seymour Martin, and Earl Raab (1995). *Jews and the New American Scene* (Cambridge, Mass.: Harvard University Press).

Livezeanu, Irina (1995). *Cultural Politics in Greater Romania: Regionalism, Nation-Building and Ethnic Struggle, 1918–1930* (Ithaca, NY: Cornell University Press).

Livingston, Donald W. (1998). *Philosophical Melancholy and Delirium: Hume's Pathology of Philosophy* (Chicago: University of Chicago Press).

Lustick, Ian S. (1993). *Unsettled States, Disputed Lands: Britain and Ireland, France and Algeria, Israel and the West Bank-Gaza* (Ithaca, NY: Cornell University Press).

Luttwak, Edward N. (1976). *The Grand Strategy of the Roman Empire from the First Century A.D. to the Third* (Baltimore, Md.: Johns Hopkins University Press).

McAdam, Doug (1982). *Political Process and the Development of Black Insurgency, 1930–1970* (Chicago: University of Chicago Press).

——John D. McCarthy, and Mayer N. Zald (1996). *Comparative Perspectives on Social Movements: Political Opportunities, Mobilizing Structures, and Cultural Framings* (New York: Cambridge University Press).

MaCardle, Dorothy (1965). *The Irish Republic* (New York: Farar, Straus & Giroux).

McCarthy, Justin (1995). *Death and Exile: The Ethnic Cleansing of Ottoman Muslims, 1821–1922* (Princeton, NJ: The Darwin Press).

MacDonagh, Oliver (1968). *Ireland* (Englewood Cliffs, NJ: Prentice-Hall).

MacDonald, David W. (1983). 'The Ecology of Carnivore Social Behavior', *Nature*, 301: 379–84.

McGarry, J., and Brendan O'Leary, eds. (1993). *The Politics of Ethnic Conflict Regulation* (London: Routledge).

McGirk, Tim (1995). 'Boys and Girls', *Independent* (London, 26 Feb.), 10–14.

MacIver, Robert (1937). *Society* (New York: Farar & Rinehart).

MacKenzie, David (1996). *Violent Solutions: Revolutions, Nationalism, and Secret Societies in Europe to 1918* (Lanham, Md.: University Press of America).

McKenzie, W. J. M., and J. W. Grove (1957). *Central Administration in Britain* (New York: Longmans, Green & Co.).

McNeill, William H. (1964). *Europe's Steppe Frontier, 1500–1800* (Chicago: University of Chicago Press).

——(1986). *Polyethnicity and National Unity in World History* (Toronto: Toronto University Press).

McRoberts, Kenneth (1980). *Quebec: Social Change and Political Crisis* (Toronto: McClelland & Stewart).

McWhiney, Grady (1988). *Cracker Culture: Celtic Ways in the Old South* (Tuscaloosa: University of Alabama Press).

Machin, Howard (1977). *The Prefect in French Public Administration* (London: Croom Helm).

Mackie, Gerald (1996). 'Ending Footbinding and Infibulation: A Convention Account', *American Sociological Review*, 61: 999–1017.

Mair, Lucy (1977). *Primitive Government* (London: Scolar Press).

Mamdani, Mahmood (1996). *Citizen and Subject: Contemporary Africa and the Legacy of Colonialism* (Princeton: Princeton University Press).

Mandle, W. F. (1987). *The Gaelic Athletic Association and Irish Nationalist Politics, 1884–1924* (London: Croom Helm).

Mann, Michael (1986). *The Sources of Social Power: A History of Power from the Beginning to A.D. 1760* (Cambridge: Cambridge University Press).

Maoz, Moshe (1982). 'Communal Conflict in Ottoman Syria During the Reform Era: The Role of Political and Economic Factors', in Benjamin Braude and Bernard Lewis (eds.), *Christians and Jews in the Ottoman Empire: The Functioning of a Plural Society* (New York: Holmes & Meier), 91–105.

Marcu, Eva Dorothea (1976). *Sixteenth Century Nationalism* (New York: Abaris Books).

Martin, Douglas (1997). 'Eager to Bite the Hands that Would Feed Them', *The New York Times* (1 June): D1.

Marwell, Gerald, and Pamela Oliver (1993). *The Critical Mass in Collective Action: A Micro-Social Theory* (Cambridge: Cambridge University Press).

Maryanski, Alexandra, and Jonathan H. Turner (1992). *The Social Cage:*

Human Nature and the Evolution of Society (Stanford, Calif.: Stanford University Press).

Maurras, Charles (1970). 'The Future of French Nationalism', in J. S. McClelland (ed.), *The French Right* (London: Jonathan Cape; originally published 1954), 295–304.

Mazzini, Giuseppe (1995). 'The Duties of Man', in Oman Dahbour and Micheline R. Ishay (eds.), *The Nationalism Reader* (Atlantic Highlands, NJ: Humanities Press; originally published 1858), 87–97.

Meadwell, Hudson (1993). 'The Politics of Nationalism in Quebec', *World Politics*, 45: 203–41.

Mettam, Colin W., and Stephen Wyn Williams (1998). 'Internal Colonialism and Cultural Divisions of Labour in the Soviet Republic of Estonia', *Nations and Nationalism*, 4: 363–88.

Migdal, Joel S. (1988). *Strong Societies and Weak States: State–Society Relations and State Capabilities in the Third World* (Princeton: Princeton University Press).

Mill, John Stuart (1861). *Considerations on Representative Government* (London: Parker, Son & Bourne).

Miller, David (1994). 'In Defence of Nationality', in Paul Gilbert and Paul Gregory (eds.), *Nations, Cultures, and Markets* (Abingdon: Avebury), 15–32.

Miller, Gary (1991). *Managerial Dilemmas* (Cambridge: Cambridge University Press).

Miller, William Ian (1990). *Bloodtaking and Peacemaking: Feud, Law, and Society in Saga Iceland* (Chicago: University of Chicago Press).

Minogue, Kenneth R. (1967). *Nationalism* (London: B. T. Batsford).

Moore, Barrington (1966). *Social Origins of Dictatorship and Democracy* (Boston, Mass.: Beacon Press).

Morgan, Kenneth O. (1963). *Wales in British Politics, 1868–1922* (Cardiff: University of Wales Press).

Morris, Aldon D. (1984). *The Origins of the Civil Rights Movement: Black Communities Organizing for Change* (New York: Free Press).

Motyl, Alexander J. (1990). *Sovietology, Rationality, Nationality: Coming to Grips with Nationalism in the USSR* (New York: Columbia University Press).

Mousnier, Roland (1958). 'Recherches sur les soulèvements populaires en France avant la Fronde', *Revue d'histoire moderne et contemporaine*, 5: 81–113.

——(1970a). 'The Fronde', in Robert Forster and Jack P. Greene (eds.), *Preconditions of Revolution in Early Modern Europe* (Baltimore, Md.: Johns Hopkins University Press), 131–60.

Mousnier, Roland (1970*b*). *Peasant Uprisings in the Seventeenth Century: France, Russia and China* (New York: Harper Torchbooks).

Mozjes, Paul (1994). *Yugoslavian Inferno: Ethnoreligious War in the Balkans* (New York: Continuum).

Mullen, Brian, Rupert Brown, and Colleen Smith (1992). 'Ingroup Bias as a Function of Salience, Relevance, and Status: An Integration', *European Journal of Social Psychology*, 22: 103–22.

Netting, Robert M. (1981). *Balancing on an Alp: Ecological Change and Continuity in a Swiss Mountain Community* (Cambridge: Cambridge University Press).

Newman, Gerald (1987). *The Rise of English Nationalism: A Cultural History* (New York: St Martin's Press).

Nightengale, Bob (1995). 'He's a Hit, from San Francisco to Osaka', *International Herald Tribune* (London, 4 May): 21.

Nordlinger, Eric A. (1972). *Conflict Regulation in Divided Societies* (Cambridge, Mass.: Harvard University Center for International Affairs).

North, Douglass C. (1981). *Structure and Change in Economic History* (New York: Norton).

Oates, Wallace E. (1972). *Fiscal Federalism* (New York: Harcourt Brace Jovanovich).

O'Donnell, Paul E. (1997). 'Language Policies and Independent Politics in Quebec', *Language Problems and Language Planning*, 21: 162–9.

Ó Gliasain, Micheal (1988). 'Bilingual Secondary Schools in Dublin, 1960–1980', *International Journal of the Sociology of Language*, 70: 89–108.

Ó Gráda, Cormac (1997). *A Rocky Road: The Irish Economy since the 1920s* (Manchester: Manchester University Press).

Ohlmeyer, Jane H. (1998). '"Civilizinge of those Rude Partes": Colonizations within Britain and Ireland, 1580s–1640s', in N. Canny (ed.), *The Oxford History of the British Empire*, i. *The Origins of Empire* (Oxford: Oxford University Press), 124–47.

Ó Laoire, Muiris (1995). 'An Historical Perspective on the Revival of Irish Outside of the Gaeltacht, 1830–1930, with Reference to the Revitalization of Hebrew', *Current Issues in Language and Society*, 2: 223–35.

Oliver, Pamela (1980). 'Rewards and Punishments as Selective Incentives for Collective Action: Theoretical Investigations', *American Journal of Sociology*, 85: 1356–75.

Olson, Mancur (1965). *The Logic of Collective Action* (Cambridge, Mass.: Harvard University Press).

——(1993). 'Dictatorship, Democracy, and Development', *American Political Science Review*, 87: 567–76.

Olzak, Susan (1992). *The Dynamics of Ethnic Competition and Conflict* (Stanford, Calif.: Stanford University Press).

Omrĉanin, Margaret (1976). *Norway, Sweden, Croatia: A Study of State Secession and Formation* (Philadelphia: Dorrance & Co.).

Østergård, Uffe (1992). 'Peasants and Danes: The National Identity and Political Culture', *Comparative Studies in Society and History*, 34: 3–27.

Ostrom, Elinor (1990). *Governing the Commons: The Evolution of Institutions for Collective Action* (Cambridge: Cambridge University Press).

Ostrom, Vincent, Charles Tiebout, and Robert Warren (1961). 'The Organization of Government in Metropolitan Areas: A Theoretical Inquiry', *American Political Science Review*, 55: 831–42.

Palmer, Robert R., and Joel Colton (1965). *A History of the Modern World* (New York: Alfred A. Knopf).

Paret, Peter (1970). 'Nationalism and the Sense of Military Obligation', *Military Affairs*, 34: 2–6.

Perlez, Jane (1998). 'A Wall Not Yet Built Casts the Shadow of Racism', *The New York Times* (2 July): A4.

Pfeiffer, John E. (1977). *The Emergence of Society: A Prehistory of the Establishment* (New York: McGraw-Hill).

Pinard, Maurice (1998). 'The Political Universe of Ambivalent Francophone Voters', *Opinion Canada*, 6 (Sept.): 1, 4–6.

—— and Richard Hamilton (1986). 'Motivational Dimensions in the Quebec Independence Movement: A Test of a New Model', *Research in Social Movements, Conflicts, and Change*, 9: 225–80.

Plamenatz, John (1976). 'Two Types of Nationalism', in Eugene Kamenka (ed.), *Nationalism: The Nature and Evolution of an Idea* (London: Edward Arnold), 23–36.

Poggi, Gianfranco (1978). *The Development of the Modern State: A Sociological Introduction* (Stanford, Calif.: Stanford University Press).

Pohl, Walter (1998). 'Telling the Difference: Signs of Ethnic Identity', in W. Pohl and Helmut Reimitz (eds.), *Strategies of Distinction: The Construction of Ethnic Communities, 300–800* (Leiden: Brill), 17–70.

Polanyi, Karl (1943). *The Great Transformation* (Boston, Mass.: Beacon Press).

Popper, Karl R. (1994). 'Models, Instruments and Truth', in Popper (ed.), *The Myth of the Framework: In Defence of Science and Rationality* (London: Routledge).

Porter, Bruce D. (1994). *War and the Rise of the State* (New York: Free Press).

228 *Bibliography*

Posen, Barry R. (1993*a*). 'Nationalism, the Mass Army, and Military Power', *International Security*, 18: 80–124.

——(1993*b*). 'The Security Dilemma and Ethnic Conflict', *Survival*, 35: 27–47.

Posner, Richard (1980). 'A Theory of Primitive Society', *Journal of Law and Economics*, 23: 1–54.

Pundeff, Marin V. (1969). 'Bulgarian Nationalism', in Peter F. Sugar and Ivo J. Lederer (eds.), *Nationalism in Eastern Europe* (Seattle: University of Washington Press), 93–165.

Putnam, Robert (1994). *Making Democracy Work* (Princeton: Princeton University Press).

——(1988). 'Diplomacy and Domestic Politics: The Logic of Two-Level Games', *International Organization*, 42: 427–60.

Québec, Assemblée nationale (1995). Bill Respecting the Future of Quebec: Including the Declaration of Sovereignty and the agreement of June 12, 1995. Quebec: Québec Official Publisher.

Québec, Conseil de la Langue Française (1995). *Indicateurs de la langue du travail au Québec*. Quebec: Gouvernment du Québec Conseil de la langue française.

Ramet, Pedro, ed. (1984). *Religion and Nationalism in Soviet and East European Politics* (Durham, NC: Duke University Press Policy Studies).

Ramet, Sabrina P. (1992). *Nationalism and Federalism in Yugoslavia, 1962–1991* (Bloomington, Ind.: Indiana University Press).

Reece, Jack E. (1979). 'Internal Colonialism: The Case of Brittany', *Ethnic and Racial Studies*, 2: 275–92.

Renan, Ernest (1994). 'Qu'est-ce qu'une nation?', in John Hutchinson and Anthony D. Smith (eds.), *Nationalism* (Oxford: Oxford University Press; originally published 1882), 17–18.

Reynolds, Andrew S. (1999). *Electoral Systems and Democratization in Southern Africa* (Oxford: Oxford University Press).

Reynolds, Vernon, Vincent Falger, and Ian Vine, eds. (1987). *The Sociobiology of Ethnocentrism* (London: Croom Helm).

Riall, Lucy (1994). *The Italian Risorgimento: State, Society, and National Unification* (London: Routledge).

Ridley, Frederick F., and Jean Blondel (1969). *Public Administration in France* (London: Routledge & Kegan Paul).

Riker, William H. (1964). *Federalism: Origin, Operation, Significance* (Boston, Mass.: Little-Brown).

Robinson, Geoffrey (1998). '*Rawan* is as *Rawan* Does: The Origins of Disorder in New Order Aceh', *Indonesia*, 66: 127–56.

Roeder, Philip G. (1991). 'Soviet Federalism and Ethnic Mobilization', *World Politics*, 43: 196–233.

Rogowski, Ronald (1985*a*). 'Causes and Varieties of Nationalism: A Rationalist Account', in Edward A. Tiryakian and Ronald Rogowski (eds.), *New Nationalisms of the Developed West* (Boston, Mass.: Allen & Unwin), 87–108.

——(1985*b*). 'Conclusion', in Edward A. Tiryakian and R. Rogowski (eds.), *New Nationalisms of the Developed West* (London: George Allen & Unwin), 374–87.

Rokkan, Stein (1970). *Citizens, Elections, Parties* (New York: David McKay).

Rothstein, Edward (1997). 'Ethnicity and Disney: It's a Whole New Myth', *The New York Times* (14 Dec.): B37.

Rusinow, Dennison (1977). *The Yugoslav Experiment, 1948–1974* (Berkeley, Calif.: Published for the Royal Institute of International Affairs, London, by the University of California Press).

Rustow, Dankwart A. (1968). 'Nation', in *International Encyclopedia of the Social Sciences*, Vol. II ed. David L. Sills (New York: Macmillan), 7–14.

Sack, Robert David (1986). *Human Territoriality: Its Theory and History* (Cambridge: Cambridge University Press).

Sacks, Oliver (1989). *Seeing Voices: A Journey into the World of the Deaf* (Berkeley, Calif.: University of California Press).

Safi, Louay (1992). 'Nationalism and the Multinational State', *American Journal of Islamic Social Sciences*, 9: 338–50.

Sahlins, Peter (1989). *Boundaries: The Making of France and Spain in the Pyrenees* (Berkeley, Calif.: University of California Press).

Sale, Kirkpatrick (1980). *Human Scale* (New York: Coward, McCann & Geoghegan).

Sampson, Robert J., Stephen W. Raudenbush, and Felton Earls (1997). 'Neighborhoods and Violent Crime: A Multilevel Study of Collective Efficacy', *Science*, 277: 918–24.

Savigear, Peter (1989). 'Autonomy and the Unitary State: The Case of Corsica', in Murray Forsyth (ed.), *Federalism and Nationalism* (Leicester: Leicester University Press), 96–114.

Sayer, Derek (1996). 'The Language of Nationality and the Nationality of Language: Prague 1780–1920', *Past and Present*, 153: 164–210.

Schein, Jerome (1989). *At Home Among Strangers* (Washington, DC: Gallaudet University Press).

Schelling, Thomas (1960). *The Strategy of Conflict* (Cambridge, Mass.: Harvard University Press).

Schulze, Hagen (1991). *The Course of German Nationalism: From Frederick the Great to Bismarck, 1763–1867* (Cambridge: Cambridge University Press).

Seabright, Paul (1996). 'Accountability and Decentralisation in Government: An Incomplete Contracts Model', *European Economic Review*, 40: 61–89.

Senelle, Robert (1989). 'Constitutional Reform in Belgium: From Unitarism Towards Federalism', in Murray G. Forsyth (ed.), *Federalism and Nationalism* (Leicester: Leicester University Press), 51–95.

Service, Elman R. (1975). *Origins of the State and Civilization* (New York: Norton).

Shaw, R. Paul, and Yuwa Wong (1989). *Genetic Seeds of Warfare* (Boston, Mass.: Unwin Hyman).

Shaw, Stanford J. (1968). 'Some Aspects of the Aims and Achievements of the Nineteenth Century Ottoman Reformers', in William R. Polk and Richard L. Chambers (eds.), *Beginnings of Modernization in the Middle East: The Nineteenth Century* (Chicago: University of Chicago Press).

——(1976). *History of the Ottoman Empire and Modern Turkey* (Cambridge: Cambridge University Press).

Sheppard, Blair H., Roy J. Lewicki, and John W. Minton (1992). *Organizational Justice: The Search for Fairness in the Workplace* (New York: Lexington Books).

Silberman, Bernard S. (1993). *Cages of Reason* (Chicago: University of Chicago Press).

Silberman, Neil (1990). *Between Past and Present: Archaeology, Ideology and Nationalism in the Modern Middle East* (New York: Anchor Books).

Simmel, Georg (1898). 'The Persistence of Groups, I.', *American Journal of Sociology*, 3: 662–98.

——(1955a). 'Conflict', in Simmel (ed.), *Conflict and the Web of Group Affiliations* (New York: Free Press; originally published 1922).

——(1955b). 'The Web of Group Affiliations', in Simmel (ed.), *Conflict and the Web of Group Affiliations* (New York: Free Press; originally published 1922).

Skinner, G. William (1977). *The City in Late Imperial China* (Stanford, Calif.: Stanford University Press).

Smith, Adam (1961). *The Wealth of Nations*, 6th edn., ed. Edwin Cannan (London: Methuen; originally published 1789).

Smith, Anthony D. (1986). *The Ethnic Origins of Nations* (Oxford: Blackwell).

——(1979). 'The "Historical Revival" in Late 18th-Century England and France.' *Art History*, 2: 156–178.

Smith, Graham (1995). 'Mapping the Federal Condition: Ideology, Political

Practice and Social Justice', in Graham Smith (ed.), *Federalism: The Multiethnic Challenge* (London: Longman), 1–28.

Smith, Vernon L. (1991). 'Economic Principles in the Emergence of Humankind: Presidential Address to the Western Economic Association, June 30, 1991', *Economic Inquiry*, 30: 1–13.

Snow, David A., and Pamela E. Oliver (1995). 'Social Movements and Collective Behavior: Social Psychological Dimensions and Considerations', in Karen Cook, Gary Fine, and James House (eds.), *Sociological Perspectives on Social Psychology* (Boston, Mass.: Allyn & Bacon), 571–600.

Snow, David A., E. Burke Rochford, jun., Steven K. Worden, and Robert D. Benford (1986). 'Frame Alignment Processes, Micromobilization, and Movement Participation', *American Sociological Review*, 51: 464–81.

Snyder, Jack, and Karen Ballentine (1996). 'Nationalism and the Marketplace of Ideas', *International Security*, 21: 5–40.

Snyder, Louis L. (1983). 'Nationalism and the Flawed Concept of Ethnicity', *Canadian Review of Studies in Nationalism*, 10: 253–66.

Sober, Elliott, and David Sloan Wilson (1998). *Unto Others: The Evolution and Psychology of Unselfish Behavior* (Cambridge, Mass.: Harvard University Press).

Sowell, Thomas (1994). *Race and Culture: A World View* (New York: Basic Books).

Sperber, Dan (1996). *Explaining Culture* (Oxford: Blackwell).

Spillman, Lyn (1997). *Nation and Commemoration: Creating National Identities in the United States and Australia* (Cambridge: Cambridge University Press).

Spruyt, Hendrik (1994). *The Sovereign State and its Competitors: An Analysis of System Change* (Princeton: Princeton University Press).

Stalin, Josef (1994). 'The Nation', in John Hutchinson and Anthony D. Smith (eds.), *Nationalism* (Oxford: Oxford University Press; originally published 1942), 18–21.

Stanovčić, Vojislav (1988). 'History and Status of Ethnic Conflicts', in Dennison Rusinow (ed.), *Yugoslavia: A Fractured Federalism* (Washington, DC: The Wilson Center), 23–40.

Steiner, Jürg (1974). *Amicable Agreement versus Majority Rule: Conflict Resolution in Switzerland* (Chapel Hill, NC: University of North Carolina Press).

Stinchcombe, Arthur L. (1965). 'Social Structure and Organizations', in James G. March (ed.), *Handbook of Organizations* (Chicago: Rand McNally).

——(1975). 'Social Structure and Politics', in Fred I. Greenstein and Nelson

232   *Bibliography*

W. Polsby (eds.), *Handbook of Political Science* (Reading, Mass.: Addison-Wesley).

——(1990). *Information and Organizations* (Berkeley, Calif.: University of California Press).

Strang, David (1996). 'Contested Sovereignty: The Social Construction of Colonial Imperalism', in Thomas J. Biersteker and Cynthia Weber (eds.), *State Sovereignty as Social Construct* (Cambridge: Cambridge University Press), 22–49.

Streeck, Wolfgang, and Philippe C. Schmitter (1991). 'From National Corporatism to Transnational Pluralism: Organized Interests in the Single European Market', *Politics and Society*, 19: 133–63.

Stringer, Keith (1994). 'Identities in Thirteenth-Century England: Frontier Society in the Far North', in Claus Bjørn, Alexander Grant, and Keith Stringer (eds.), *Social and Political Identities in Western History* (Copenhagen: Academic Press Copenhagen), 28–66.

Stürmer, Michael (1987). 'France and German Unification', in Hagen Schulze (ed.), *Nation-Building in Central Europe* (Leamington Spa: Berg), 135–49.

Sugar, Peter F. (1969). 'External and Domestic Roots of Eastern European Nationalism', in Peter F. Sugar and Ivo G. Lederer (eds.), *Nationalism in Eastern Europe* (Seattle: University of Washington Press), 3–54.

Suny, Ronald Grigor (1993). *Looking Toward Ararat: Armenia in Modern History* (Bloomington, Ind.: Indiana University Press).

Szporluk, Roman (1993). 'Belarus, Ukraine, and the Russian Question: A Comment', *Post-Soviet Affairs*, 9: 366–74.

Tachau, Frank (1984). *Turkey: The Politics of Authority, Democracy, and Development* (New York: Praeger).

Tajfel, Henri (1981). *Human Groups and Social Categories: Studies in Social Psychology* (Cambridge: Cambridge University Press).

——ed. (1982). *Social Identity and Intergroup Relations* (Cambridge: Cambridge University Press).

Tambiah, Stanley J. (1996). *Leveling Crowds: Ethnonationalist Conflicts and Collective Violence in South Asia* (Berkeley, Calif.: University of California Press).

Tarrow, Sidney (1977). *Between Center and Periphery* (New Haven, Conn.: Yale University Press).

Taylor, Deems, and Russell Kerr, eds. (1954). *Music Lovers' Encyclopedia* (Garden City, NY: Garden City Books).

Te Brake, Wayne (1998). *Shaping History: Ordinary People in European Politics, 1500–1700* (Berkeley, Calif: University of California Press).

Thibaut, John, and Laurens Walker (1975). *Procedural Justice: A Psychological Analysis* (Hillsdale, NJ: Lawrence Erlbaum Associates).

Tilly, Charles (1985). 'War Making and State Making as Organized Crime', in Peter B. Evans, Dietrich Rueschmeyer, and Theda Skocpol (eds.), *Bringing the State Back in* (Cambridge: Cambridge University Press), 169–91.

——(1990). *Coercion, Capital, and European States, AD 990–1990* (Cambridge, Mass.: B. Blackwell).

——(1993). 'National Self-Determination as a Problem for All of Us', *Daedalus*, 122: 29–36.

——(1998). *Durable Inequality* (Berkeley, Calif.: University of California Press).

Tiryakian, Edward A., and Ronald Rogowski, eds. (1985). *New Nationalisms of the Developed West* (Boston, Mass.: Allen & Unwin).

Tocqueville, Alexis de (1955). *The Old Régime and the French Revolution*, trans. Stuart Gilbert (Garden City, NY: Anchor Books; originally published 1858).

——(1969). *Democracy in America*, trans. George Lawrence (Garden City, NY: Anchor Books; originally published 1835).

Tollefson, James W. (1991). *Planning Language, Planning Inequality: Language Policy in the Community* (London: Longman).

Treisman, Daniel S. (1997). 'Russia's "Ethnic Revival": The Separatist Activism of Regional Leaders in a Postcommunist Order', *World Politics*, 49: 212–49.

Trigger, Bruce (1984). 'Alternative Archaeologies: Nationalist, Colonialist, Imperialist', *Man*, 19: 355–70.

Trudeau, Pierre Eliot (1968). *Federalism and the French Canadians* (Toronto: Macmillan & Canada).

Tsebelis, George (1990). *Nested Games: Rational Choice in Comparative Politics* (Berkeley, Calif.: University of California Press).

Tully, James (1995). *Multiplicity: Constitutionalism in an Age of Diversity* (Cambridge: Cambridge University Press).

Turner, John C., Michael A. Hogg, Penelope J. Oakes, Stephen D. Reicher, and Margaret S. Wetherell (1987). *Rediscovering the Social Group: A Self-Categorization Theory* (New York: Basil Blackwell).

Tyler, Patrick E. (1997). 'Ethnic Strain in China's Far West Flares with Bombs and Rioting', *The New York Times* (28 Feb.): A1, A7.

Tyler, Tom R. (1990). *Why People Obey the Law* (New Haven, Conn.: Yale University Press).

Udéhn, Lars (1996). *The Limits of Public Choice* (London: Routledge).

Vail, Leroy (1989). *The Creation of Tribalism in Southern Africa* (Berkeley, Calif.: University of California Press).

Van den Berghe, Pierre L. (1979). *Human Family Systems: An Evolutionary View* (New York: Elsevier).

——(1981). *The Ethnic Phenomenon* (New York: Elsevier).

Van Knippenberg, A., and Naomi Ellemers (1993). 'Strategies in Intergroup Relations', in Michael A. Hogg and Dominic Abrams (eds.), *Group Motivation: Social Psychological Perspectives* (New York: Harvester Wheatsheaf), 17–32.

Van Leeuwen, Marco H. D. (1997). 'Trade Unions and the Provision of Welfare in the Netherlands, 1910–1960', *Economic History Review*, 50: 764–91.

Wallerstein, Immanuel (1961). *Africa: The Politics of Independence* (New York: Vintage).

——(1974). *The Modern World System: Capitalist Agriculture and the Origins of the European World-Economy in the Sixteenth Century* (New York: Academic Press).

——(1991). *Geopolitics and Geoculture: Essays on the Changing World-System* (Cambridge: Cambridge University Press).

Watt, T. (1991). *Cheap Print and Popular Piety, 1550–1640* (Cambridge: Cambridge University Press).

Weakliem, David L., and Anthony F. Heath (1994). 'Rational Choice and Class Voting', *Rationality and Society*, 6: 243–70.

Weber, Eugen (1976). *The Making of Modern France* (Stanford, Calif.: Stanford University Press).

Weber, Max (1978). *Economy and Society*, ed. Guenther Roth and Claus Wittich (Berkeley, Calif.: University of California Press; originally published 1922).

Weingast, Barry R. (1995). 'The Economic Role of Political Institutions: Market-Preserving Federalism and Economic Growth', *Journal of Law, Economics and Organization*, 11: 1–31.

——(1998). 'Political Stability and Civil War: Institutions, Commitment, and American Democracy', in Robert H. Bates, Avner Greif, Margaret Levi, Jean-Laurent Rosenthal, and Barry R. Weingast (eds.), *Analytic Narratives* (Princeton: Princeton University Press), 148–93.

Welch, Michael, and Jennifer L. Bryan (1996–7). 'Flag Desecration in American Culture: Offenses against Civil Religion and a Consecrated Symbol of Nationalism', *Crime, Law and Social Change*, 26: 77–93.

Western, Bruce (1997). *Between Class and Market: Postwar Unionization in the Capitalist Democracies* (Princeton: Princeton University Press).

White, Wilbur W. (1937). *The Process of Change in the Ottoman Empire* (Chicago: University of Chicago Press).

Williams, Rory (1994). 'Britain's Regional Mortality: A Legacy from Disaster in the Celtic Periphery?', *Social Science and Medicine*, 39: 189–99.

——and B. Ecob (1999). 'Regional Mortality and the Irish in Britain: Findings from the ONS Longitudinal Study', *Sociology of Health and Illness*, 21: 344–67.

Wittman, Donald (1991). 'Nations and States: Mergers and Acquisitions; Dissolutions and Divorce', *American Economic Review*, 81: 126–9.

Wolff, Kurt H. (1950). *The Sociology of Georg Simmel* (New York: Free Press).

Wong, R. Bin (1997). *China Transformed: Historical Change and the Limits of European Experience* (Ithaca, NY: Cornell University Press).

Wood, J. R. (1981). 'Secession: A Comparative Analytical Framework', *Canadian Journal of Political Science*, 14: 107–34.

Wood, Robert E. (1984). 'Ethnic Tourism, the State, and Cultural Change in Southeast Asia', *Annals of Tourism Research*, 11: 353–74.

Woodward, Susan L. (1995). *Balkan Tragedy: Chaos and Dissolution After the Cold War* (Washington, DC: Brookings Institution).

Woolfson, Jonathan (1999). *Padua and the Tudors: English Students in Italy, 1485–1603* (Cambridge: James Clarke).

Wright, Stephen C., Donald M. Taylor, and Fathali M. Moghaddam (1990). 'Responding to Membership in a Disadvantaged Group: From Acceptance to Collective Protest', *Journal of Personality and Social Psychology*, 58: 994–1003.

Yack, Bernard (1996). 'The Myth of the Civic Nation', *Critical Review*, 10: 193–211.

Yamagishi, Toshio, Karen S. Cook, and Motoki Watabe (1998). 'Uncertainty, Trust, and Commitment Formation in the United States and Japan', *American Journal of Sociology*, 104: 165–94.

Young, Crawford (1976). *The Politics of Cultural Pluralism* (Madison, Wis.: University of Wisconsin Press).

Young, Robert A. (1994). 'The Political Economy, of Secession: The Case of Quebec', *Constitutional Political Economy* 5: 221–45.

——(1995). *The Secession of Quebec and the Future of Canada* (Montreal and Kingston: Published for The Institute of Intergovernmental Relations, Queen's University, Kingston, by McGill-Queen's University Press).

Zagorin, Perez (1982). *Rebels and Rulers, 1500–1660* (Cambridge: Cambridge University Press).

Zajac, Edward (1995). *Political Economy of Fairness* (Cambridge, Mass.: MIT Press).

INDEX

12 group consciousness ⟶ homogeneity
   nationalism vs <u>Kinship</u> or face-to-face
                                    interaction
13 These statements could be supplemented by...
   the idea that nationalism is owed to
   <u>objective differentia</u>
14 Weber: Nation: intersubjective (cf Durkheim
    Durkheim's sacred ≈ intersubjective

    Nation = subset of ethnic group
Nation ⟶ territoriality
15 sleeping beauty vs Frankenstein
6 Nationalism ⟹ far more political than
                         literary, musical,
                         artistic --

  E pluribus Unum

P.3 This book focuses on 3 of them?

62 Direct Rule

28 State-building nationalism erodes peripher
groups nations by fostering cultural
homogeneity

29 Nap, soviet tun collapse of Soviet
Union exposed the weakness of
indirect rule
indirect rule ——sometimes——> secession
direct rule ———————> secession

30 who are the nationalists?
Ans: usual suspects

180 National educational systems policy.

long Titles 2 Emperor of Austria
182 Khanate (Crimea
Aceh vs Kosovo

171: Clans: 1- a political body,
"military"
Quebec 1) no one knows whether it be stable
2) no "   "   "

178 Gypsies tongue cut in Inquisition for
goal of   speaking their lan,
196 authentic national identity may conflict
with state sovereignty

196 ethnic proportionality & territorialism

186 Exogenous shock = Impetus for unifications in
Italy & Germany

88 German Romanticism —> a rxn against French

84 Irredenta = Italian

89 ... in the eyes of the world ... Victor Emmanuel's wife
90 Viva Italia — Victor Emmanuel's wife
91 unification —> indoctrination in schools Hebrew
196 Why did Israel succeed in reviving Hebrew
whereas Ireland failed in
reviving Gaelic